PHARMACEUTICAL PRODUCT DEVELOPMENT

ESSENTIAL INSIGHTS ON EXCIPIENTS, FORMULATION TECHNIQUES, AND REGULATORY COMPLIANCE

DR. M. RAMAKRISHNA, M. SANTHOSH ARUNA,
G. LAKSHMI DEVI, DR. G. RAGHAVENDRA

Made with ♥ on the Notion Press Platform
www.notionpress.com

Contents

Pharmaceutical Product Development

Essential Insights on Excipients, Formulation Techniques, and Regulatory Compliance
AUTHORS
Dr. Ramakrishna Malepati, M.Pharm., Ph.D
Vice Principal & Associate Professor,
Department of Pharmaceutical Analysis,
Narasaraopeta Institute of Pharmaceutical Sciences (Autonomous),
Narasaraopet, Palnadu (Dt), Andhra Pradesh – 522601, India
Mrs. Santhosh Aruna Mamidi, M.Pharm., (Ph.D)
Associate Professor,
Department of Pharmaceutics,
SIMS College of Pharmacy,
Guntur, Andhra Pradesh – 522001, India
Mrs. Lakshmi Devi Gottemukkula, M.Pharm., (Ph.D)
Associate Professor,
Department of Pharmaceutics,
Joginpally B.R. Pharmacy College,
Hyderabad, Telangana – 500075, India
Dr. Raghavendra Kumar Gunda, M.Pharm., Ph.D., FCEM
Associate Professor,
Department of Pharmaceutics,
Narasaraopeta Institute of Pharmaceutical Sciences (Autonomous),
Narasaraopet, Palnadu (Dt), Andhra Pradesh – 522601, India

Editor
Dr. A. Muralidhar Rao, M.Pharm., Ph.D
Principal,
St. Mary's College of Pharmacy,
Secunderabad, Telangana, India

Published by Notion Press
Notion Press, Inc.
800, West El Camino Real #180,
California, USA 94040
Notion Press Media Pvt Ltd
#7, Red Cross Road,
Egmore, Chennai, Tamil Nadu 600008
Email ID: publish@notionpress.com
Phone Number: +91 44 46315631

Preface

Pharmaceutical Product Development: Essential Insights on Excipients, Formulation Techniques, and Regulatory Compliance" is a comprehensive guide designed to provide students, researchers, and professionals with a thorough understanding of the various stages involved in pharmaceutical product development. The process of transforming an idea into a marketable drug product requires extensive knowledge and careful consideration of several factors, including excipients, formulation techniques, and regulatory frameworks. This book aims to bridge the gap by offering practical insights and scientific principles essential for successful pharmaceutical product development. In the pharmaceutical industry, excipients play a vital role in the effectiveness, stability, and bioavailability of drug formulations. Understanding the various excipients, their functions, and how they interact with Active Pharmaceutical Ingredients (APIs) is critical to optimizing formulations. Throughout this book, we delve into the detailed types of excipients and their roles in the design of various dosage forms, helping professionals make informed decisions in formulation development. The book also covers the formulation techniques that are the cornerstone of the development process. From early-stage preformulation studies to the final manufacturing stages, this text highlights the importance of optimizing processes such as granulation, compression, and coating to achieve high-quality drug products. With examples of different dosage forms, including oral, injectable, and topical formulations, the book provides in-depth knowledge to help develop the most suitable formulation for each type of drug. Regulatory compliance is a critical component of pharmaceutical product development, ensuring that drugs are not only safe and effective but also meet the rigorous standards set by regulatory agencies. This book offers a detailed overview of global regulatory guidelines and their impact on the development, approval, and commercialization of pharmaceutical products. From the FDA and EMA to ICH guidelines, we explore how packaging, labeling, and testing procedures must align with regulatory standards to facilitate market approval. This book is an essential resource for students studying pharmaceutical sciences, as well as industry professionals involved in formulation development, regulatory affairs, and quality control. It presents an integrated approach to understanding the key elements of pharmaceutical product development, ensuring that readers are well-equipped to navigate the complexities of the industry. We hope that this book will serve as an informative guide to those working in the field and inspire the next generation of pharmaceutical scientists to innovate and contribute to the ongoing advancement of drug development processes. Dr. M. Ramakrishna M. Santhosh Aruna G. Lakshmi Devi Dr. Raghavendra Kumar

Pharmaceutical Product Development: Essential Insights on Excipients, Formulation Techniques, and Regulatory Compliance" is a comprehensive guide designed to provide students, researchers, and professionals with a thorough understanding of the various stages involved in pharmaceutical product development. The process of transforming an idea into a marketable drug product requires extensive knowledge and careful consideration of several factors, including **excipients, formulation techniques**, and **regulatory frameworks**. This book aims to bridge the gap by offering **practical insights** and **scientific principles** essential for successful pharmaceutical product development.

In the pharmaceutical industry, excipients play a vital role in the effectiveness, stability, and bioavailability of drug formulations. Understanding the various excipients, their functions, and how they interact with Active Pharmaceutical Ingredients (APIs) is critical to optimizing formulations. Throughout this book, we delve into the detailed **types of excipients** and their roles in the design of various dosage forms, helping professionals make informed decisions in formulation development.

The book also covers the **formulation techniques** that are the cornerstone of the development process. From early-stage **preformulation studies** to the final manufacturing stages, this text highlights the importance of optimizing processes such as **granulation**, **compression**, and **coating** to achieve high-quality drug products. With examples of different dosage forms, including **oral**, **injectable**, and **topical formulations**, the book provides in-depth knowledge to help develop the most suitable formulation for each type of drug.

Regulatory compliance is a critical component of pharmaceutical product development, ensuring that drugs are not only safe and effective but also meet the rigorous standards set by regulatory agencies. This book offers a detailed overview of global regulatory guidelines and their impact on the development, approval, and commercialization of pharmaceutical products. From the **FDA** and **EMA** to **ICH** guidelines, we explore how packaging, labeling, and testing procedures must align with regulatory standards to facilitate market approval.

This book is an essential resource for students studying **pharmaceutical sciences**, as well as industry professionals involved in **formulation development**, **regulatory affairs**, and **quality control**. It presents an integrated approach to understanding the key elements of pharmaceutical product development, ensuring that readers are well-equipped to navigate the complexities of the industry.

We hope that this book will serve as an informative guide to those working in the field and inspire the next generation of pharmaceutical scientists to innovate and contribute to the ongoing advancement of drug development processes.

Dr. M. Ramakrishna
M. Santhosh Aruna
G. Lakshmi Devi
Dr. Raghavendra Kumar

CHAPTER ONE

Introduction to Pharmaceutical Product Development

1.1 Objectives of Pharmaceutical Product Development

Pharmaceutical product development plays a crucial role in ensuring the availability of safe, effective, and high-quality medicines to the public. It involves a series of steps and processes, from the discovery of new drug candidates to the development and commercialization of the final product. These efforts aim to improve public health by providing treatments for various diseases, conditions, and disorders.

In the pharmaceutical industry, product development is significant for several reasons. It ensures that medications are developed with scientific rigor, regulatory compliance, and ethical standards. The main objectives of pharmaceutical product development include:

1. **Ensuring Safety and Efficacy**: One of the primary objectives is to develop medicines that are both safe and effective for human use. This involves rigorous testing and clinical trials to evaluate the safety profile of the drug and its therapeutic effectiveness. Safety checks help identify potential side effects, while efficacy studies ensure that the drug works as intended.

2. **Compliance with Regulatory Standards**: Pharmaceutical product development must comply with various regulatory requirements set by health authorities like the Food and Drug Administration (FDA), European Medicines Agency (EMA), and the Indian Drug Regulatory Authority. These regulations ensure that products are safe for public

consumption and that they meet quality standards.

3. **Innovation in Medicine**: A significant part of pharmaceutical development is driven by the need to address unmet medical needs. Researchers constantly explore new drug candidates, formulations, and delivery methods to improve the quality of life for patients. Innovation in medicine helps in treating diseases that currently have no effective treatments or in improving the current treatment options.

4. **Optimization of Drug Formulation**: In the development of pharmaceutical products, optimizing the drug formulation is crucial. This includes selecting the appropriate ingredients, excipients, and dosage forms (such as tablets, injections, or topical formulations) to ensure the drug's stability, bioavailability, and patient acceptability.

5. **Cost-Effectiveness**: Pharmaceutical companies aim to develop products that are not only effective but also affordable. Balancing production costs and the cost of research and development is essential to make drugs accessible to the broader population, especially in lower-income regions.

6. **Market Success and Sustainability**: Another important objective is ensuring the commercial success and sustainability of the product in the market. This involves identifying the target patient population, understanding market demands, and effectively marketing the product once it is ready for commercialization.

7. **Patient-Centric Approach**: Product development also involves considering the needs and preferences of patients. This includes factors like ease of administration, taste, and the ability to provide relief from symptoms in a convenient and effective manner.

Pharmaceutical product development is not just about creating new medicines; it is a process of continuous learning, innovation, and adaptation. It is about ensuring that the final product will provide therapeutic benefits, meet regulatory standards, and, most importantly, improve the lives of those who need it the most.

Major Stages Involved

Pharmaceutical product development is a multi-step process that requires careful planning and execution. The major stages involved are as follows:

1. **Discovery and Preclinical Research**: The first stage of pharmaceutical development is discovering new drug candidates. Researchers identify

potential compounds through laboratory research and screening. Once a promising candidate is found, preclinical studies are conducted to test its safety and effectiveness in laboratory settings, using cell cultures and animal models. This helps to identify any harmful effects before human trials.

2. **Clinical Trials**: After preclinical research, clinical trials are conducted to test the drug in humans. Clinical trials are typically divided into three phases:

   - **Phase I**: This phase tests the drug on a small group of healthy volunteers to assess safety, dosage, and side effects.
   - **Phase II**: In this phase, the drug is tested on a larger group of patients with the target disease to evaluate its effectiveness and monitor for any side effects.
   - **Phase III**: This phase involves even larger groups of patients and aims to confirm the drug's effectiveness, monitor side effects, and compare it to existing treatments. Successful completion of Phase III allows for regulatory approval.

3. **Regulatory Approval**: Once clinical trials are completed successfully, the pharmaceutical company submits the data to regulatory bodies (such as the FDA, EMA, or the Indian Drug Authority) for approval. These agencies review the data to ensure the drug is safe, effective, and meets all necessary standards for market release.

4. **Manufacturing and Scale-Up**: After obtaining regulatory approval, the drug moves to large-scale manufacturing. This phase focuses on producing the drug in large quantities while ensuring it maintains its quality, stability, and consistency. The scale-up process includes optimizing production techniques and ensuring the drug can be manufactured at a cost-effective price.

5. **Market Launch and Post-Market Surveillance**: Once the drug is available in the market, companies monitor its performance through post-market surveillance. This includes tracking any new side effects or issues that may arise once the drug is used by the general population. Post-market surveillance helps companies make adjustments if necessary and ensures the ongoing safety of the product.

Key Considerations for Effective Development

To ensure successful pharmaceutical product development, several key considerations must be taken into account at each stage:

1. **Regulatory Compliance**: Adhering to local and international regulations is critical for ensuring the safety, efficacy, and quality of the product. Regulatory bodies like the FDA, EMA, and local authorities in India set stringent guidelines for clinical trials, manufacturing processes, and labeling. Compliance ensures that the drug is safe for public use and meets the required standards.
2. **Safety and Efficacy**: The safety and efficacy of a drug are the top priorities in its development. Throughout the clinical trial phases, it is essential to assess the potential risks and benefits of the drug. This includes monitoring for side effects, drug interactions, and any long-term health impacts.
3. **Quality Control**: Consistent quality is a key consideration for pharmaceutical products. From the raw materials used in manufacturing to the final packaged product, every step of the process must meet strict quality control standards. This ensures that the drug is safe, effective, and free from contaminants.
4. **Cost Management**: Developing a new pharmaceutical product can be an expensive process. Therefore, it is important to manage costs effectively throughout the development stages. This includes optimizing research and development resources, improving manufacturing processes, and reducing production costs without compromising the quality of the drug.
5. **Patient-Centric Design**: Understanding the needs of patients is essential for the success of the product. This includes considering factors like the drug's form (e.g., tablet, injection, or liquid), dosage regimen, ease of administration, and potential side effects. The goal is to create a product that is not only effective but also easy for patients to use.
6. **Collaboration and Partnerships**: Effective pharmaceutical product development often involves collaboration between research teams, regulatory experts, contract manufacturers, and marketing teams. Building strong partnerships helps in efficiently navigating the complex development process and bringing the product to market faster.
7. **Market Demand and Competition**: Assessing market demand and the competitive landscape is crucial for understanding the commercial viability of a new drug. Market research helps determine the target

population, pricing strategy, and potential market share. It also helps in identifying existing treatments and ensuring that the new product offers a better or more efficient solution.

8. **Sustainability and Environmental Impact**: Sustainability has become an important consideration in pharmaceutical product development. Companies are now focused on reducing the environmental impact of manufacturing processes, such as waste generation and energy consumption. Green chemistry and sustainable practices are increasingly being integrated into drug development and production.

By carefully considering these key factors and following the appropriate stages of development, pharmaceutical companies can create drugs that are safe, effective, and meet the needs of both patients and healthcare providers. This comprehensive approach ensures that new pharmaceutical products successfully reach the market and provide meaningful benefits to society.

1.2 Regulations in Pharmaceutical Product Development
Overview of Global/Regional Frameworks (FDA, EMA, CDSCO)

Regulations play a vital role in pharmaceutical product development as they ensure that drugs are safe, effective, and of high quality before they reach patients. Various regulatory bodies across the world set standards and guidelines for the development, testing, approval, and monitoring of pharmaceutical products. Some of the key regulatory frameworks include the Food and Drug Administration (FDA) in the United States, the European Medicines Agency (EMA) in Europe, and the Central Drugs Standard Control Organization (CDSCO) in India.

Food and Drug Administration (FDA) - USA

The FDA is one of the most influential regulatory bodies globally. It is responsible for ensuring that drugs and medical devices are safe and effective for public use in the United States. The FDA's role in pharmaceutical product development includes:

- **Preclinical and Clinical Trials Oversight**: The FDA sets guidelines for the approval process, which includes preclinical studies, clinical trials, and the submission of data for evaluation. Before clinical trials can begin in humans, companies must submit an Investigational New Drug (IND) application to the FDA, detailing the results of preclinical studies and the proposed trial design.
- **Approval Process**: The FDA reviews the data from clinical trials and assesses whether the drug should be approved for public use. This process involves evaluating the drug's safety, efficacy, and manufacturing quality. If the data is satisfactory, the FDA grants approval, allowing the drug to be marketed in the U.S.
- **Post-Market Surveillance**: After a drug is approved, the FDA continues to monitor its safety and efficacy through post-market surveillance. This involves tracking adverse drug reactions (ADRs) and ensuring the drug remains safe for long-term use.
- **Good Manufacturing Practices (GMP)**: The FDA enforces GMP guidelines to ensure that drugs are manufactured under strict quality standards. These regulations cover everything from raw material testing to packaging, ensuring that drugs are consistently produced and controlled.

European Medicines Agency (EMA) - Europe

The EMA is the central regulatory authority for pharmaceutical products in Europe. It works with national regulatory bodies in European Union (EU) member states to evaluate and supervise medicines. The EMA's key responsibilities include:

- **Centralized Procedure for Drug Approval**: The EMA provides a centralized process for drug approval within the EU. Companies can submit a single marketing authorization application to the EMA, which can then be used to gain approval across all EU member states. This reduces duplication and speeds up the approval process.
- **Scientific Advice and Guidelines**: The EMA offers scientific advice to pharmaceutical companies on the development of medicines. This includes guidance on clinical trial design, manufacturing standards, and regulatory requirements. The agency helps ensure that drugs meet EU standards before they are submitted for approval.
- **Safety and Risk Management**: Similar to the FDA, the EMA monitors the safety of medicines after they are approved and marketed. The agency issues warnings, recalls, and additional guidelines if new safety concerns arise. The EMA works with national authorities to manage risks and protect public health.
- **Pharmacovigilance**: The EMA plays a critical role in pharmacovigilance, the practice of monitoring the effects of drugs after they have been approved for use. The agency collects and evaluates information about the safety of medicines and can take actions such as revising labeling or even withdrawing a drug from the market if necessary.

Central Drugs Standard Control Organization (CDSCO) - India

The CDSCO is the national regulatory authority responsible for regulating pharmaceuticals and medical devices in India. It ensures that drugs are safe, effective, and of the required quality before they are marketed in the country. The CDSCO's functions include:

- **Approval and Licensing**: The CDSCO is responsible for approving new drugs in India. This process includes evaluating clinical trial data, manufacturing practices, and labeling standards. The CDSCO also licenses pharmaceutical companies to manufacture, sell, and distribute drugs in India.

- **Clinical Trials Regulations**: The CDSCO sets guidelines for the conduct of clinical trials in India, ensuring that trials are carried out in an ethical and scientific manner. The organization ensures that the rights and safety of clinical trial participants are protected through informed consent and strict monitoring.
- **Pharmacovigilance and Post-Marketing Surveillance**: Like the FDA and EMA, the CDSCO monitors the safety of drugs after they are approved. It tracks adverse drug reactions (ADRs) and ensures that any issues related to the safety or efficacy of medicines are addressed promptly.
- **Quality Control and GMP**: The CDSCO enforces Good Manufacturing Practices (GMP) standards in India. This ensures that drugs manufactured in the country, as well as those imported, meet the necessary quality standards. The organization also conducts inspections to verify compliance with GMP.
- **Regulation of Over-the-Counter (OTC) and Prescription Drugs**: The CDSCO plays a key role in regulating both prescription and over-the-counter drugs, ensuring they meet safety standards and that they are marketed appropriately.

Global Harmonization of Regulations

In recent years, there has been a significant push towards harmonizing regulations across different regions to streamline the approval process for pharmaceutical products. Organizations such as the **International Council for Harmonisation (ICH)** work to align regulatory standards across major markets like the U.S., Europe, and Japan. This helps reduce the time and cost involved in drug development, as companies can use the same data to gain approval in multiple countries.

Key Takeaways

- **FDA (USA)**: Focuses on rigorous preclinical and clinical trial approval processes, ensuring drug safety, efficacy, and quality.
- **EMA (Europe)**: Offers a centralized drug approval process for the EU, provides scientific advice, and ensures drug safety post-market.
- **CDSCO (India)**: Regulates clinical trials, ensures drug quality, and enforces GMP within India while monitoring post-market safety.

These regulatory bodies work to ensure that drugs developed and marketed worldwide meet the highest safety and efficacy standards. By adhering to their guidelines, pharmaceutical companies can contribute to public health while complying with the legal requirements of different markets.

Regulatory Requirements at Each Stage (Preformulation, Formulation, Manufacturing)

Pharmaceutical product development involves several stages, and at each stage, regulatory requirements are put in place to ensure the safety, efficacy, and quality of the product. These requirements differ depending on the phase of development. Below are the key regulatory requirements for each stage:

1. Preformulation Stage

The preformulation stage is the initial phase where the characteristics of the drug compound are studied before developing the actual formulation. The primary objective is to understand the drug's physical and chemical properties to decide on the most suitable formulation.

- **Regulatory Requirements:**

  - **Drug Substance Characterization**: The drug substance must be carefully characterized, which includes determining its solubility, stability, pH, and other relevant physical-chemical properties. Regulatory bodies require comprehensive data on the drug substance's structure, impurities, and stability before the formulation stage begins.
  - **Good Laboratory Practices (GLP)**: The preclinical research should be conducted following GLP guidelines to ensure the reliability and integrity of the data. This includes safety testing, animal studies, and validation of analytical techniques.
  - **Regulatory Documentation**: Before progressing to the formulation stage, developers must prepare and submit detailed documentation (such as an Investigational New Drug (IND) application) to regulatory agencies like the FDA or CDSCO. This documentation includes the results of preclinical studies, proposed dosing, and initial safety data.

2. Formulation Stage

The formulation stage is where the active pharmaceutical ingredient (API) is combined with excipients to create the drug product. This step is critical to ensure the drug is delivered to the patient in the right dosage form (e.g., tablet, injection, etc.).

- **Regulatory Requirements:**

  - **Formulation Development and Stability Testing**: Regulatory bodies require data on the stability of the formulation, which involves testing the product under various conditions (e.g., temperature, humidity, light) to ensure it remains stable throughout its shelf life.
  - **Excipients Selection**: The choice of excipients (inactive ingredients) must comply with regulatory standards to ensure that they are safe and do not interfere with the drug's efficacy.
  - **Good Manufacturing Practice (GMP)**: The formulation process must adhere to GMP guidelines to ensure consistency, reproducibility, and quality of the drug product.
  - **Filing of Investigational New Drug (IND)**: Before clinical trials, an IND application is filed with regulatory agencies to gain approval for testing the drug in humans. This includes data on the drug formulation, proposed dosing regimens, and any preclinical testing results.

3. Manufacturing Stage

The manufacturing stage involves the large-scale production of the drug product. Regulatory bodies require strict compliance with quality standards and practices to ensure the drug is manufactured consistently and safely.

- **Regulatory Requirements:**

  - **GMP Compliance**: One of the most critical regulatory requirements during the manufacturing phase is compliance with Good Manufacturing Practices (GMP). This includes maintaining a controlled manufacturing environment, using validated equipment, and ensuring that every batch of the product meets established specifications.
  - **Batch Release and Testing**: Every batch of the drug must undergo rigorous testing to ensure it meets the required standards for identity,

strength, purity, and quality. Regulatory authorities often require batch records to be maintained, along with full documentation of quality control (QC) tests.

- **Licensing**: Pharmaceutical manufacturers must obtain licenses to operate from the relevant regulatory authorities (e.g., FDA, CDSCO). This ensures that the manufacturing facility is compliant with the required standards for drug production.
- **Post-Approval Inspections**: After market approval, regulatory bodies continue to monitor the manufacturing processes through inspections and audits. These inspections verify compliance with GMP and ensure that manufacturing practices remain consistent.

Regulatory Bodies and Their Roles

Regulatory bodies are responsible for overseeing pharmaceutical product development to ensure public safety and the integrity of the healthcare system. These bodies establish regulations that guide each stage of the drug development process. Below are some of the key regulatory bodies and their roles:

1. Food and Drug Administration (FDA) - USA

The FDA is the central regulatory body for pharmaceutical products in the United States. Its role includes overseeing the safety, efficacy, and quality of drugs throughout their development and commercialization.

- **Role**:

  - **Preclinical and Clinical Evaluation**: The FDA reviews all clinical trial applications, including Investigational New Drug (IND) submissions, ensuring that trials are scientifically sound and ethically conducted.
  - **Approval and Marketing**: The FDA evaluates the data from clinical trials and, if the drug is found to be safe and effective, grants approval for it to be marketed in the U.S. This includes evaluating the drug's labeling, usage instructions, and advertising.
  - **Regulation of Manufacturing**: The FDA enforces GMP requirements in manufacturing and regularly inspects facilities to ensure compliance.
  - **Pharmacovigilance**: The FDA monitors drugs after they are approved, tracking adverse effects and ensuring patient safety.

2. European Medicines Agency (EMA) - Europe

The EMA is responsible for the regulation of medicines in the European Union (EU) and ensures that pharmaceuticals are safe, effective, and of high quality.

- **Role:**

  - **Centralized Drug Approval**: The EMA provides a centralized procedure for drug approval, allowing a single application to be submitted for approval in all EU member states.
  - **Scientific Advice and Guidelines**: The EMA provides guidance to pharmaceutical companies on clinical trial design, manufacturing standards, and regulatory requirements to help ensure compliance with EU standards.
  - **Post-Market Surveillance**: The EMA monitors the safety of medicines after approval and takes action when necessary, including issuing warnings or withdrawing products from the market.

3. Central Drugs Standard Control Organization (CDSCO) - India

The CDSCO is the national regulatory authority in India that oversees the approval and regulation of drugs and medical devices.

- **Role:**

  - **Approval of New Drugs**: The CDSCO evaluates the safety and efficacy data for new drugs and grants marketing approval in India.
  - **Clinical Trials Regulation**: The CDSCO establishes guidelines for conducting clinical trials in India, ensuring they are conducted ethically and in compliance with Indian laws.
  - **Manufacturing Oversight**: The CDSCO ensures that pharmaceutical manufacturing facilities comply with GMP to maintain high standards of quality and safety in drug production.
  - **Pharmacovigilance**: Like other regulatory bodies, the CDSCO monitors the safety of drugs post-approval and takes action to protect public health.

Key Takeaways

- **Preformulation Stage**: Regulatory requirements include drug characterization, safety testing, and IND submissions.
- **Formulation Stage**: Regulatory guidelines ensure the stability, quality, and safety of the formulation through GMP and clinical trial approvals.
- **Manufacturing Stage**: Strict GMP compliance, batch testing, and licensing are essential at this stage to ensure the drug's quality and consistency.

Regulatory Bodies: The FDA (USA), EMA (Europe), and CDSCO (India) each play significant roles in the regulation and approval of pharmaceutical products, ensuring safety and efficacy at every stage.

CHAPTER TWO

Preformulation and Formulation Development

2.1 Preformulation Studies

Importance in Product Development

Defining the Role of Preformulation Studies

Preformulation studies are a critical initial step in the development of any pharmaceutical product. Before a drug can be formulated into its final dosage form (such as tablets, capsules, or injections), it is essential to understand the physical and chemical properties of the Active Pharmaceutical Ingredient (API). The primary role of preformulation studies is to assess the characteristics of the API and use this information to guide the selection of the most suitable formulation strategy.

The main objective of preformulation studies is to identify any challenges that might arise in the later stages of development. By studying the drug's solubility, stability, and compatibility with excipients (inactive ingredients), researchers can predict how the API will behave during manufacturing, storage, and in the body once administered. These studies help create a well-balanced formulation that is not only stable and effective but also suitable for the targeted drug delivery system.

Understanding the API's physical and chemical properties, such as particle size, solubility, and stability, is crucial because these factors influence the drug's bioavailability and the effectiveness of the treatment. Bioavailability refers to the proportion of the drug that enters the bloodstream when administered and is made available to the site of action. If the API is poorly soluble or unstable, it may not be absorbed adequately, which can lead to treatment failure.

Preformulation studies also play a vital role in identifying potential interactions between the API and excipients. Excipients are included in formulations to serve various purposes, such as to stabilize the drug, facilitate its absorption, or improve patient compliance. However, some excipients may interact with the API, causing degradation, reduced effectiveness, or even safety concerns. Identifying such issues early helps avoid costly delays or product failures.

Thus, preformulation studies lay the foundation for the successful development of a pharmaceutical product. The data generated from these studies not only provides insights into how to optimize the formulation but also guides decisions on the most appropriate route of administration (oral, parenteral, topical, etc.) based on the API's characteristics.

Risk Mitigation

Preformulation studies are crucial for mitigating risks during the later stages of drug development. The early identification of potential issues related to the API's solubility, stability, and excipient compatibility can significantly reduce the chances of failure in subsequent stages, such as clinical trials or large-scale manufacturing.

For instance, if solubility issues are identified early, formulation scientists can explore strategies to improve the API's solubility, such as altering the particle size, using solubilizing agents, or changing the dosage form (e.g., from a tablet to a solution). Likewise, if the API is found to be unstable under certain conditions (e.g., heat, light, or moisture), the formulation can be adjusted to incorporate stabilizing agents or packaging that protects the drug from these environmental factors.

By addressing these challenges early in the process, companies can save time and resources that would otherwise be spent on reformulating or recalling products later. Identifying and addressing risks in the preformulation phase allows developers to move more confidently into the formulation and manufacturing stages, as they already have a solid understanding of the potential issues and how to address them.

Moreover, preformulation studies also help identify potential issues related to scale-up during manufacturing. Understanding the physical properties of the drug at a small scale enables developers to predict how the formulation will behave when produced in larger batches, ensuring that production remains consistent, cost-effective, and meets regulatory standards.

In addition to improving the stability and performance of the drug, these studies also help in the development of an appropriate dosage form that ensures patient safety and adherence. By minimizing the risk of formulation failure, preformulation studies significantly contribute to the overall success of pharmaceutical product development.

Foundation for Formulation Development

Preformulation studies serve as the foundation for the entire formulation development process. The data collected during this phase guide the selection of excipients, the choice of the dosage form, and the development of an effective drug delivery system.

1. **Excipients Selection**: The selection of excipients plays a pivotal role in the formulation of a drug product. Excipients are substances used in the formulation to support the API and help in the processing and delivery of the drug. Examples include binders (which hold the tablet together), disintegrants (which help the tablet break down in the stomach), and stabilizers (which enhance the shelf life of the drug).

Preformulation studies provide critical data about the chemical and physical properties of the API, which is used to choose the most compatible excipients. For instance, if an API is sensitive to moisture, excipients with moisture-absorbing properties may be chosen to prevent degradation. Likewise, if the drug is prone to oxidation, excipients with antioxidant properties can be incorporated.

1. **Suitable Dosage Form**: Based on the preformulation data, the most appropriate dosage form is selected. For example, a drug with poor solubility may be better formulated into a liquid form or as a nanoparticle formulation to enhance its absorption. On the other hand, a drug that requires controlled release may be formulated as a sustained-release tablet or capsule.

Preformulation studies help determine how the drug will be absorbed in the body, whether it will be effective when taken orally, or if it needs to be administered through a different route, such as injection or topical application. These studies guide the overall drug delivery strategy, ensuring that the formulation provides the required therapeutic effect.

3. **Feasibility of Large-Scale Production**: Preformulation studies also provide the data needed to assess the feasibility of large-scale production. For example, understanding the solubility and stability of the API at the preformulation stage allows manufacturers to design production processes that can be scaled up efficiently without compromising quality or consistency.

Additionally, these studies provide insights into the manufacturing challenges that may arise, such as the need for specialized equipment or processes. By identifying such issues early, developers can plan accordingly, reducing the chances of production delays or failures during large-scale manufacturing.

Key Aspects of Preformulation:

1. Solubility

Importance:

Solubility is one of the most critical factors in determining the bioavailability of a drug. Bioavailability refers to the fraction of the administered dose of the drug that reaches the systemic circulation and is available to exert its therapeutic effect. Poor solubility of an Active Pharmaceutical Ingredient (API) can significantly impact its absorption in the body, leading to low bioavailability and, in turn, reduced therapeutic efficacy.

When a drug is administered, it must first dissolve in the fluids in the gastrointestinal tract before it can be absorbed into the bloodstream. If the drug does not dissolve adequately, it may not be absorbed in sufficient quantities to produce the desired effect. This is particularly relevant for orally administered drugs, where solubility directly influences how much of the drug reaches the bloodstream.

Drugs with poor solubility often experience challenges in development, especially when they are intended for oral administration. In such cases, special strategies need to be employed during formulation development to enhance solubility and ensure the drug performs effectively.

Poor solubility can also lead to variability in drug absorption, which can cause inconsistent therapeutic outcomes. This becomes especially problematic in drugs that require precise dosing or are used for chronic conditions. Therefore, understanding and optimizing solubility during preformulation studies is crucial for successful drug development.

Tests and Techniques:

To evaluate the solubility of an API, various tests and techniques are used in preformulation studies. These tests help identify the solubility profile of the drug in different solvents and under different conditions, such as temperature and pH. Some of the common techniques used for solubility testing include:

1. **Shake-Flask Method**:
   This is one of the most widely used methods to determine the solubility of a drug in a given solvent. In this method, a known amount of API is added to a solvent, and the mixture is shaken to allow dissolution. The solution is then filtered, and the concentration of the dissolved API is measured, usually by UV spectroscopy or HPLC. The shake-flask method provides a simple and reliable way to measure solubility in different solvents or under varying conditions.

2. **High-Performance Liquid Chromatography (HPLC)**:
   HPLC is a highly sensitive technique used to measure the concentration of a drug in solution. In the context of solubility testing, HPLC can be used to assess the amount of API that has dissolved in a solvent after the drug has been subjected to the shake-flask method or other dissolution techniques. It is particularly useful when testing solubility in complex solvents or when precise quantification is required.

3. **Dissolution Testing**:
   Dissolution testing is a process where a drug's rate of dissolution in a given medium (e.g., simulated gastric or intestinal fluid) is measured. This is particularly important for oral dosage forms such as tablets or capsules, as the rate at which a drug dissolves in the stomach or intestine directly impacts its absorption. The dissolution rate is measured using a dissolution apparatus, which mimics the conditions in the human gastrointestinal tract. The test helps predict how quickly the drug will become available for absorption and how its solubility might impact its overall effectiveness.

4. **Solubility in Different pH Conditions**:
   Solubility can vary significantly depending on the pH of the medium. For example, some drugs may be more soluble in acidic conditions, while others may be more soluble in alkaline conditions. Preformulation studies often involve testing the drug in solutions with varying pH levels to understand how the solubility changes and to identify the most suitable formulation conditions.

5. **Solubility in Different Solvents:**
   The solubility of a drug can differ when tested in various solvents (such as water, ethanol, or phosphate buffer). In preformulation studies, solubility testing is done using a range of solvents to identify which one best suits the intended formulation. This helps in selecting the right formulation technique, such as using solubilizers or co-solvents to improve the solubility of poorly soluble drugs.

6. **Saturation Solubility:**
   Saturation solubility is the maximum concentration of the API that can dissolve in a given solvent at a specific temperature. This test helps determine whether the API is highly soluble or poorly soluble, which in turn influences decisions about formulation strategies. If the API is found to have low saturation solubility, the development team may need to explore techniques such as particle size reduction or the use of surfactants to improve solubility.

Strategies to Enhance Solubility:

In cases where poor solubility is identified, there are several strategies that can be used during formulation development to improve the solubility of the drug:

- **Particle Size Reduction**: Smaller particles have a larger surface area, which can lead to increased solubility. Techniques such as micronization or nanonization can reduce the size of the API particles, allowing for faster dissolution and better absorption.
- **Use of Solubilizing Agents**: Surfactants or co-solvents are often added to the formulation to increase solubility. For example, cyclodextrins, which are cyclic oligosaccharides, can form inclusion complexes with poorly soluble drugs, improving their solubility and bioavailability.
- **Solid Dispersion**: This technique involves dispersing the API in a solid state with excipients that enhance solubility. This is often used for drugs that are poorly soluble in water.
- **Use of Lipid-Based Formulations**: Lipid-based formulations, such as self-emulsifying drug delivery systems (SEDDS), are employed for lipophilic drugs that are poorly soluble in water. These formulations improve solubility by utilizing lipid vehicles to solubilize the drug.

2. Stability

Importance:

The stability of a drug is crucial to its effectiveness, safety, and quality throughout its shelf life. Stability studies ensure that the Active Pharmaceutical Ingredient (API) and the final drug product maintain their potency, purity, and safety from the time they are manufactured to when they are used by patients. Drugs that degrade over time, due to exposure to environmental factors such as temperature, light, or humidity, may lose their therapeutic effectiveness, potentially leading to treatment failure. Additionally, degradation can result in the formation of harmful by-products that may pose safety risks to patients.

Stability is a key factor in determining the expiration date and storage conditions of a drug. It is also an essential requirement for regulatory approval. Regulatory authorities such as the FDA, EMA, and CDSCO require manufacturers to provide stability data to ensure that the drug product will remain safe and effective until the end of its shelf life. This is especially important for drugs that are used over long periods, such as chronic disease treatments, and for biologic products, which may be more sensitive to degradation.

Several aspects of stability need to be evaluated during the drug development process:

- **Chemical Stability**: Ensures that the drug does not degrade chemically over time into inactive or harmful substances. Chemical degradation may occur due to oxidation, hydrolysis, or photodegradation.
- **Physical Stability**: Refers to the drug's ability to maintain its physical characteristics, such as appearance, texture, and integrity, throughout its shelf life. For example, tablets should not break down, and solutions should not precipitate over time.
- **Microbiological Stability**: Ensures that the drug remains free from microbial contamination throughout its shelf life, particularly for liquid formulations, injectables, or products that do not contain preservatives.

The goal of stability studies is to determine the optimal conditions for storage, identify any degradation pathways, and establish an appropriate shelf-life for the product.

Techniques:

To assess the stability of the drug, a variety of testing techniques are used, each designed to simulate different conditions and provide insights into how the drug will behave over time. The key techniques used for stability testing include:

1. **Accelerated Stability Testing:**

   - **Purpose**: Accelerated stability testing is conducted to predict the long-term stability of a drug product in a short period by exposing the product to extreme conditions, such as higher temperatures, humidity, and light.
   - **How It Works**: In accelerated testing, the drug is subjected to stress conditions that would normally shorten its shelf life. For example, samples may be stored at elevated temperatures (e.g., 40°C or higher) or higher humidity levels for a specified time period. The rate of degradation is expected to be faster under these conditions, allowing researchers to observe any changes in the product's physical, chemical, or microbiological properties more quickly.
   - **Outcome**: The data obtained from accelerated stability testing can be used to estimate the shelf life of the drug at normal storage conditions. It also helps identify any immediate degradation pathways and provides early warnings of potential stability issues.

2. **Real-Time Stability Studies:**

   - **Purpose**: Real-time stability studies involve storing drug samples under normal storage conditions for extended periods to monitor how they change over time.
   - **How It Works**: Unlike accelerated testing, real-time stability studies are conducted at standard temperature and humidity conditions that the drug is expected to be stored under, such as 25°C and 60% relative humidity (for most drugs). Samples are tested at regular intervals (e.g., 3, 6, 12, and 24 months) to assess changes in the API's potency, physical appearance, and any microbial contamination.
   - **Outcome**: Real-time testing provides the most accurate data for determining a drug's shelf life and expiration date. It also gives insight into the stability of the drug under conditions that reflect actual usage. However, real-time stability studies require a longer period of time to yield results, often taking several months or years, depending on the expected shelf life of the drug.

3. **Stress Testing**:

   - **Purpose**: Stress testing is designed to evaluate the drug's stability under extreme conditions that may accelerate its degradation process. This is useful for understanding the potential breakdown of the drug in various stressful conditions, such as exposure to high temperatures, extreme pH levels, light, and oxidative environments.
   - **How It Works**: The drug product is subjected to stress conditions that are beyond typical storage conditions. This includes exposure to high or low temperatures, variations in pH (acidic or alkaline), and oxidative agents (e.g., hydrogen peroxide). By subjecting the drug to these extreme conditions, the goal is to identify any chemical degradation products and to understand how the drug's formulation will hold up under these stresses.
   - **Outcome**: Stress testing can reveal any potential degradation pathways, such as hydrolysis, oxidation, or photodegradation. This data is valuable for formulating products that are more stable and can withstand challenges that may occur during storage or transport. It also helps in designing packaging that protects the drug from light or air exposure.

4. **Shelf-Life Testing**:

   - **Purpose**: Shelf-life testing is a final assessment performed after stability data has been gathered to determine the drug's effective expiration date.
   - **How It Works**: During shelf-life testing, the drug is continuously stored under controlled environmental conditions (e.g., room temperature, humidity) for the entirety of its predicted shelf life. The API's stability is monitored periodically through various tests, such as potency testing, dissolution, and appearance.
   - **Outcome**: The results from this study provide a clear indication of the maximum time period the drug can be used before its quality is compromised. Shelf-life testing is required by regulatory authorities to ensure the drug remains effective and safe throughout its lifespan.

5. **Packaging Compatibility Studies**:

- ◦ **Purpose**: Packaging plays an essential role in maintaining the stability of a drug by protecting it from environmental factors such as light, moisture, and oxygen.
- ◦ **How It Works**: In these studies, drug products are stored in different types of packaging (e.g., bottles, blisters, vials) to determine if the packaging material interacts with the drug or affects its stability. The study includes assessing the integrity of the packaging as well as the protection it provides against external factors.
- ◦ **Outcome**: Packaging compatibility studies help identify the ideal packaging material that will protect the drug from degradation while ensuring that the drug maintains its safety and efficacy over time.

3. Excipient Compatibility

Importance:

Excipients are inactive ingredients that are added to drug formulations to support the Active Pharmaceutical Ingredient (API). While excipients do not have any therapeutic effect, they play a crucial role in the formulation process by ensuring that the API performs effectively, remains stable, and is easy for patients to administer. The compatibility between the API and excipients is critical, as any chemical or physical interaction between the two can affect the drug's stability, bioavailability, and overall performance.

The main roles of excipients include:

- **Stability**: Excipients help stabilize the API, protecting it from degradation due to environmental factors such as heat, light, or moisture. They can also prevent interactions that might lead to chemical changes in the API.
- **Bioavailability**: Excipients can improve the solubility of poorly soluble drugs or enhance the rate at which the drug is absorbed in the body. They help ensure that the API reaches the target site in an effective concentration.
- **Ease of Administration**: Excipients help improve the formulation's physical properties, such as taste masking, texture, or viscosity, making the drug more palatable or easier to handle (e.g., in the case of liquid formulations or topical creams).
- **Patient Compliance**: Proper formulation with compatible excipients ensures that the drug is easy for patients to take. For example, excipients are used to form tablets, which can make administration easier compared

to liquid or injectable formulations, especially for patients who need long-term medication.

During the preformulation phase, assessing the compatibility of the API with different excipients is essential to avoid potential issues that could arise during formulation development. Unfavorable interactions between the API and excipients can lead to problems like reduced drug stability, changes in the drug's efficacy, or unwanted side effects. For example, some excipients might accelerate the degradation of the drug, alter its absorption characteristics, or cause precipitation or discoloration. Therefore, identifying and addressing such interactions early is vital for the success of the formulation.

Techniques:

Several analytical techniques are employed to assess the compatibility of excipients with the API in preformulation studies. These techniques help determine whether the excipients will maintain the drug's stability and efficacy over time.

1. **Differential Scanning Calorimetry (DSC):**

   - **Purpose**: DSC is a technique used to study the thermal behavior of substances. It measures the heat flow into or out of a sample as it is heated, providing information about the melting points, crystallization, and thermal stability of both the API and excipients.
   - **How It Works**: In DSC, both the API and excipients are subjected to controlled heating, and the changes in heat flow are recorded. The technique identifies any thermal interactions that may occur between the API and excipients, such as the formation of new compounds or the alteration of melting points. These interactions could suggest incompatibility that may affect the drug's stability.
   - **Outcome**: DSC can identify any shifts in the melting point of the API or excipients, which may indicate that a chemical interaction has occurred. For example, if the API undergoes a change in thermal behavior when mixed with a particular excipient, it might suggest that degradation or a chemical reaction is occurring. This helps in selecting excipients that do not interfere with the API's stability.

2. **Fourier Transform Infrared Spectroscopy (FTIR):**

- ○ **Purpose**: FTIR is a technique that provides information about the molecular structure of a substance by analyzing its infrared absorption spectrum. It is widely used to study functional groups and chemical bonds in both the API and excipients.
- ○ **How It Works**: FTIR measures the absorption of infrared light by the sample, producing a spectrum that shows the presence of different chemical bonds, such as carbon-hydrogen, carbon-oxygen, or nitrogen-hydrogen bonds. By comparing the FTIR spectra of the API and excipients before and after mixing, researchers can identify any new peaks or changes in the spectrum, indicating possible chemical interactions.
- ○ **Outcome**: FTIR helps detect any changes in the functional groups of the API or excipients that may indicate a reaction or incompatibility. For example, a new peak in the FTIR spectrum after mixing the API with an excipient might suggest the formation of a new compound, which could affect the drug's performance or stability.

3. **Stability Studies:**

- ○ **Purpose**: Stability studies are designed to assess how the API interacts with excipients over time under various environmental conditions (e.g., temperature, humidity, light). These studies help determine if any chemical or physical changes occur in the drug formulation due to excipient interactions.
- ○ **How It Works**: Stability studies involve storing the drug formulation (API plus excipients) under controlled conditions, such as elevated temperature and humidity. The samples are tested at regular intervals to evaluate any changes in the physical appearance, chemical composition, or microbial contamination. These studies can also involve monitoring for signs of degradation, such as color changes, precipitation, or the formation of harmful by-products.
- ○ **Outcome**: Stability testing can help determine the shelf life of the drug product and identify which excipients are suitable for use in the formulation. If degradation is observed, researchers can either modify the formulation or choose different excipients to ensure long-term stability.

Techniques Used in Preformulation

1. Physical Characterization

Particle Size and Morphology:

The size, shape, and surface area of particles are important physical properties that can significantly influence the solubility and dissolution rates of the Active Pharmaceutical Ingredient (API). The larger the surface area of the particles, the greater the potential for the drug to dissolve and be absorbed in the body. Smaller particles, with their increased surface area, often dissolve more quickly than larger particles, which can improve the rate at which the drug is absorbed.

Particle size affects not only the dissolution rate but also the stability and bioavailability of the drug. A drug that dissolves rapidly is more likely to be absorbed quickly in the gastrointestinal tract, leading to higher bioavailability. On the other hand, a drug that dissolves slowly may have delayed absorption, potentially reducing its effectiveness in treating the condition.

Morphology, or the shape of the particles, can also impact the behavior of the drug. Irregularly shaped particles may not pack as efficiently, leading to poor flow properties in powder formulations and affecting the uniformity of the drug dose. Spherical particles, in contrast, tend to flow more easily and can provide a more uniform mix in formulations.

Several techniques can be used to measure particle size and morphology:

- **Laser Diffraction**: This technique measures the scattering of light by particles in a sample, allowing the determination of particle size distribution.
- **Scanning Electron Microscopy (SEM)**: SEM provides detailed images of the particle surface, allowing the characterization of the shape and surface features of the particles.
- **Dynamic Light Scattering (DLS)**: DLS is used to measure the size of nanoparticles or colloidal suspensions by analyzing the fluctuations in the scattering light intensity caused by Brownian motion.

Polymorphism:

Polymorphism refers to the occurrence of different crystalline forms of the same compound. These different crystalline forms, known as polymorphs, can exhibit significantly different physical properties, including solubility, stability, and dissolution rate. Even though the chemical structure of the compound remains the same, the arrangement of molecules in the crystal lattice differs, which can lead to variations in the drug's behavior.

The solubility and dissolution rates of different polymorphs can vary widely. Some polymorphs may be more soluble, leading to faster absorption and higher bioavailability, while others may be less soluble and have slower dissolution rates. The more soluble polymorphs are often preferred for oral formulations because they improve the drug's effectiveness by ensuring faster absorption into the bloodstream.

In addition to solubility, polymorphism can also impact the stability of the drug. Some polymorphs are more stable under normal storage conditions, while others may be more prone to degradation over time. For instance, one polymorph might be more sensitive to temperature or humidity, leading to instability and reduced shelf life of the drug.

Several techniques are used to identify and characterize polymorphs:

- **X-Ray Diffraction (XRD)**: This is the most widely used method for identifying polymorphs, as different polymorphs of the same drug will have distinct X-ray diffraction patterns.
- **Differential Scanning Calorimetry (DSC)**: DSC can be used to measure the melting points of different polymorphs, which helps identify and differentiate them based on thermal properties.
- **Fourier Transform Infrared Spectroscopy (FTIR)**: FTIR is used to analyze the functional groups and bonding in different polymorphs, providing insight into the structural differences.

By identifying the polymorphs early in the preformulation stage, researchers can select the most suitable polymorph for the formulation, optimizing the drug's solubility, stability, and overall performance.

2. Chemical Characterization

pKa Determination:

The pKa of a compound refers to the pH at which half of the molecules of that compound are ionized and half are non-ionized. It is an important parameter in understanding the behavior of the compound in different environments, especially in terms of solubility and bioavailability. The ionization state of a compound can significantly influence its solubility, absorption, and distribution in the body.

At different pH levels, the solubility of a drug may change, depending on whether the drug is in its ionized or non-ionized form. Ionized molecules generally have higher solubility in aqueous environments, while non-ionized molecules are more likely to cross biological membranes, such as the intestinal wall, during absorption. Therefore, understanding the pKa of a drug helps predict how it will behave under various physiological conditions, such as in the stomach (acidic pH) and in the intestines (more neutral to slightly alkaline pH).

pKa determination is especially important when formulating oral dosage forms. For example, if a drug is weakly acidic or basic, its solubility in the stomach and intestines may differ, affecting its absorption. By knowing the pKa, formulators can design dosage forms that optimize drug solubility and bioavailability at the site of absorption.

The pKa of a drug is typically determined through various laboratory techniques, including:

- **Potentiometric Titration**: In this method, a known concentration of acid or base is added to the drug solution while the pH is measured. The pKa is determined by analyzing the inflection points in the titration curve, where the drug changes from its non-ionized to ionized form.
- **UV-Visible Spectroscopy**: Some compounds undergo changes in their UV-absorption spectra when they ionize. This change can be used to determine the pKa value by measuring the absorption at different pH levels.
- **NMR Spectroscopy**: Nuclear Magnetic Resonance (NMR) can be used to observe chemical shifts associated with ionization, helping in determining the pKa.

Stability Studies:

Stability studies are critical in evaluating the chemical stability of a drug, identifying degradation pathways, and predicting its shelf-life. Stability testing helps ensure that a drug remains effective, safe, and free from harmful degradation products throughout its storage and use by patients.

Drugs can undergo various types of chemical degradation, such as oxidation, hydrolysis, photodegradation, and racemization. These degradation processes can alter the drug's chemical structure, potentially leading to a loss of therapeutic effect, the formation of toxic metabolites, or a decrease in product quality.

Several aspects are assessed during stability studies:

- **Degradation Pathways**: Stability studies help identify the chemical reactions through which the API degrades over time. For example, a drug might degrade due to exposure to light, oxygen, or moisture. Identifying these pathways is critical in developing strategies to stabilize the drug and ensure its long-term effectiveness.
- **Shelf-Life Prediction**: Stability studies provide data on how long the drug will remain safe and effective. The shelf-life of a drug is typically determined by testing it under accelerated conditions (e.g., higher temperatures, humidity) and extrapolating the results to estimate its behavior under normal storage conditions. This allows manufacturers to assign an expiration date to the drug.
- **Formulation and Packaging Impact**: The stability of a drug is not only dependent on the API but also on the excipients used in the formulation and the type of packaging. Some excipients might promote degradation, or the packaging might not protect the drug from environmental factors. Stability studies assess how the combination of drug, excipients, and packaging materials affects the overall stability of the product.

Stability studies include various techniques to monitor the chemical integrity of the drug:

- **Accelerated Stability Testing**: This technique involves storing drug samples under high temperature, humidity, or light conditions to speed up degradation reactions. The results help predict the drug's long-term stability.
- **Real-Time Stability Testing**: In real-time testing, drug samples are stored under normal conditions (e.g., room temperature) over an extended period. This provides data on how the drug will behave in typical storage environments and helps determine its shelf-life.
- **High-Performance Liquid Chromatography (HPLC)**: HPLC is used to measure the concentration of the drug over time and to detect any degradation products. By comparing the amount of API in the drug formulation over time, researchers can identify whether the drug is breaking down into unwanted by-products.
- **Mass Spectrometry (MS)**: Mass spectrometry can be used to detect the molecular weight of degradation products, helping to identify the specific chemical changes that have occurred during the stability testing.

3. Spectroscopic Techniques

FTIR (Fourier Transform Infrared Spectroscopy):

Fourier Transform Infrared Spectroscopy (FTIR) is a powerful analytical technique used to identify the functional groups present in a compound and to study interactions between the Active Pharmaceutical Ingredient (API) and excipients. FTIR works by passing infrared light through a sample and measuring the absorption of specific wavelengths by different bonds and functional groups in the sample. The result is an infrared spectrum that provides detailed information about the molecular structure of the compound.

Importance in Pharmaceutical Development:

- **Identification of Functional Groups**: FTIR is widely used in the pharmaceutical industry to identify the presence of specific functional groups in the API and excipients. These functional groups, such as hydroxyl, carbonyl, and amine groups, play a significant role in the chemical behavior of a compound. For example, the presence of an amine group could indicate that the compound might be susceptible to oxidation or undergo certain chemical reactions.

- **Characterization of API and Excipients**: FTIR helps in understanding the molecular composition of both the API and the excipients, providing insight into how they interact. For instance, if the API and an excipient form a new bond or undergo any chemical changes during mixing, FTIR can detect these interactions, which may impact the formulation's stability and performance.

- **Study of Drug-Excipient Interactions**: In preformulation studies, FTIR is used to assess the compatibility of the API with various excipients. Excipients are often added to formulations to improve drug solubility, stability, or ease of administration. However, certain excipients might chemically interact with the API, leading to degradation or altered drug performance. FTIR helps identify such interactions by providing spectral data that shows changes in the molecular vibrations of the API and excipient when they are mixed.

How It Works:

- FTIR measures the absorption of infrared light by a sample across a range of wavelengths. The resulting absorption spectrum provides a "fingerprint" for the compound, which can be compared to known reference spectra to identify functional groups.

- By analyzing shifts in the absorption peaks, it is possible to detect any chemical changes or interactions in the drug-excipient mixture. For example, if a new peak appears or an existing peak shifts after mixing, this may indicate a chemical reaction or interaction.

Applications:

- **Drug Identification**: FTIR is often used to confirm the identity of a compound by comparing its spectra with reference spectra from known compounds.
- **Monitoring Drug Stability**: FTIR can be used in stability studies to monitor any chemical changes in the drug over time by comparing the spectra of the drug at different time intervals.
- **Quality Control**: FTIR is also useful in ensuring the consistency of a drug's formulation, as it can detect any deviations in the drug's chemical composition.

NMR (Nuclear Magnetic Resonance):

Nuclear Magnetic Resonance (NMR) spectroscopy is another critical technique used in pharmaceutical development to determine the molecular structure, purity, and interactions of the API. NMR is based on the principle that nuclei in a magnetic field resonate at specific frequencies depending on their chemical environment. By analyzing the signals produced, NMR provides detailed information about the molecular structure of a compound, including the arrangement of atoms and the presence of different functional groups.

Importance in Pharmaceutical Development:

- **Molecular Structure Determination**: NMR is one of the most powerful techniques for determining the detailed molecular structure of an API. It helps identify the arrangement of atoms in a molecule, providing information about chemical bonds, functional groups, and the overall architecture of the compound.
- **Purity Assessment**: NMR can be used to assess the purity of the API. Impurities, such as residual solvents or by-products from the synthesis, will produce additional signals in the NMR spectrum. By comparing the

intensity of these signals to the signals of the main API, the level of purity can be determined.

- **Characterization of Drug-Excipient Interactions**: NMR can also be used to study interactions between the API and excipients. This technique provides insights into how the drug molecules are affected by their environment, and it can detect the formation of new chemical bonds or interactions that might affect the stability, solubility, or bioavailability of the drug.

How It Works:

- NMR spectroscopy involves placing the sample in a strong magnetic field and irradiating it with radiofrequency radiation. The nuclei in the sample absorb energy at specific frequencies based on their chemical environment. These frequencies are recorded as peaks in the NMR spectrum, which is then analyzed to determine the structure of the molecule.
- The resulting NMR spectrum provides information on the number and type of hydrogen (proton NMR) or carbon (carbon-13 NMR) atoms in the molecule. By analyzing the shifts in these signals, researchers can deduce how the atoms are connected within the molecule.

Applications:

- **Structure Elucidation**: NMR is often the method of choice for determining the detailed structure of complex molecules. It can provide unambiguous structural data, especially for large or complex molecules like biologics or peptides.
- **Quantitative Analysis**: NMR can be used for quantitative analysis, such as determining the concentration of the API in a formulation or quantifying impurities in a sample.
- **Stability Studies**: NMR is also useful for studying the stability of drugs over time. Changes in the NMR spectrum can indicate chemical degradation or the formation of by-products.

4. Dissolution Testing

Dissolution testing is a critical part of the pharmaceutical development process, particularly for oral dosage forms such as tablets and capsules.

This test evaluates how quickly and efficiently the Active Pharmaceutical Ingredient (API) releases its active substance into the bloodstream when administered. The rate at which the drug dissolves in the gastrointestinal tract directly impacts its bioavailability, which is a key determinant of the drug's therapeutic effectiveness.

Importance:

Dissolution testing is essential for the following reasons:

1. **Bioavailability Prediction:** The dissolution rate of a drug is often a good indicator of how well it will be absorbed in the body. A faster dissolution rate generally correlates with quicker absorption and higher bioavailability, which can lead to a faster onset of action. On the other hand, slow dissolution may result in delayed drug absorption, potentially reducing its therapeutic effect.

2. **Formulation Development:** During the preformulation and formulation stages, dissolution testing helps in selecting the right excipients and dosage form to optimize the release of the API. If a drug does not dissolve adequately, formulations such as solubility enhancers or controlled-release systems may be employed to improve its release profile.

3. **Quality Control:** Dissolution testing serves as a quality control measure to ensure batch-to-batch consistency in drug release. It helps verify that every batch of the drug product behaves similarly in terms of drug release, providing confidence that the drug will work consistently in patients.

4. **Regulatory Requirements:** Regulatory bodies such as the FDA, EMA, and CDSCO require dissolution testing as part of the drug approval process. It is used to demonstrate that the drug product performs as expected under conditions that simulate the human gastrointestinal tract.

5. **Comparative Studies:** Dissolution testing is used to compare different formulations of the same drug. For example, immediate-release formulations may be compared with extended-release or controlled-release formulations to determine which one provides the most effective release profile. It can also be used to compare the brand-name drug with generic formulations to ensure that the generic product releases the API at the same rate.

Techniques:

Dissolution testing involves placing a drug formulation into a dissolution medium that simulates the conditions of the human gastrointestinal tract. The key techniques include:

1. **Dissolution Apparatus:**

    ○ **Apparatus 1 (Basket Method):** In this method, the drug formulation is placed inside a small basket, which is then submerged in a dissolution medium (usually water or a buffer solution). The basket rotates at a constant speed, mimicking the movement of the drug in the stomach and intestines. This method is commonly used for capsules, tablets, and other solid dosage forms.

    ○ **Apparatus 2 (Paddle Method):** In this method, the drug formulation is placed in a vessel with a rotating paddle at the top. The paddle stirs the dissolution medium, helping to release the API from the dosage form. This method is often used for tablets and other solid oral dosage forms that are not contained in a basket.

2. **Sampling and Measurement:**

    ○ During the dissolution test, samples are withdrawn at predefined time intervals to measure the amount of the API that has dissolved. The concentration of the drug in the dissolution medium is determined using techniques such as UV-Visible Spectroscopy or HPLC (High-Performance Liquid Chromatography).

    ○ The dissolution profile is plotted, showing the percentage of the API released over time. This helps to assess the rate of dissolution and provides valuable information about the formulation's performance.

3. **Simulated Gastric and Intestinal Fluid:**

    ○ To closely mimic the conditions in the human gastrointestinal tract, dissolution testing is often performed using media that replicate the pH of the stomach (pH 1.2) and the intestines (pH 6.8 to 7.4). Different dissolution media are used to evaluate how the drug will perform in different environments within the GI tract.

4. **Factors Affecting Dissolution Testing:**

- **Temperature**: The dissolution medium is typically maintained at a temperature of 37°C, which approximates the temperature of the human body.
- **Rotation Speed**: The speed of rotation of the basket or paddle influences the rate at which the drug is released into the dissolution medium. The standard rotation speeds are typically 50 or 100 rpm, but this may vary depending on the drug and formulation.

5. **Dissolution Profile Comparison:**

- Dissolution profiles can be compared between different formulations of the same drug or between different brands to assess bioequivalence. For example, a generic version of a drug must show similar dissolution characteristics to the branded product to ensure that it will deliver the same therapeutic effect.

Applications:

1. **Formulation Optimization**: Dissolution testing is used to optimize the formulation during the early stages of development. For example, if a drug is found to dissolve too slowly, formulation scientists may adjust the particle size, use solubilizing agents, or modify the excipients to enhance dissolution.
2. **Bioequivalence Studies**: In the case of generic drugs, dissolution testing is crucial for demonstrating that the generic formulation releases the active ingredient at the same rate as the innovator product. Regulatory agencies typically require dissolution testing to establish that generic drugs are bioequivalent to the reference product.
3. **Stability Studies**: Dissolution testing can also be used in stability studies to monitor changes in the dissolution profile over time. If the dissolution rate changes during storage, this could indicate that the drug is degrading or that the formulation is unstable.
4. **In Vitro-In Vivo Correlation (IVIVC)**: Dissolution testing can be used to predict how the drug will behave in the body. In certain cases, dissolution data can be correlated with in vivo data (i.e., the actual absorption of the drug in humans) to establish a relationship between

the rate of drug dissolution and its absorption.

Dissolution testing is a vital tool in drug development that helps ensure that a drug is absorbed properly and performs as expected in the body. By evaluating how quickly a drug releases its active ingredient, dissolution testing provides essential information about the drug's bioavailability, formulation quality, and potential therapeutic efficacy.

2.2 Formulation Development

Strategies for Developing Various Dosage Forms:

1. Oral Dosage Forms:

Oral dosage forms, including tablets, capsules, solutions, and suspensions, are among the most common methods of drug administration. Developing an effective oral dosage form requires careful consideration of various factors such as the drug's solubility, stability, release profile, and patient compliance. Below are the strategies used in the development of two major types of oral dosage forms: tablets and capsules, and solutions and suspensions.

Tablets and Capsules:

Tablets and capsules are the most widely used forms of oral drug delivery. Tablets are solid dosage forms that typically contain the API along with excipients, and they are designed for oral ingestion. Capsules are similar, but they contain the drug inside a gelatin or other soluble shell. Both tablets and capsules must be formulated to ensure that the drug is released in the body in a controlled and effective manner.

Strategies for Tablets and Capsules Formulation:

- **Optimizing Excipients for Tablet Compression:**

  - Excipients are necessary for tablet formulation to ensure that the tablet can be compressed into a uniform shape and remain stable. Excipients such as binders (e.g., starch, cellulose) help the tablet hold together, while disintegrants (e.g., croscarmellose sodium) ensure the tablet breaks apart properly when ingested, aiding in drug release.
  - Lubricants like magnesium stearate prevent sticking during tablet compression, and fillers (e.g., lactose, microcrystalline cellulose) are added to adjust the tablet's weight and bulk.

- **Ensuring Uniform Distribution of the API:**

  - Achieving uniform distribution of the API in a tablet or capsule is critical to ensure consistent dosing. This requires precise mixing of the API with excipients to avoid variations in the drug content in individual doses. Granulation (wet or dry) is often used to improve the flow properties and uniformity of the powder mix.

- **Achieving Desired Release Profiles (Immediate-Release vs. Sustained-Release):**

  - **Immediate-Release (IR):** Immediate-release tablets are designed to release the API rapidly into the bloodstream. Strategies include using fast-dissolving excipients or selecting the right particle size of the API to ensure rapid dissolution.
  - **Sustained-Release (SR) or Controlled-Release (CR):** Sustained-release formulations release the drug gradually over a prolonged period. To achieve this, different excipients are used to control the drug's release rate, such as polymers (e.g., hydroxypropyl methylcellulose) that form a gel when exposed to water, allowing for the slow release of the drug.
  - Other release-modifying techniques include matrix tablets (where the drug is embedded in a polymeric matrix), coating the drug with a polymer film, and using osmotic pumps.

Solutions and Suspensions:
While tablets and capsules are solid dosage forms, solutions and suspensions are liquid dosage forms used when a drug needs to be delivered in a liquid form for better bioavailability or easier administration, especially in patients who have difficulty swallowing pills.

Formulation Strategies for Solutions and Suspensions:

- **Ensuring Solubility of the Drug:**

  - The solubility of the API is the primary factor in the formulation of solutions. If the API is poorly soluble in water, solubilizing agents, such as surfactants or co-solvents (e.g., alcohol, glycerin), may be used to improve the solubility.
  - For poorly water-soluble drugs, techniques like micronization (reducing the particle size) or the use of complexing agents like cyclodextrins may be used to increase the solubility and thus improve the drug's bioavailability.

- **Stabilizing the Suspension:**

- Suspensions contain solid particles dispersed in a liquid. The primary challenge in suspension formulations is ensuring that the solid particles remain evenly distributed and do not settle over time. To achieve this, suspensions require stabilizers, such as suspending agents (e.g., xanthan gum, cellulose derivatives) that prevent settling and aggregation of particles.
- Preservatives, such as sodium benzoate, may also be added to prevent microbial growth in liquid formulations, particularly for oral solutions or suspensions intended for long-term use.

- **Ensuring Ease of Administration:**

  - Liquid dosage forms, such as solutions and suspensions, need to be formulated to ensure ease of administration. This includes optimizing the viscosity and taste of the formulation. For example, sweeteners and flavoring agents (e.g., sucrose, citric acid, menthol) are added to mask the unpleasant taste of bitter drugs.
  - For suspensions, the particle size should be controlled to prevent a gritty texture, and the formulation should have the right viscosity to make it easy for patients to swallow. The formulation should also flow easily without being too thin or too thick.

- **Preservative-Free Formulations**: Some oral solutions and suspensions are designed to be preservative-free to avoid potential irritation or allergic reactions. In these cases, the solution or suspension is typically packed in single-dose units or stored in sealed containers to prevent contamination.

2. Parenteral Dosage Forms

Parenteral dosage forms, particularly injectables, are designed for the administration of drugs by routes other than the digestive tract. These forms include intravenous (IV), intramuscular (IM), subcutaneous (SC), and other injection methods. Parenteral formulations require stringent control of multiple factors to ensure the drug is delivered safely, effectively, and consistently. Two of the main challenges in developing parenteral formulations are **sterility** and **stability**, which are essential for ensuring the safety and efficacy of the drug.

Injectables:

Injectables are used for the rapid and precise delivery of drugs, often in emergency situations or when rapid onset of action is required. These formulations are highly effective for drugs that are poorly absorbed via oral administration or when a high level of bioavailability is necessary.

Key Considerations for Injectables:

- **Sterility:**

  - Sterility is the most critical requirement for injectable formulations. Any microbial contamination in parenteral products can cause serious infections, potentially leading to life-threatening conditions. To ensure sterility, parenteral formulations are subjected to **aseptic manufacturing** processes, including sterilization of both the product and the containers (e.g., vials, syringes). Sterilization techniques such as **autoclaving, dry heat sterilization**, or **filtration** (for heat-sensitive drugs) are employed.
  - The formulation must also be packaged in sterile containers, and the final product should remain free from microbial contamination throughout its shelf life. Preservatives (e.g., benzyl alcohol, phenol) may be added to prevent microbial growth in multi-dose vials or other packaging types that are intended to be opened multiple times.
  - The packaging itself must be sealed in a way that ensures sterility is maintained during storage and transportation. The final container closure system is critical in protecting the formulation from contamination.

- **Stability:**

  - The stability of injectable formulations is another major concern. Drugs in parenteral dosage forms are susceptible to degradation due to factors such as temperature, light, pH, and the nature of excipients used in the formulation. Chemical degradation can lead to reduced drug efficacy, formation of harmful degradation products, or loss of sterility.
  - Stability testing is crucial to ensure that the API remains effective over time. Accelerated stability studies, real-time testing, and stress testing under various conditions (e.g., varying temperatures, humidity, and light exposure) are used to predict the shelf life of

injectable products.

- Special care is taken to ensure that the drug maintains its intended therapeutic effect throughout the product's lifecycle, even under storage conditions.

Formulation Challenges:

Formulating parenteral drugs presents several challenges that must be addressed to ensure the product is safe, effective, and stable.

1. **pH Control:**

   - pH is an essential parameter in injectable formulations. The pH of the formulation can affect the solubility of the drug, the stability of the API, and the comfort of the injection. A pH that is too acidic or too alkaline may cause irritation at the injection site or lead to precipitation of the drug, making it ineffective.
   - pH control is often achieved by using buffer systems. A buffer is a solution that resists changes in pH when small amounts of acids or bases are added. The selection of the buffer system depends on the drug's characteristics and the desired pH for optimal drug solubility and stability. For instance, a phosphate buffer or citrate buffer may be used to maintain the pH within a specific range that is suitable for the drug.
   - Ensuring that the pH is within the optimal range also minimizes the risk of causing irritation or damage to tissues when the drug is injected.

2. **Osmolality:**

   - Osmolality refers to the concentration of solute particles in a solution. It is a critical factor in injectable formulations because if the osmolality of the drug formulation differs too much from the osmolality of the body's fluids (e.g., blood or interstitial fluid), it can lead to **pain, irritation**, or **hemolysis** (rupture of red blood cells).
   - Injectable formulations need to be isotonic, meaning their osmolality must be similar to that of bodily fluids, to ensure they are well-tolerated by the body. If the formulation is hypertonic (higher osmolality), it may cause pain or swelling at the injection site.

Hypotonic (lower osmolality) formulations can cause cell rupture or discomfort.

- To control osmolality, formulators use **osmotic agents** like sodium chloride (salts), dextrose, or other tonicity-adjusting excipients. The exact osmotic pressure is calculated to match physiological conditions to prevent adverse effects.

3. **Buffer Systems:**

- Buffer systems are essential for maintaining the desired pH and preventing fluctuations in the formulation's acidity or alkalinity. They are designed to resist changes in pH upon dilution or administration, ensuring that the drug remains stable and effective.
- The selection of buffer systems is based on the pH stability range of the API. For instance, weak acids or bases with their conjugate salts are typically used as buffers (e.g., phosphate buffer, acetate buffer, citrate buffer).
- Buffer systems also help stabilize the formulation against degradation and prevent the precipitation of the drug. A stable pH and buffering capacity contribute to the long-term stability of the injectable product, ensuring that the drug remains effective and safe throughout its shelf life.

4. **Solubility Enhancers:**

- Some APIs, particularly those that are poorly soluble in water, require solubility enhancers to ensure that the drug can be dissolved and delivered effectively via injection. Techniques such as **complexation, co-solvency,** or **use of surfactants** may be used to improve solubility and prevent precipitation at the injection site.
- Solubility enhancers, such as cyclodextrins (which form inclusion complexes with the drug) or surfactants (e.g., polysorbates), are often included in parenteral formulations to improve drug solubility and stability, particularly for hydrophobic or lipophilic drugs.

5. **Sterile Filtration and Packaging:**

- ○ Sterile filtration is an important process in the preparation of parenteral products. Since parenteral formulations are delivered directly into the bloodstream, they must be free from microbial contamination. Filtration through 0.22-micron filters is commonly used to remove bacterial contaminants.
- ○ The final packaging of injectables, such as vials or prefilled syringes, must also maintain the sterility of the product. The packaging material and closure system are designed to prevent contamination, leakage, and degradation, while also being compatible with the drug formulation.

3. Topical Dosage Forms

Topical dosage forms are used for the application of drugs directly to the skin or mucous membranes. These formulations are designed to deliver the drug locally at the site of application or, in some cases, for systemic absorption. Common types of topical dosage forms include creams, ointments, gels, and lotions. Each of these formulations has distinct characteristics and formulation challenges. A key aspect of formulating these products is ensuring compatibility between the Active Pharmaceutical Ingredient (API) and excipients, as well as ensuring the drug is effectively absorbed through the skin.

Creams, Ointments, Gels, and Lotions:

Topical dosage forms include various types such as creams, ointments, gels, and lotions. Each of these formulations has specific benefits depending on the therapeutic application, the skin condition being treated, and the desired effect of the API.

- **Creams:**

  - ○ Creams are semisolid emulsions that consist of water and oil phases. They are designed to provide a cooling, soothing effect on the skin, and they can be used for a variety of conditions, from hydrating dry skin to delivering APIs for conditions such as fungal infections or eczema.
  - ○ **Formulation Considerations:** Creams need to be formulated with excipients that stabilize the emulsion and provide proper consistency. The ratio of oil to water is critical for ensuring the appropriate texture and spreadability of the cream. Surfactants are often used to keep the

emulsion stable and prevent separation of the oil and water phases.

- **Ointments:**

  - Ointments are greasy, hydrophobic formulations that contain little or no water. They are typically used for their occlusive properties, as they create a barrier that helps retain moisture and can be used to treat dry skin conditions, inflammation, and localized infections.
  - **Formulation Considerations**: Ointments need to be formulated with lipophilic excipients, such as petroleum jelly or beeswax, to create a stable, thick base. The API is incorporated into these fatty bases, which allows for controlled, sustained release of the drug over time.

- **Gels:**

  - Gels are semisolid systems that contain a gelling agent, such as carbomer or hydroxyethyl cellulose, which provides a jelly-like consistency. Gels are often used for their cooling effect and are ideal for conditions that require a non-greasy feel on the skin.
  - **Formulation Considerations**: Gels are typically clear or translucent and are formulated with aqueous solvents, often containing alcohol. This provides a refreshing sensation, but care must be taken to ensure that the alcohol does not irritate sensitive skin. Gels are ideal for delivering APIs that need to be absorbed quickly.

- **Lotions:**

  - Lotions are liquid emulsions that are easier to spread over large areas of skin. They are typically used for conditions that require hydration or to treat conditions like rashes or sunburn.
  - **Formulation Considerations**: Lotions are less greasy than creams or ointments and are generally water-based. Excipients such as emulsifiers and stabilizers are used to maintain the uniformity of the lotion and prevent separation. Lotions are often formulated to be easy to apply and absorb quickly, making them ideal for patients who prefer lightweight formulations.

Bioavailability Considerations:

Bioavailability is a critical factor in the formulation of topical drugs, as it refers to the extent and rate at which the active ingredient is absorbed through the skin and becomes available at the site of action or systemically. For topical formulations, achieving adequate bioavailability depends on several factors:

1. **Skin Penetration:**

   - The skin acts as a barrier that prevents the entry of most substances. Therefore, ensuring that the API can penetrate this barrier is crucial for the efficacy of the topical formulation. The stratum corneum (the outermost layer of the skin) is a particularly important barrier that must be overcome for the drug to be absorbed.
   - **Strategies for Enhancing Skin Penetration:**

     - **Use of Permeation Enhancers:** Certain excipients can be added to the formulation to enhance the permeability of the skin. These enhancers, such as alcohols (e.g., ethanol), surfactants, and fatty acids, work by temporarily disrupting the skin's barrier function, allowing the drug to penetrate more easily.
     - **Nanotechnology**: The use of nanoparticles and nanocarriers, such as liposomes or micelles, is increasingly popular in topical formulations. These carriers can encapsulate the drug and help it pass through the skin more effectively.

2. **Partition Coefficient (Lipophilicity vs. Hydrophilicity):**

   - The partition coefficient of the drug (the ratio of the drug's concentration in oil to its concentration in water) plays an important role in its absorption. Lipophilic drugs tend to permeate the skin better than hydrophilic drugs. Therefore, the solubility of the API in the skin's lipid-rich environment is a key factor in determining how well it is absorbed.
   - **Formulation Strategy**: For drugs that are hydrophilic, formulators may use oil-in-water emulsions (such as creams) or use penetration enhancers to increase drug solubility in the skin's lipophilic layers. Lipophilic drugs, on the other hand, may be formulated into ointments or oils for better absorption.

3. **Vehicle Selection:**

- The vehicle in which the API is dissolved or dispersed plays a significant role in skin penetration. The vehicle must not only help in solubilizing the API but also act as a medium that supports its effective delivery through the skin.
- **Appropriate Vehicle for the Drug**: For example, a lipophilic API may be best suited for an ointment base that is thick and greasy, allowing the drug to remain in contact with the skin longer and enhancing absorption. In contrast, a hydrophilic API may be better formulated in a water-based gel or cream that facilitates faster absorption.
- The choice of excipients is crucial for maintaining the integrity of the formulation and ensuring that the drug remains stable while also being able to penetrate the skin barrier effectively.

4. **Localized vs. Systemic Delivery:**

- **Localized Delivery**: Some topical formulations are designed to deliver the drug only at the site of application (e.g., treating a skin infection or inflammation). In these cases, the drug's absorption into the bloodstream is not a primary concern. Instead, the focus is on ensuring the drug remains at the site for sustained action.
- **Systemic Delivery**: Some topical formulations, such as transdermal patches or other delivery systems designed for systemic drug delivery, are intended to release the drug slowly over time for absorption through the skin into the bloodstream. For systemic delivery, it is essential to ensure that the drug can penetrate deep enough into the skin to reach the bloodstream and exert a therapeutic effect.

Steps Involved in Formulating a New Product
1. Selection of Drug Formulation Type:
The first step in formulating a new pharmaceutical product is selecting the most appropriate drug formulation type. This decision is primarily based on the physical and chemical properties of the Active Pharmaceutical Ingredient (API), as well as the intended therapeutic use of the drug. The selected dosage form must be suitable for achieving the desired therapeutic effect while maintaining the drug's stability, bioavailability, and ease of

administration.

Factors to Consider for Selecting the Formulation Type:

1. **Solubility**:

   - Solubility plays a critical role in determining the dosage form. For instance, poorly soluble drugs may be better formulated as solutions or suspensions to improve absorption. On the other hand, drugs with good solubility might be formulated as tablets or capsules for convenience.
   - Drugs with low solubility may require specialized formulations, such as **lipid-based formulations**, **solid dispersions**, or **nanotechnology** approaches to enhance bioavailability.

2. **Stability**:

   - The chemical and physical stability of the API must be considered. Some drugs are sensitive to light, heat, or moisture and may require specialized packaging or a formulation that shields them from environmental factors.
   - If a drug is unstable in the gastrointestinal tract, for example, a parenteral or transdermal form might be preferred to ensure more controlled and stable delivery.

3. **Therapeutic Target**:

   - The therapeutic target also influences the selection of the formulation type. For local effects (e.g., treating skin conditions, eye infections, or inflammation), topical formulations (creams, ointments, gels) are ideal. For systemic effects, oral, parenteral, or transdermal formulations may be more appropriate depending on the drug's absorption characteristics and desired release profile.

4. **Route of Administration**:

   - **Oral Formulations**: If the drug is intended for systemic action and has good solubility and stability, oral formulations such as tablets, capsules, or liquids are commonly chosen. Oral tablets and capsules are preferred for patient convenience and ease of use.

- **Injectables**: If rapid action is needed, or if the drug is poorly absorbed through the gastrointestinal tract, parenteral formulations (e.g., intravenous injections or subcutaneous injections) may be the preferred route. Injectable formulations require careful consideration of sterility, stability, and dosage precision.
- **Topical Formulations**: For localized therapeutic effects, topical creams, ointments, gels, or lotions are selected. These are suitable for treating skin conditions or providing localized relief without systemic absorption.

5. **Patient Compliance:**

- The ease of administration is another important factor. Oral tablets or capsules are convenient and easy to take, which enhances patient adherence. In contrast, injectable drugs may require administration by healthcare professionals, which could affect patient compliance. Topical formulations, though simple to apply, may require careful consideration of skin sensitivity and application frequency.
- The dosage form chosen must also take into account factors like taste, frequency of administration, and the possibility of dose adjustment.

6. **Release Profile:**

- The desired release profile is another deciding factor. Immediate-release formulations are suitable when rapid onset of action is required, whereas sustained-release or controlled-release formulations are used when prolonged therapeutic action is needed. For instance, sustained-release tablets release the drug gradually over time, providing a longer duration of action, which is often preferred for chronic conditions.

7. **Cost Considerations:**

- The manufacturing cost of the dosage form should also be taken into account. Tablets and capsules are relatively easy and cost-effective to manufacture, whereas injectables and complex formulations (e.g., biologics) can be more expensive to produce.

- Cost-effective formulation strategies must be balanced with the therapeutic needs of the drug, especially when the target market includes populations in low-resource settings.

The careful selection of the drug formulation type ensures that the drug can be delivered effectively and efficiently to the patient, with maximum therapeutic benefit and minimal side effects. This selection also guides the subsequent stages of product development, including preformulation studies, formulation design, and scale-up for manufacturing.

2. Selection of Excipients

The selection of excipients is a critical step in the formulation development process. Excipients are inactive substances that are added to the drug formulation to facilitate the manufacturing process, enhance the stability and efficacy of the drug, and improve patient acceptance. Excipients do not have therapeutic effects, but they play an important role in ensuring that the drug product performs as expected and remains safe for use.

Excipients are chosen based on the drug's specific requirements and the type of formulation being developed. They must be compatible with the Active Pharmaceutical Ingredient (API) and should support the desired release profile, stability, and bioavailability of the drug.

Key Types of Excipients and Their Roles:

1. **Binders:**

   - **Role**: Binders are excipients used to hold the components of a tablet together. They ensure that the tablet maintains its integrity during handling and storage. Binders help in tablet compression by allowing the API and excipients to form a cohesive mass.
   - **Selection Criteria**: The choice of binder depends on the formulation type, such as whether the drug requires immediate release or controlled release. For example, **hydroxypropyl methylcellulose (HPMC)** is often used in sustained-release formulations, while **starch** and **polyvinylpyrrolidone (PVP)** are common in immediate-release tablets.

2. **Stabilizers:**

- ○ **Role:** Stabilizers are used to maintain the chemical and physical stability of the drug during manufacturing, storage, and throughout the product's shelf life. These excipients help prevent degradation of the drug due to exposure to environmental factors such as light, heat, oxygen, and moisture.
- ○ **Selection Criteria:** The stabilizer should be selected based on the type of drug and its degradation pathway. For example, antioxidants like **ascorbic acid** or **sodium metabisulfite** are used to prevent oxidative degradation of sensitive APIs. Similarly, stabilizers like **citric acid** may be used to maintain the pH of the formulation.

3. **Preservatives:**

- ○ **Role:** Preservatives are added to formulations to prevent microbial contamination and growth. This is particularly important in liquid formulations, where the risk of microbial contamination is higher.
- ○ **Selection Criteria:** The choice of preservative depends on the type of formulation and its intended shelf life. Common preservatives include **benzyl alcohol**, **sodium benzoate**, and **parabens**. Preservatives must be chosen carefully to ensure they do not interact with the API and compromise the drug's safety and effectiveness.

4. **Flavoring Agents:**

- ○ **Role:** Flavoring agents are used in liquid formulations, particularly for oral solutions or suspensions, to mask the bitter taste of the API and make the drug more palatable, improving patient compliance, especially in pediatric or geriatric populations.
- ○ **Selection Criteria:** Flavoring agents should be chosen based on the drug's taste profile and the target patient group. For instance, sweeteners like **sucrose, xylitol,** or **sorbitol** are commonly used in oral formulations to improve taste. Additionally, flavoring agents like **orange, cherry,** or **mint** are selected to improve the sensory appeal of the drug.

5. **Disintegrants:**

- ○ **Role**: Disintegrants are added to solid dosage forms like tablets to facilitate their breakup in the gastrointestinal tract, ensuring that the drug is released and absorbed effectively. Disintegrants promote the rapid disintegration of tablets when they come into contact with water or gastric fluids.
- ○ **Selection Criteria**: The choice of disintegrant depends on the type of tablet and the desired release rate. Examples of disintegrants include **croscarmellose sodium**, **sodium starch glycolate**, and **crospovidone**.

6. **Lubricants:**

- ○ **Role**: Lubricants are added to formulations to reduce friction during tablet compression and to improve the flow of powder during manufacturing. Lubricants ensure that tablets are formed easily and do not stick to the equipment, leading to more uniform and consistent tablets.
- ○ **Selection Criteria**: The most commonly used lubricants are **magnesium stearate** and **stearic acid**, which are effective at low concentrations. It is essential to use the right amount of lubricant, as excessive amounts can affect tablet dissolution.

7. **Solvents and Co-Solvents:**

- ○ **Role**: In liquid formulations such as solutions, solvents and co-solvents are used to dissolve the API and improve its solubility. These excipients help in the formulation of solutions, suspensions, and injectable products.
- ○ **Selection Criteria**: The solvent should be chosen based on its ability to dissolve the API without causing any degradation. **Water, ethanol,** and **propylene glycol** are commonly used solvents. For poorly soluble drugs, co-solvents like **glycerin** or **ethanol** may be used to improve solubility.

8. **Emulsifiers:**

- ○ **Role**: Emulsifiers are used in the formulation of emulsions, where one liquid is dispersed in another (e.g., oil in water or water in oil). Emulsifiers stabilize the mixture by reducing the surface tension between the two immiscible phases, preventing phase separation.

- **Selection Criteria**: The choice of emulsifier depends on the type of emulsion required. **Polysorbates (e.g., Tween 80)** are commonly used for oil-in-water emulsions, while **cetyl alcohol** and **sorbitan esters** are used for water-in-oil emulsions.

9. **Surfactants**:

- **Role**: Surfactants are used to modify the surface tension of liquids, which helps improve the solubility of poorly soluble drugs. They are also used in topical formulations to enhance drug penetration through the skin.
- **Selection Criteria**: Surfactants are often chosen for their ability to solubilize the drug or enhance absorption. For example, **polysorbates** and **sodium lauryl sulfate** are commonly used surfactants in oral and injectable formulations.

Selection Process:

The selection of excipients depends on the formulation's specific requirements and the nature of the drug. The excipient must be compatible with the API to prevent chemical interactions that could affect the drug's stability, efficacy, or safety. Additionally, excipients should be chosen based on their ability to perform their intended function without interfering with the drug's pharmacological action.

When selecting excipients, formulators consider factors such as:

- **Compatibility**: Ensuring that excipients do not chemically interact with the API, leading to degradation or reduced efficacy.
- **Functionality**: The excipient must serve its intended purpose, such as enhancing solubility, stabilizing the formulation, or improving drug release.
- **Patient Acceptance**: Excipients should be chosen to ensure that the final product is well-tolerated by patients, with minimal risk of adverse effects.

The careful selection of excipients plays a vital role in ensuring that the drug product is safe, stable, effective, and well-accepted by patients, leading to better therapeutic outcomes and improved patient compliance.

3. Preformulation Studies

Preformulation studies are the foundational phase in the development of a new pharmaceutical product. During this stage, the physical, chemical, and compatibility characteristics of the drug (Active Pharmaceutical Ingredient or API) and excipients are carefully assessed. This helps in determining how the drug will behave during formulation, manufacturing, and after administration. The primary goal of preformulation is to optimize the formulation by understanding the properties of the API and selecting the right excipients that will ensure the stability, bioavailability, and effectiveness of the drug.

Understanding the Physical Characteristics of the Drug:

The physical characteristics of the API play a significant role in its solubility, dissolution rate, and absorption. By understanding these properties early on, formulators can identify potential challenges that may affect the drug's performance. Some of the key physical characteristics assessed during preformulation include:

1. **Particle Size and Surface Area**: The size and surface area of the particles of the API affect its solubility and dissolution rate. Smaller particles typically have a larger surface area, which enhances dissolution and bioavailability. Understanding the particle size distribution allows formulators to optimize the drug's release and absorption rates.

2. **Polymorphism**: Polymorphism refers to the existence of different crystalline forms of the same drug, each with distinct physical properties, including solubility and stability. Identifying the most stable and soluble polymorph is critical for selecting the right form of the drug for formulation.

3. **Solubility**: The solubility of the drug determines how much of it will dissolve in bodily fluids to be absorbed. Preformulation studies help in assessing the solubility of the API in different solvents and under various conditions (e.g., pH, temperature) to determine the best formulation strategy.

4. **Melting Point**: The melting point of the drug is an important indicator of its purity and stability. Drugs with a high melting point are often more stable and easier to handle during manufacturing, while those with lower melting points may require special storage or formulation conditions.

5. **Hygroscopicity**: Some drugs absorb moisture from the air, which can lead to instability or degradation. Determining the hygroscopic nature of the API helps in selecting the proper packaging and storage conditions to maintain its integrity.

Understanding the Chemical Characteristics of the Drug:

The chemical properties of the API influence its stability, solubility, and interactions with excipients. By evaluating the chemical nature of the drug, formulators can predict potential degradation pathways and identify the best approach to enhance its stability. Some of the key chemical properties assessed include:

1. **pKa and Ionization**: The pKa of the API provides information about its ionization at different pH levels, which affects its solubility and absorption. Knowledge of the pKa helps in designing formulations that optimize solubility and bioavailability, particularly in the gastrointestinal tract, where pH varies.
2. **Stability and Degradation Pathways**: Identifying the chemical stability of the drug is essential to ensure that it remains effective over time. Preformulation studies help in understanding how the drug degrades under various environmental conditions such as temperature, light, and humidity. This allows formulators to design stable formulations with appropriate shelf lives.
3. **Chemical Interactions with Excipients**: The chemical compatibility between the API and excipients is crucial to avoid unwanted reactions that could affect the drug's performance. Preformulation studies assess how the API interacts with different excipients (such as binders, stabilizers, and preservatives) to ensure that there are no adverse chemical reactions during the formulation process.

Assessing Compatibility with Excipients:

Excipients are used to support the formulation and delivery of the drug, and their compatibility with the API is critical for ensuring the drug's stability, bioavailability, and safety. Preformulation studies help assess whether the excipients will interact with the API and whether these interactions could lead to issues like reduced efficacy or drug degradation.

1. **Excipients Selection**: Based on the drug's properties, suitable excipients are selected to enhance the drug's solubility, stability, and bioavailability. For example, solubilizing agents or surfactants may be used to improve the solubility of a poorly water-soluble drug, while stabilizers may be needed for drugs prone to degradation.

2. **Chemical Interactions**: Studies such as **Fourier Transform Infrared Spectroscopy (FTIR)** or **Differential Scanning Calorimetry (DSC)** are used to detect any chemical interactions between the drug and excipients. If any reaction occurs, it could impact the drug's stability, solubility, or overall performance. For instance, certain excipients might accelerate the degradation of the drug, leading to reduced therapeutic efficacy or safety concerns.

3. **Physical Compatibility**: In addition to chemical interactions, physical compatibility is also crucial. Some excipients may affect the API's physical properties, such as its solubility or stability under specific conditions (e.g., temperature, humidity). For example, an excipient that forms a gel or sticky residue might impair the release of the drug from a tablet or capsule.

By performing these preformulation tests, formulators can identify and address potential compatibility issues early in the development process, reducing the risk of failure in later stages of formulation and manufacturing.

4. Prototype Formulation

The **prototype formulation** is a critical early-stage step in the development of a pharmaceutical product. It involves the preparation of a preliminary version of the drug formulation using the selected excipients, based on the findings from preformulation studies. This prototype is used to evaluate how the Active Pharmaceutical Ingredient (API) behaves within the chosen formulation and provides insight into the feasibility of scaling up the formulation for commercial production.

Creating a prototype formulation allows formulators to test and optimize various parameters, ensuring that the final product will meet the required quality standards. These initial formulations are typically small-scale and are tested for a range of important characteristics that influence the drug's efficacy, safety, and patient acceptance.

Steps Involved in Creating and Testing the Prototype Formulation:

1. **Selection of Excipients:**

○ Based on the preformulation data, excipients such as binders, disintegrants, lubricants, stabilizers, and preservatives are chosen to support the desired formulation type (e.g., tablet, suspension, or cream). The excipients selected must be compatible with the API and capable of achieving the desired drug release profile and stability.

2. **Formulation Preparation**:

   ○ Once the excipients are selected, the prototype formulation is prepared. The preparation process involves blending the API with the excipients to create a homogenous mixture. The formulation may undergo additional processes, such as granulation (wet or dry), mixing, and compression (for tablet formulations), or homogenization (for liquid formulations).
   ○ During this stage, special attention is given to ensuring uniform distribution of the API throughout the formulation. This ensures that each dose contains the correct amount of the active ingredient.

3. **Quality Control Testing**:

   ○ After the prototype formulation is prepared, it is subjected to a series of quality control tests to evaluate its characteristics and performance. These tests are designed to ensure that the formulation meets the required standards for stability, safety, and efficacy.

Key Quality Control Parameters Tested in Prototype Formulation:

- **Dissolution Rate:**

   ○ Dissolution testing is one of the most important tests conducted on the prototype formulation. This test evaluates how quickly the API is released from the dosage form into the dissolution medium. It simulates the conditions the drug will face in the human body, particularly in the gastrointestinal tract. A consistent and predictable dissolution rate is essential for ensuring that the drug is absorbed effectively after administration.
   ○ For example, immediate-release tablets are tested to ensure they dissolve rapidly, while controlled-release formulations are tested to

assess the rate of drug release over time.

- **Stability:**

  - Stability studies are conducted to assess how the prototype formulation performs under various environmental conditions, such as changes in temperature, humidity, and light. The goal is to determine if the formulation maintains its integrity, efficacy, and safety over time.
  - Stability tests can include **accelerated stability testing** (exposing the formulation to extreme conditions to speed up degradation) and **real-time stability testing** (storing the formulation at standard conditions to observe long-term stability).
  - The stability of both the API and the excipients in the formulation is tested to identify potential degradation pathways, such as hydrolysis, oxidation, or the formation of unwanted by-products.

- **Content Uniformity:**

  - Content uniformity is a critical parameter that ensures each dose of the formulation contains the correct amount of API. This test ensures that there is no significant variation in the amount of drug in each individual tablet, capsule, or unit dose. Inconsistent content could lead to either subtherapeutic or toxic doses, both of which would be problematic.
  - Typically, content uniformity is tested by randomly selecting samples from different batches of the formulation and measuring the API content using methods such as **High-Performance Liquid Chromatography (HPLC)** or **UV spectrophotometry.**

- **Physical Characteristics:**

  - Physical properties of the prototype formulation, such as hardness, friability, and dissolution time, are also tested to ensure that the dosage form can withstand handling, storage, and transportation without breaking or losing its integrity.
  - For tablets, **hardness testing** is done to measure the tablet's ability to withstand pressure. **Friability testing** is used to evaluate the tablet's

resistance to breaking under stress (e.g., when it is dropped).

- ○ For liquid formulations, viscosity and particle size distribution may be assessed to ensure the consistency and stability of the formulation.

- **Appearance and Texture:**

  - ○ The appearance of the prototype formulation is important for patient acceptance. The final product should be uniform in size, shape, and color. In the case of topical formulations like creams or ointments, the texture and spreadability are also evaluated. The formulation should not be too greasy or too watery and should be easy to apply without irritation.

- **Microbial Testing:**

  - ○ In the case of formulations that are intended to be used over time or are prone to microbial contamination (e.g., liquid formulations), microbial testing is essential to ensure the product is free from harmful pathogens. This is especially important for formulations like oral liquids, injectables, and creams, which can be prone to microbial growth if not properly preserved.

Optimization and Adjustments:
Once the prototype formulation has been tested, any issues that arise during the testing phase (such as instability, poor dissolution, or inconsistent content uniformity) can be addressed. Based on the results, the formulation may be adjusted by altering the excipient concentrations, using different excipients, or changing the processing conditions (e.g., altering the granulation method or tablet compression force).

5. Optimization
Optimization is a critical step in the development of pharmaceutical formulations. After the initial prototype formulation is prepared and tested for various quality control parameters, the next phase involves refining and improving the formulation to meet specific performance, safety, and regulatory standards. The goal of optimization is to enhance the drug's effectiveness, stability, and patient acceptability by modifying the excipient composition, drug release profile, and production methods.

Key Aspects of Formulation Optimization:

1. Modifying the Excipients Composition:

Excipients are essential to the formulation process as they support the API and help deliver it effectively to the intended site of action. After testing the initial formulation, modifications to the excipient composition may be necessary to improve the product's characteristics, such as solubility, stability, and drug release rate.

- **Enhancing Drug Solubility**: If the API has poor solubility, excipients such as solubilizers, surfactants, or co-solvents (e.g., polyethylene glycol, ethanol) may be added to improve its solubility. For poorly water-soluble drugs, strategies like the use of **cyclodextrins** (which form inclusion complexes) or **solid dispersions** may be explored to enhance solubility and bioavailability.
- **Stability Modifications**: If stability issues are identified, excipients that improve the stability of the formulation may be selected or altered. For example, antioxidants (e.g., **ascorbic acid, sodium metabisulfite**) can be added to prevent oxidative degradation, while **chelation agents** (e.g., **EDTA**) can be used to prevent metal-catalyzed degradation. Excipients may also be modified to protect the drug from light or moisture by altering the packaging or using moisture-absorbing excipients.
- **Improving Bioavailability**: Excipients like **penetration enhancers** can be incorporated into topical formulations to improve the skin's permeability to the drug. In oral formulations, excipients that enhance dissolution and drug absorption, such as **disintegrants** (e.g., **sodium starch glycolate**) or **lubricants**, may be optimized for faster drug release.
- **Taste Masking**: For oral liquid formulations, especially those for children or the elderly, taste masking may be necessary. Sweeteners and flavoring agents (e.g., **sorbitol, saccharin**) are added to improve patient compliance by masking the unpleasant taste of the drug.

2. Modifying the Drug Release Profile:

The release rate of the drug is an important consideration, especially for controlled-release or sustained-release formulations. Optimization of the drug release profile ensures that the drug is delivered at the right rate to achieve therapeutic effectiveness while minimizing side effects.

- **Immediate-Release Formulations**: If the initial formulation shows slower-than-desired drug release, optimization may involve adjusting the excipient concentration or using different excipients to increase dissolution speed. For example, **disintegrants** like **croscarmellose sodium** or **crospovidone** can be added to facilitate rapid disintegration of the tablet in the stomach.

- **Sustained-Release or Controlled-Release Formulations**: Optimization of sustained-release formulations involves modifying the excipients that control the rate of drug release. Common strategies include using **polymers** (e.g., **hydroxypropyl methylcellulose**) that form a gel layer when exposed to water, controlling the release of the drug. Another strategy is the use of **matrix tablets**, where the drug is embedded in a polymer matrix that gradually releases the API over time.

- **Formulation of Multiparticulate Systems**: For achieving uniform drug release, multiparticulate systems like pellets, beads, or microspheres can be developed. These systems allow for more predictable drug release, reducing the peak-to-trough fluctuation in plasma drug concentrations, which is common with traditional formulations.

- **Dissolution Rate Testing**: Continuous optimization of the formulation is guided by dissolution testing to ensure the drug's release profile matches the intended therapeutic effect. The dissolution rate should be consistent and reproducible across different batches and storage conditions.

3. Modifying the Production Methods:

The manufacturing process plays a key role in determining the final quality and consistency of the drug product. During optimization, adjustments to the production methods may be necessary to improve batch-to-batch consistency, reduce production costs, or ensure that the formulation is suitable for large-scale manufacturing.

- **Granulation Process**: For solid dosage forms like tablets, optimizing the granulation process (either **wet granulation** or **dry granulation**) may be necessary. Wet granulation helps improve flow properties and uniformity of the powder blend, while dry granulation is suitable for heat-sensitive drugs.

- **Compression and Tablet Formation**: Optimizing the tablet compression process helps achieve the desired hardness and friability of tablets. If the initial batch of tablets is too hard or too soft, adjustments in compression force and excipient composition are made. Also, optimizing **tablet coating** (for controlled-release formulations) ensures uniform drug release.

- **Spray Drying and Lyophilization for Injectable Formulations**: For injectables, spray drying or lyophilization (freeze-drying) processes may be used to create stable formulations. Spray drying can be used for creating fine powders of the API, which can then be reconstituted into a liquid before administration. Lyophilization is often used for biologics to create stable, dry formulations that are reconstituted just before use.
- **Scaling Up for Commercial Production**: During optimization, the formulation must also be adjusted for scalability, ensuring that the formulation process can be replicated in larger batches without compromising quality. For example, adjusting mixing times, granulation processes, or drying methods may be required to maintain consistency at larger production scales.

4. Analytical Testing for Optimization:

Optimization is not only about modifying the formulation and production processes but also about testing the resulting changes through rigorous analytical testing. The modified formulation is tested for the following parameters:

- **Dissolution Rate**: Ensuring that the modified formulation meets the desired drug release profile.
- **Stability**: Stability testing ensures that the optimized formulation retains its efficacy and safety over time.
- **Content Uniformity**: Optimizing the formulation should not affect the consistency of the drug content in each dose.
- **Compatibility**: Testing excipient compatibility again after any changes is important to ensure that there are no new chemical interactions.
- **Microbial Testing**: For liquid formulations or those that may be prone to contamination, it's essential to ensure that the modified formulation remains free from microbial contamination.

6. Scale-Up

Scale-up is the process of transferring the final formulation from small-scale development to large-scale production. It involves adjusting the formulation and manufacturing processes to ensure that the drug can be produced in larger quantities while maintaining the same quality, safety, and effectiveness as the small-scale prototype. The primary goal of scale-up is to ensure that the production process is reproducible, efficient, and suitable for commercial manufacturing.

Key Aspects of Scale-Up:

1. Transition from Laboratory to Pilot and Full-Scale Production:

During the initial development phases, the formulation is typically prepared in small quantities for testing and optimization. Once the formulation has been finalized, it must be scaled up to produce larger batches for clinical trials, stability studies, and eventual commercial distribution. This transition requires careful planning to ensure that the process remains consistent, and the final product meets the required quality standards.

- **Pilot-Scale Production**: This stage involves producing larger batches (typically hundreds of kilograms) under conditions that simulate commercial production but on a smaller scale. Pilot-scale production is used to evaluate the scalability of the formulation and the manufacturing process. Any adjustments needed in terms of excipient concentrations, process parameters, or equipment are identified and addressed during this phase.

- **Full-Scale Commercial Production**: Following successful pilot-scale production, the formulation is moved to full-scale production, where it is manufactured in much larger quantities. This phase requires careful control over manufacturing variables to ensure that each batch meets the required specifications for consistency, purity, and potency.

2. Reproducibility of the Process:

One of the most important aspects of scale-up is ensuring that the manufacturing process remains reproducible. Variability in the manufacturing process can lead to differences in the quality and effectiveness of the final product. Several factors must be closely monitored and controlled during scale-up to maintain reproducibility:

- **Batch Consistency:** The formulation must be consistent in terms of API content, excipient composition, and drug release profile across all batches. To achieve this, critical process parameters such as mixing time, granulation, drying, and compression force need to be optimized and standardized.

- **Equipment Validation**: The equipment used in small-scale development may differ from the equipment used in large-scale production, so it is important to ensure that the new equipment can replicate the results achieved in smaller batches. Equipment such as tablet presses, granulators, and mixers must be validated to ensure that they can handle the increased scale without compromising the quality of the drug product.
- **In-Process Controls**: During scale-up, it is essential to maintain in-process controls such as temperature, humidity, pH, and mixing speed. These factors must be monitored and controlled to ensure that they do not cause variability in the formulation's quality.

3. Process Optimization for Large-Scale Production:

Scaling up requires optimizing the production process to accommodate larger volumes of the formulation. Some aspects that require adjustment and optimization during scale-up include:

- **Mixing and Granulation**: On a larger scale, the mixing and granulation processes may behave differently due to the increased volume of materials. For example, the residence time in the granulator may change, or the mixing process may need to be optimized to ensure uniform distribution of the API and excipients.
- **Drying**: In many formulations, drying is a critical step in the process. On a larger scale, it may be necessary to adjust drying times or temperatures to ensure that the moisture content of the final product is consistent and within acceptable limits.
- **Compression and Tablet Coating**: Scaling up tablet compression requires adjusting the compression force and speed to ensure consistent tablet hardness, friability, and weight. Additionally, for coated tablets, the coating process must be adjusted to maintain uniformity in the film thickness and appearance.

4. Quality Assurance and Control:

During scale-up, quality assurance (QA) and quality control (QC) are critical to ensuring that the product remains consistent and meets regulatory standards. Several activities are involved in maintaining quality during large-scale production:

- **Stability Testing**: Stability testing is performed on large-scale batches to ensure that the formulation remains stable over time. This helps determine the shelf life and storage conditions for the drug.
- **Validation of Analytical Methods**: Analytical methods used to test the API, excipients, and final product must be validated for large-scale production. This includes ensuring that the methods used to test for drug content, dissolution, and impurities are accurate and reproducible.
- **End-Product Testing**: Routine testing of the final product is necessary to ensure that it meets the required specifications. This includes tests for drug content uniformity, dissolution, stability, microbial contamination, and physical appearance (e.g., hardness, friability for tablets, or viscosity for liquids).

5. Cost Considerations:

As the production scale increases, so do the costs. Scaling up must be done with efficiency in mind to keep costs manageable while maintaining product quality. Key factors affecting cost include:

- **Raw Material Costs**: The amount of API and excipients used in large-scale production can significantly impact the overall cost of the drug. Efficient sourcing and formulation adjustments can help minimize these costs.
- **Manufacturing Efficiency**: Streamlining manufacturing processes and reducing waste during production can help lower costs. This may involve investing in more efficient equipment, improving process workflows, or reducing the number of manufacturing steps.
- **Packaging**: Packaging must also be optimized for large-scale production. Packaging materials (e.g., bottles, blisters, vials) must be sourced in bulk, and automated systems must be in place to ensure efficient filling and sealing.

6. Regulatory Compliance:

As the formulation is scaled up for commercial production, it must meet regulatory requirements established by agencies such as the FDA, EMA, or CDSCO. Regulatory agencies require extensive documentation for all stages of production, including scale-up. This includes providing data on:

- **Process Validation**: Regulatory bodies require evidence that the manufacturing process is capable of producing consistent, high-quality batches. This includes process validation studies, which demonstrate that the scaling up process can be performed consistently with no loss in quality.
- **Manufacturing Site Inspections**: Regulatory authorities will often inspect manufacturing facilities to ensure compliance with Good Manufacturing Practices (GMP). The facility must be capable of handling large-scale production while adhering to quality control and sterility standards.

7. Stability and Testing

Stability Testing is a critical component of the pharmaceutical product development process. It helps determine the shelf-life of a drug product, ensuring that it remains safe, effective, and of high quality throughout its storage and use. Stability testing is conducted by exposing the product to various environmental conditions such as temperature, humidity, and light, and monitoring its performance over time. This process helps identify potential degradation pathways, enabling formulation adjustments to maintain the drug's integrity.

Importance of Stability Testing:

1. **Shelf-Life Determination**:

   - Stability testing is essential to determine the shelf-life of a drug, which is the time period during which the product maintains its safety, efficacy, and quality when stored under specified conditions. Regulatory authorities require stability data to approve a product's shelf life. The shelf life is determined based on the degradation rate observed under stability testing conditions, and it is used to establish the product's expiration date.

2. **Understanding Degradation Mechanisms**:

   - Stability testing helps identify how and why a drug degrades over time. Common degradation processes include **oxidation, hydrolysis, photodegradation**, and **thermolysis**. Identifying these pathways is crucial for making formulation adjustments that can prevent or minimize degradation. For example, drugs that are sensitive to light may need to be packaged in opaque containers, while those prone to oxidation may require the addition of antioxidants.

3. **Formulation Optimization:**

   ◦ Data from stability testing guides formulators in optimizing the drug formulation. For example, if a formulation shows signs of instability under humid conditions, the use of moisture-absorbing excipients or improved packaging may be necessary. Stability data can also help determine the ideal packaging materials that protect the drug from environmental factors like light and oxygen.

4. **Regulatory Compliance:**

   ◦ Stability testing is a regulatory requirement. Agencies such as the **FDA, EMA,** and **CDSCO** require stability studies to ensure that the product remains safe and effective during its shelf life. The results of stability tests are submitted as part of the drug approval process, and they play a significant role in determining product labeling, storage instructions, and expiration dates.

Key Types of Stability Studies:

1. **Accelerated Stability Testing:**

   ◦ **Purpose:** Accelerated stability testing is designed to speed up the degradation process by exposing the product to extreme conditions (e.g., higher temperatures, increased humidity). This allows formulators to predict the product's stability and estimate its shelf-life in a shorter period.
   ◦ **Conditions:** Common conditions for accelerated stability testing include temperatures of 40°C or higher and humidity levels of 75% or greater.
   ◦ **Outcome:** The data from these tests are used to predict the long-term stability of the product. The results are extrapolated to estimate how the drug will behave under normal storage conditions. Accelerated testing is particularly useful for identifying potential degradation

pathways that may require formulation adjustments.

2. **Real-Time Stability Testing:**

- **Purpose:** Real-time stability testing involves storing the drug at normal conditions (e.g., room temperature, 60% humidity) for an extended period to evaluate its stability over the product's intended shelf life.
- **Conditions:** The product is stored under recommended storage conditions (such as at 25°C/60% relative humidity for many pharmaceutical products). Stability tests are conducted periodically at different time intervals (e.g., 3 months, 6 months, 12 months).
- **Outcome:** Real-time stability testing provides the most accurate prediction of the product's shelf life and ensures that the product remains stable during its expected usage period. This data is critical for determining the expiration date and labeling requirements.

3. **Stress Testing:**

- **Purpose:** Stress testing is designed to evaluate the stability of the drug under extreme conditions, such as high temperature, high humidity, and light exposure. The goal is to identify potential degradation pathways that may not be detected under normal storage conditions.
- **Conditions:** Stress conditions may include exposing the drug to temperatures higher than the normal storage range, subjecting it to ultraviolet (UV) light, or introducing oxidative agents.
- **Outcome:** Stress testing helps determine how sensitive the drug is to environmental factors and can identify any chemical reactions that may occur, such as oxidation or photodegradation. This data allows formulators to design packaging or formulation changes to mitigate degradation.

4. **Packaging Studies:**

- **Purpose:** Stability testing also includes evaluating the interaction between the drug formulation and packaging materials. Packaging can significantly impact the stability of the drug, as it must protect the drug from external factors such as light, moisture, and oxygen.

- ◦ **Conditions**: Different packaging materials, such as bottles, vials, or blisters, are tested for their ability to protect the drug. The stability of the product is assessed both before and after exposure to conditions like temperature fluctuations, moisture, and light.
- ◦ **Outcome**: Packaging studies provide valuable information on the best materials to use for drug packaging, ensuring that the final product remains stable and effective until the expiration date.

Key Parameters Evaluated in Stability Testing:

1. **Chemical Stability:**

   - ◦ Chemical stability testing evaluates the integrity of the API over time, monitoring for any degradation products or changes in the molecular structure of the drug. Methods such as **High-Performance Liquid Chromatography (HPLC)** or **Gas Chromatography (GC)** are used to measure the concentration of the active ingredient and detect degradation products.

2. **Physical Stability:**

   - ◦ Physical stability testing assesses changes in the drug's appearance, texture, and physical properties. This includes testing for changes in color, crystallization, phase separation, or viscosity. In solid formulations like tablets, testing is done for hardness, friability, and disintegration time.

3. **Microbial Stability:**

   - ◦ Microbial stability is important for liquid formulations, especially those without preservatives. Microbial testing evaluates the drug's ability to resist microbial contamination and growth over time. This is crucial for products like oral liquids, injectables, and creams, where contamination can compromise the drug's safety.

4. **Dissolution Profile:**

○ The dissolution rate is monitored throughout stability testing to ensure that the drug continues to dissolve at the desired rate over its shelf life. Changes in the dissolution profile could indicate issues with the formulation, such as crystallization or improper release of the API.

Challenges and Innovations in Formulation Development

Formulation development is a complex and multifaceted process that faces several challenges. These challenges can impact the success of a pharmaceutical product, but there are also innovations and strategies to overcome these hurdles and improve the drug's performance. Below are the key challenges and the innovative approaches being used to address them.

1. Challenges:

a. Solubility Issues:

Many drugs, particularly those with poor water solubility, face significant challenges in terms of bioavailability. Poor solubility means that a large proportion of the drug is unable to dissolve sufficiently in the gastrointestinal fluids to be absorbed into the bloodstream, resulting in reduced therapeutic effects.

- **Impact**: Poor solubility leads to low bioavailability, meaning that less of the active ingredient reaches the target site in the body. This is especially problematic for orally administered drugs, as they rely on solubility for absorption in the gastrointestinal tract.

Innovative Approaches to Overcome Solubility Issues:

- **Nanotechnology**: The use of nanoparticles has emerged as a promising technique to enhance the solubility of poorly soluble drugs. Nanoparticles have a large surface area, which can significantly improve the dissolution rate and bioavailability of the drug. Technologies like **nanocrystal formulations** are gaining popularity for drugs with poor solubility.
- **Lipid-Based Formulations**: Lipid-based drug delivery systems, such as **liposomes, solid lipid nanoparticles (SLNs),** and **self-emulsifying drug delivery systems (SEDDS),** are used to improve the solubility of lipophilic drugs. These systems enhance solubility by increasing the dissolution rate and the absorption of the API in the intestinal tract.

- **Solubility Enhancers**: The incorporation of solubilizing agents like **cyclodextrins** or **surfactants** can improve the solubility of hydrophobic drugs. Cyclodextrins can form inclusion complexes with the API, increasing its aqueous solubility.

b. Stability Problems:

Stability is another significant challenge in formulation development. Some drugs are unstable under normal conditions and may degrade over time, which can lead to reduced potency, formation of harmful degradation products, or changes in physical properties (e.g., discoloration, precipitation).

- **Impact**: Degradation can affect the safety, efficacy, and shelf-life of the drug, ultimately leading to product failure or recall. The degradation may occur due to environmental factors such as **heat, light, moisture**, or **oxidation**.

Innovative Approaches to Overcome Stability Problems:

- **Specialized Formulations**: For drugs prone to degradation, specialized formulations can be developed. This may include the use of **stabilizing agents** (e.g., antioxidants or chelating agents), which help prevent chemical breakdown during storage. For example, adding **ascorbic acid** as an antioxidant can protect drugs from oxidative degradation.
- **Packaging Innovations**: Packaging plays a crucial role in protecting drugs from environmental stressors. **Light-protective packaging** (e.g., amber vials) is used to protect drugs from light-induced degradation, while **moisture-resistant packaging** (e.g., desiccant packs) is used for drugs sensitive to moisture. **Aseptic packaging** also ensures that microbial contamination is prevented in injectable formulations.
- **Lyophilization (Freeze-Drying)**: Lyophilization is an effective technique for improving the stability of biologics and heat-sensitive drugs. This process removes water from the drug formulation by sublimation, leaving a stable, dry product that can be reconstituted when needed, thus increasing the shelf life.

c. Bioavailability:

Achieving the desired bioavailability is a major challenge for many drugs, especially those with low solubility or poor permeability. Bioavailability refers to the proportion of the drug that enters the bloodstream and reaches the target tissue. If the API is not sufficiently absorbed or delivered to the site of action, the drug's therapeutic effects may be diminished.

- **Impact**: Poor bioavailability can lead to inconsistent or suboptimal therapeutic effects, making it difficult to achieve the desired clinical outcomes, particularly for oral drugs.

Innovative Approaches to Improve Bioavailability:

- **Sustained-Release Formulations**: Sustained-release or controlled-release formulations can improve bioavailability by ensuring a gradual release of the drug over time. These formulations are designed to maintain therapeutic drug levels for a prolonged period, reducing the frequency of dosing and improving patient compliance.
- **Advanced Drug Delivery Systems**: Techniques such as **liposomes, microspheres, nanoparticles**, and **transdermal patches** are being explored for their ability to enhance the bioavailability of drugs. These systems can provide controlled drug release, targeted delivery, or improved absorption, ensuring that the API reaches the desired site of action in an efficient manner.
- **Permeation Enhancers**: For drugs that are poorly absorbed due to low permeability across biological membranes, permeation enhancers can be used. These include **surfactants** or **penetration enhancers** that temporarily open tight junctions in the intestinal wall or enhance the drug's ability to cross the skin barrier in the case of topical formulations.

d. Regulatory Challenges:

One of the significant challenges faced by pharmaceutical manufacturers is navigating the complex and varying regulatory requirements across different global markets, such as the **FDA** (U.S.), **EMA** (Europe), and **CDSCO** (India). Each regulatory body has its own set of guidelines for drug development, testing, and approval, which can lead to delays and increased costs.

- **Impact**: Meeting the regulatory requirements for approval in multiple regions can be time-consuming and expensive. Differences in clinical trial protocols, stability testing conditions, and documentation requirements can result in delays in the drug's market entry.

Innovative Approaches to Overcome Regulatory Challenges:

- **Harmonization of Guidelines**: Efforts by international regulatory bodies to harmonize guidelines, such as those under the **International Council for Harmonisation (ICH),** help streamline the approval process. This ensures that drug development processes are consistent across regions and that the regulatory burden is reduced.
- **Adaptive Clinical Trial Designs**: To accelerate the regulatory approval process, innovative trial designs such as **adaptive clinical trials** are being used. These trials allow for modifications to the trial protocol based on interim results, which can reduce time and costs associated with clinical testing.
- **Pre-Submission Consultations**: Some regulatory agencies, such as the FDA, offer **pre-submission consultations**, where pharmaceutical companies can discuss their development plans and seek advice on regulatory requirements. This helps avoid misunderstandings and potential delays during the review process.

2. Innovations in Formulation Development

Innovations in pharmaceutical formulation development are continually evolving to meet the growing needs of patients and improve therapeutic outcomes. These innovations focus on enhancing drug solubility, stability, bioavailability, and patient compliance. Below are some of the key innovations in drug formulation that are transforming the pharmaceutical industry:

1. Nanotechnology

Nanotechnology refers to the use of nanoparticles—particles sized between 1 and 100 nanometers—in drug delivery systems. These tiny particles have unique physical and chemical properties that can significantly enhance the solubility, stability, and bioavailability of drugs, especially those that are poorly soluble in water.

- **Enhancement of Solubility and Bioavailability:**

- ○ Nanoparticles offer a larger surface area, which improves the dissolution rate of poorly soluble drugs, allowing for faster absorption into the bloodstream. This enhancement of solubility directly improves the bioavailability of the drug.

- ○ **Nanocarriers**, such as liposomes, solid lipid nanoparticles (SLNs), and dendrimers, can encapsulate the drug, protecting it from degradation and improving its stability. These carriers can also enhance drug absorption by overcoming biological barriers such as the gastrointestinal tract.

- **Targeted Drug Delivery**:

  - ○ Nanoparticles can be engineered to target specific cells or tissues in the body. For example, surface modifications can allow nanoparticles to recognize and bind to cancer cells, delivering the drug directly to the site of action and minimizing systemic side effects.

  - ○ This targeted approach not only enhances therapeutic efficacy but also reduces the risk of toxicity, making nanotechnology particularly beneficial for cancer therapy and other precision medicine applications.

- **Applications**:

  - ○ Nanotechnology is being used to improve the delivery of a variety of drugs, including anticancer agents, vaccines, and poorly soluble small molecules. It also holds promise in the development of **nanoparticle-based vaccines** and **drug-eluting nanoparticles** for sustained drug release.

2. Biologics and Biosimilars

Biologics are a class of complex drugs derived from living organisms, including **monoclonal antibodies, recombinant proteins, vaccines,** and **gene therapies**. These drugs are used to treat a variety of conditions, including cancer, autoimmune diseases, and genetic disorders.

- **Challenges with Biologics**:

- ◦ Biologics are typically large, complex molecules that are difficult to manufacture and require specialized formulation techniques. They are often administered via injection or infusion due to their large molecular size and instability in oral formulations.
- ◦ The production of biologics involves biotechnology techniques such as **cell culture, genetic engineering**, and **protein purification**. Due to their complexity, biologics require stringent handling and storage conditions to maintain their stability, such as refrigeration or lyophilization (freeze-drying).

- **Biosimilars:**

- ◦ Biosimilars are biologic products that are highly similar to an already-approved reference biologic, with no clinically meaningful differences in safety, potency, and efficacy. The development of biosimilars allows for increased access to biologic therapies by reducing treatment costs.
- ◦ Formulation techniques for biosimilars are crucial to ensure they maintain the same therapeutic effect as the reference product. The manufacturing processes for biosimilars must meet stringent regulatory requirements and demonstrate that the product is as safe and effective as the original biologic.

- **Applications:**

- ◦ Biologics are used in a range of therapeutic areas, including oncology (e.g., monoclonal antibodies), immunology (e.g., TNF inhibitors), and hematology (e.g., erythropoietin). Biosimilars are becoming increasingly popular as cost-effective alternatives to expensive biologic drugs.

3. 3D Printing

3D printing, also known as **additive manufacturing**, is a revolutionary technology that allows the creation of personalized drug formulations by building up the material layer by layer.

- **Customization of Dosage Forms:**

- ○ 3D printing enables the production of **personalized dosage forms,** such as tablets or capsules, that can be tailored to individual patients. This customization allows for the precise adjustment of the drug dosage, release profile, and even the shape of the tablet, which can improve patient compliance.
- ○ For instance, patients with specific dosage needs, such as children or elderly patients who may require smaller or differently shaped tablets, can benefit from 3D-printed personalized tablets.

- **Controlled Release Profiles:**

  - ○ 3D printing can also be used to create complex dosage forms that release the drug in a controlled manner. By varying the composition and structure of the printed material, formulators can create tablets with **multilayered** or **multi-compartment designs,** which can release the drug at different rates over time (e.g., immediate-release and sustained-release components in one tablet).
  - ○ This allows for more precise control over drug delivery, reducing the need for multiple doses throughout the day.

- **Applications:**

  - ○ 3D printing is particularly useful in the development of personalized medicines, where exact dosing is critical. It also has applications in the development of **orodispersible tablets, tablet implants,** and **multidose systems.**

4. Smart Drug Delivery Systems

Smart drug delivery systems are advanced formulations designed to release the drug at the right time, at the right site, and in the right amount. These systems are capable of responding to specific triggers, such as changes in pH, temperature, or the presence of specific enzymes, to release the drug only when needed.

- **Responsive Drug Delivery:**

  - ○ **pH-Responsive Systems:** Some drugs require a specific pH for optimal absorption. pH-sensitive formulations can release the drug in the stomach (acidic pH) or intestines (neutral to alkaline pH) based on the pH changes in different parts of the gastrointestinal tract.

- **Temperature-Responsive Systems**: Certain drugs, especially biologics, are sensitive to temperature. Temperature-responsive delivery systems can release the drug when the body reaches a certain temperature, making them ideal for thermosensitive drugs or localized treatments like **heat-triggered release.**
- **Enzyme-Responsive Systems**: Enzyme-triggered delivery is used for controlled release of drugs in specific areas, such as targeting the release of an API in the small intestine, where certain enzymes are present.

- **Targeted Delivery:**

  - Smart drug delivery systems can also be used for **targeted drug delivery**, where the drug is directed to a specific site in the body, such as cancer cells, while minimizing systemic side effects. **Nanoparticles** and **liposomes** are often used in these systems to achieve controlled and targeted release.

- **Applications:**

  - These systems have applications in **cancer therapy**, where drugs need to be delivered directly to tumor sites, as well as in **diabetes management** (e.g., insulin release based on blood sugar levels) and **antibiotic therapy** for localized infections.

CHAPTER THREE

Stability Assessment and Manufacturing

3.1 Stability Assessment

Importance of Stability Studies

Definition of Stability and Its Significance in Drug Product Development:

Stability refers to the ability of a drug product to retain its desired physical, chemical, therapeutic, and microbiological properties throughout its shelf life when stored under specified conditions. Stability studies are essential in drug development as they provide vital information about how the Active Pharmaceutical Ingredient (API) and the entire drug formulation will behave over time.

Stability is not just about the chemical integrity of the API but also concerns its physical state, dissolution, and bioavailability in the body. A stable drug product maintains its intended therapeutic effect and ensures safety throughout its lifecycle—from production to patient use. Stability studies ensure that the drug is safe to use, effective, and retains the same characteristics throughout the period it is expected to be in storage and distribution.

Role in Determining Shelf-Life and Expiration Date:

One of the primary outcomes of stability studies is the determination of a drug's **shelf-life**, which refers to the period during which the product remains effective and safe for use. This is closely tied to the **expiration date** of the product, which is the date after which the manufacturer can no longer guarantee the quality, safety, or efficacy of the drug.

The **shelf-life** is determined through testing the product under various conditions, such as accelerated stability testing (high temperature, humidity, and light) and real-time stability testing (under normal storage conditions). The degradation rate of the drug is assessed, and based on these results, an appropriate expiration date is assigned. The shelf-life reflects the duration for which the drug will maintain its quality under recommended storage conditions.

Impact on Drug Safety, Efficacy, and Regulatory Approval:

Stability studies are critical for ensuring that a drug remains **safe** and **effective** for use over its intended shelf life. Degradation of the API or the formulation can lead to a loss of potency, the formation of harmful by-products, or a change in the drug's effectiveness.

For example, a drug that is not chemically stable may break down into potentially toxic metabolites, or it may become ineffective before the expiration date. Stability studies ensure that any degradation pathways are identified early, allowing for formulation adjustments to prevent these issues.

In addition, stability studies are a **regulatory requirement** for drug approval. Regulatory agencies such as the **FDA**, **EMA**, and **CDSCO** require data from stability studies to ensure that the drug meets specific quality standards before it is approved for market release. This testing verifies that the drug will remain safe and effective through its entire shelf life and under various conditions during shipping, storage, and use.

Importance in Ensuring Consistent Drug Quality Over Time:

Consistency in drug quality is essential for **patient safety** and **therapeutic efficacy**. A formulation that is unstable can vary in its composition over time, leading to potential therapeutic failures or side effects. Stability testing ensures that each batch of the drug, over its shelf life, maintains the same **chemical composition**, **dissolution characteristics**, and **bioavailability**, resulting in a consistent effect on the patient.

For instance, if a drug loses its potency over time due to instability, patients may receive suboptimal doses, leading to treatment failure. Conversely, if the drug degrades into harmful by-products, patients may face toxicity. Stability studies, therefore, are vital for ensuring that the drug performs consistently and safely over time.

Overall, stability assessments provide the evidence needed to determine the appropriate **storage conditions**, **expiration date**, and **packaging**

requirements to ensure that the drug remains **safe, effective**, and of **high quality** throughout its shelf life. These studies are fundamental for product development, regulatory approval, and market acceptance.

Factors Influencing Stability

The stability of a pharmaceutical product is influenced by a range of environmental and formulation factors. These factors can impact the **chemical, physical**, and **microbiological stability** of the drug over time. Understanding how these factors affect stability is crucial for developing drug products that maintain their quality, safety, and efficacy throughout their shelf life.

1. Temperature: Effects of High or Low Temperatures on Drug Degradation and Stability

Temperature is one of the most significant environmental factors influencing drug stability. **High temperatures** can accelerate the degradation of drugs by increasing the rate of chemical reactions, while **low temperatures** can lead to changes in the physical properties of certain formulations, such as crystallization or phase separation.

- **High Temperatures**: Elevated temperatures can lead to accelerated **chemical degradation** through processes such as **oxidation, hydrolysis,** and **decarboxylation**. For example, some drugs may undergo **thermal degradation** where the API may lose its potency or produce harmful by-products when exposed to high temperatures.
- **Low Temperatures**: While low temperatures generally slow down degradation, they may cause certain formulations to become unstable. For instance, emulsions may separate, or liquids may freeze, affecting the solubility and bioavailability of the drug. Drugs that are sensitive to freezing, such as some biological products, may lose activity or undergo denaturation at low temperatures.

Temperature-Controlled Packaging: To mitigate temperature-related stability issues, drugs are often stored in temperature-controlled environments, and packaging materials are selected to protect against extreme temperature fluctuations.

2. Light: Impact of Light Exposure on Photosensitive Drugs and the Need for Protective Packaging

Light, particularly **ultraviolet (UV) radiation**, can cause degradation in **photosensitive drugs**. Many drugs, including certain antibiotics, vitamins, and anticancer agents, are sensitive to light exposure, which can lead to **photodegradation**—a process where the chemical structure of the API is altered, reducing its efficacy and potentially producing harmful by-products.

- **Photodegradation**: UV light can break the bonds in the drug molecule, leading to chemical changes that may render the drug ineffective or toxic. For example, **nitrofurantoin** and **methotrexate** are drugs known to be susceptible to light degradation.

Protective Packaging: To prevent light-induced degradation, drugs that are sensitive to light are often packaged in **amber-colored vials, opaque containers**, or **light-protective blister packs**. These packaging materials block UV light and help preserve the drug's integrity during storage and transport.

3. Humidity: Effects of Moisture on the Stability of Hygroscopic Drugs and Formulations

Moisture or **humidity** can have a significant impact on the stability of drugs, particularly **hygroscopic** drugs, which readily absorb moisture from the air. Moisture absorption can lead to **physical changes** (e.g., caking or clumping of powders), **chemical degradation** (e.g., hydrolysis of certain drugs), or the growth of microorganisms in liquid formulations.

- **Hygroscopicity**: Drugs like **lithium carbonate, morphine sulfate**, and many **antibiotics** are hygroscopic and may absorb moisture, resulting in reduced stability or altered pharmacokinetics.

Solutions for Moisture Sensitivity:

- **Desiccants**: Moisture-absorbing materials (e.g., silica gel) are used in packaging to prevent moisture exposure.
- **Moisture-Proof Packaging**: Blister packs, bottles with tight seals, and foil pouches can be used to shield drugs from moisture.
- **Lyophilization (Freeze-Drying)**: For liquid formulations that are sensitive to moisture, lyophilization is often used to remove water content, allowing for stable, dry formulations.

4. Oxygen and Air: Oxidative Degradation and Packaging Solutions to Mitigate Air Exposure

Oxidative degradation occurs when oxygen reacts with the drug, leading to the formation of degradation products that can reduce the drug's potency or produce toxic by-products. Oxygen can also affect the stability of excipients, particularly in formulations like **liquids** or **inhalers**, where exposure to air can cause chemical reactions such as **oxidation** or **peroxide formation**.

- **Oxidation**: Many drugs, especially those with **unsaturated bonds** or **phenolic groups**, are susceptible to oxidation. For example, **vitamin A**, **asparaginase**, and **adrenaline** undergo oxidation when exposed to air, leading to loss of efficacy.

Packaging Solutions:

- **Nitrogen Purging**: For sensitive products, nitrogen or other inert gases are often used to displace oxygen in the packaging. This creates an oxygen-free environment, preventing oxidative reactions.
- **Airtight Packaging**: **Vacuum-sealed** or **airtight** packaging can be used to prevent exposure to air and maintain drug stability.
- **Antioxidants**: Adding antioxidants (e.g., **ascorbic acid** or **tocopherols**) to the formulation helps prevent oxidation by scavenging free radicals and oxygen.

5. pH and Chemical Interactions: How pH Variations and Interactions Between the Drug and Excipients Affect Stability

The **pH** of a drug formulation plays a critical role in its **solubility**, **stability**, and **bioavailability**. Many drugs are pH-sensitive, meaning their stability can be significantly affected by changes in pH during manufacturing, storage, or in the body. Additionally, the **interaction between the drug and excipients** can lead to instability, including precipitation, degradation, or the formation of insoluble complexes.

- **pH-Sensitive Drugs**: For example, **aspirin** (acetylsalicylic acid) is unstable at high pH, leading to hydrolysis into salicylic acid. Similarly, some **biologic drugs** are sensitive to changes in pH and can denature when exposed to unfavorable pH conditions.

Solutions:

- **Buffer Systems:** Buffers are used in formulations to maintain a stable pH and prevent pH-induced degradation. Common buffer systems include **phosphate buffers, citrate buffers**, and **acetate buffers.**
- **Formulation Adjustments:** By selecting excipients that maintain the required pH and prevent chemical interactions, formulators can stabilize the drug and prevent degradation.

6. Physical State of the Drug: Influence of Polymorphism, Crystallization, and Particle Size on Stability

The **physical state** of the drug significantly impacts its **stability** and **performance**. Changes in the crystalline form of the drug, such as the occurrence of different **polymorphs**, can affect solubility, dissolution rate, and stability.

- **Polymorphism:** Different polymorphs of the same drug can have different solubility and stability profiles. For example, one polymorph may be more soluble and dissolve more quickly, improving bioavailability, while another may be more stable but dissolve more slowly.
- **Crystallization and Particle Size:** The size and shape of the drug particles influence the rate at which the drug dissolves. **Smaller particles** typically have a larger surface area and can dissolve more quickly, improving bioavailability. However, the physical properties of smaller particles can sometimes lead to issues like **agglomeration** or **caking** during storage, affecting formulation stability.

Solutions:

- **Polymorph Selection:** The most stable and soluble polymorph should be selected during preformulation studies to ensure optimal stability and performance.
- **Nanotechnology:** By reducing the particle size to the nanoscale, formulations can enhance solubility and bioavailability, especially for poorly soluble drugs.
- **Crystallization Control:** Methods such as **controlled crystallization** or **solid dispersion** techniques can be used to maintain the stability and

desired dissolution characteristics of the drug.

Stability Testing Protocols and Regulatory Guidelines

Stability testing is a critical component of the drug development process. It ensures that a pharmaceutical product remains safe, effective, and of high quality throughout its shelf life. Regulatory agencies require stability studies to evaluate the effects of various environmental factors, such as temperature, humidity, and light, on the stability of a drug product. Stability testing helps determine the **expiration date, storage conditions**, and **packaging requirements**. Below are the key aspects of stability testing protocols and the associated regulatory guidelines.

1. Accelerated Stability Testing: Methods and Conditions (Temperature, Humidity) Used to Predict Long-Term Stability

Accelerated stability testing is a method used to simulate long-term storage conditions by exposing the product to higher-than-normal temperatures and humidity levels. This approach helps predict how the drug will behave over time under normal storage conditions, accelerating the process of determining its shelf life.

- **Testing Conditions:**

  - **Temperature**: The drug product is stored at elevated temperatures, typically **40°C ± 2°C** or **50°C ± 2°C**, to accelerate degradation. These conditions are chosen based on the specific properties of the drug and are designed to speed up chemical reactions that may occur over time.

  - **Humidity**: The stability of the drug under high-humidity conditions is also tested, with **75% ± 5% relative humidity** being a common standard.

  - **Duration**: The accelerated stability test usually lasts for a shorter period (e.g., 3 to 6 months) compared to real-time stability testing, with the results being extrapolated to predict the long-term stability (usually 2 to 5 years).

- **Purpose:**

  - This testing allows formulators to identify degradation pathways (e.g., hydrolysis, oxidation) that could potentially affect the drug's efficacy or safety.

- ○ It also helps estimate the **shelf life** by extrapolating the data to normal conditions (e.g., **25°C ± 2°C, 60% RH**).

2. Real-Time Stability Testing: Guidelines for Testing Under Normal Storage Conditions Over Extended Periods

Real-time stability testing involves storing the drug product under normal conditions (i.e., standard temperature and humidity) to evaluate how it performs over a long period. This method provides the most accurate data regarding the drug's shelf life.

- **Testing Conditions:**

  - ○ The drug is stored at standard storage conditions, typically at **25°C ± 2°C** and **60% ± 5% relative humidity**, which are considered typical for commercial storage.
  - ○ The duration of real-time stability testing can vary from **12 months to 60 months** depending on the type of drug, its expected shelf life, and regulatory requirements.

- **Purpose:**

  - ○ This testing simulates the product's actual storage and usage conditions, helping to assess the **physical, chemical, and microbiological stability** of the drug over time.
  - ○ Real-time testing results are used to determine the **expiration date** and ensure the product maintains its **therapeutic efficacy, safety,** and **quality** up to the end of its shelf life.

3. International Regulatory Requirements: Stability Testing Requirements Set by the FDA, EMA, CDSCO, and Other Regulatory Agencies

Regulatory agencies require extensive stability testing to ensure that a drug product meets quality standards before it is approved for market release. Different agencies may have slightly varied requirements for stability testing, but there are key common standards that manufacturers must meet.

- **FDA (Food and Drug Administration, USA):**

  - The FDA follows guidelines outlined in the **ICH (International Council for Harmonisation)** guidelines, which include stability testing requirements for the **US Pharmacopeia (USP)**.
  - The FDA typically requires **accelerated testing** and **real-time testing** to assess the stability of drug products.

- **EMA (European Medicines Agency):**

  - The EMA follows ICH guidelines and requires **long-term stability studies** under standard conditions (25°C ± 2°C, 60% RH) and accelerated stability studies (40°C ± 2°C, 75% RH).
  - The stability testing protocols must be aligned with the **European Pharmacopoeia** standards, and the testing duration is typically longer for biologics and complex formulations.

- **CDSCO (Central Drugs Standard Control Organization, India):**

  - The CDSCO follows similar ICH stability testing guidelines as the FDA and EMA.
  - **Accelerated stability studies** and **long-term testing** are required for **new drug approvals** in India, with specific emphasis on conditions relevant to the local environment (e.g., higher ambient temperatures).

- **Other Regulatory Agencies:**

  - Other regulatory bodies, including those in **Japan**, **Australia**, and **Brazil**, also follow ICH guidelines or have adapted their own based on international standards. However, local climate conditions and storage practices can influence specific testing protocols.

4. Good Stability Practices: Best Practices for Conducting Stability Studies and Documenting Results

Good Stability Practices (GSP) are essential for ensuring the reliability and integrity of stability data. These practices ensure that stability studies are conducted systematically and consistently, and that the data is properly documented for regulatory submission.

- **Documentation**: Proper **documentation** is critical to provide a clear and reproducible record of all stability studies. This includes the storage conditions, testing methods, results, and any deviations observed during testing. Detailed records also ensure traceability and compliance with regulatory guidelines.
- **Controlled Environments**: Stability studies must be conducted in **controlled environments**, such as **stability chambers** or **climatic test chambers**, where temperature, humidity, and light can be accurately monitored and maintained.
- **Sample Size and Sampling Frequency**: The **sample size** and **sampling frequency** should be appropriate to represent batch-to-batch variations and to detect degradation over time. Samples are typically tested at **3-month intervals** for the first year and then at **6-month intervals** thereafter.
- **Reporting Results**: Stability results should be clearly reported, including detailed data on **API content**, **dissolution rates**, **appearance**, **pH**, **microbial load**, and **any observed changes** in the formulation. This data is used to assess whether the drug remains within acceptable quality standards throughout its shelf life.

5. Storage Conditions and Packaging: Regulatory Guidelines for Packaging Materials, Labeling, and Storage Instructions

Regulatory agencies provide guidelines on **packaging**, **labeling**, and **storage conditions** to protect the drug from environmental factors such as light, heat, and moisture. These guidelines are critical to maintaining the drug's stability during transportation, storage, and use.

- **Packaging**: Packaging materials must be selected to protect the drug from external factors that could affect stability. For instance, **amber glass bottles** are used to protect drugs from light, while **moisture-proof containers** (e.g., blister packs or desiccant packets) are used for hygroscopic drugs.
- **Labeling**: Labeling must clearly state the **storage conditions** (e.g., "store at room temperature" or "refrigerate after opening") and **expiration date**. It also includes any special instructions for the patient or healthcare provider, such as **sensitive-to-light** instructions or **discard**

after opening information.

- **Storage Guidelines:** The storage conditions outlined on the label must be aligned with the **real-time stability testing** results. These conditions typically specify temperature, humidity, and protection from light to ensure that the drug remains stable during its shelf life. In some cases, specific storage instructions are required, such as **freezing, cool storage,** or **room temperature** storage.

3.2 Manufacturing of Dosage Forms

The manufacturing of dosage forms involves a series of carefully controlled processes that ensure the drug is delivered in the appropriate form, at the right dose, and with the desired release profile. Below is an overview of the manufacturing processes for various dosage forms, including tablets, capsules, injectables, topical forms, liquid dosage forms, and controlled-release systems.

1. Tablets: Overview of the Manufacturing Process

Tablets are one of the most common dosage forms and are produced through a series of well-established processes. The goal is to create a stable, effective, and easily administered drug product.

Manufacturing Process:

- **Granulation**: This process is used to convert the powder blend of the Active Pharmaceutical Ingredient (API) and excipients into granules, which are easier to compress into tablets. Granulation can be wet or dry.

  - **Wet Granulation**: The drug powder is mixed with a binder solution, then moistened, and passed through a granulator to form wet granules. These are then dried and sieved to obtain uniform-sized granules.
  - **Dry Granulation**: This method is used for drugs that are sensitive to moisture or heat. The powder mixture is compacted into large chunks and then broken down into granules.

- **Compression**: Granules are compressed into tablets using a tablet press. The amount of force applied during compression determines the tablet's hardness and uniformity.
- **Coating**: Tablets may be coated to protect the drug from degradation, mask the taste, or control the release rate of the drug. Coating can be achieved through **sugar coating** or **film coating**, where a thin layer of polymer is applied to the tablet.
- **Packaging**: After compression and coating, tablets are packaged into bottles, blister packs, or foil strips. Packaging ensures the tablets are protected from moisture, light, and air.
- **2. Capsules: Processes Involved in Filling Hard and Soft Gel Capsules**

Capsules are solid dosage forms in which the API is enclosed in a gelatin or other suitable shell. Capsules can be filled with powders, granules, liquids, or semi-solids.

Manufacturing Process:

- **Filling Hard Gel Capsules:**

  - **Powder/Granule Filling**: The API and excipients are blended together and filled into the hard gelatin capsule shell using an automatic capsule-filling machine. The capsule shells are typically **two-piece hard gelatin** or **HPMC** capsules.
  - **Sealing**: The two capsule halves are sealed together using a banding process to prevent leakage.

- **Filling Soft Gel Capsules:**

  - **Liquid Filling**: Soft gel capsules are typically filled with a liquid formulation, such as oils or liquid APIs, which are enclosed in a gelatin shell. This process involves **sealing** the soft capsules using a heat and pressure process to ensure the integrity of the capsule.

- **Liquid-Filled Capsules**: These capsules are designed to contain liquid formulations. The formulation is typically filled under controlled conditions to avoid air bubbles or leakage, and the capsules are sealed to prevent moisture ingress.
- **Packaging**: Capsules are packaged in blister packs or bottles. Special care is taken to ensure moisture-sensitive capsules are stored in **airtight** and **moisture-resistant packaging**.
- **3. Injectables: Sterile Formulation Processes, Aseptic Filling, Lyophilization, and Packaging Considerations**

  Injectables are pharmaceutical products designed for administration via injection (intravenous, intramuscular, subcutaneous). The manufacturing process for injectables is highly controlled to ensure sterility and the maintenance of drug stability.

  Manufacturing Process:
- **Sterile Formulation**: The API and excipients are dissolved or suspended in a sterile solvent, ensuring that the formulation is free from contaminants.

- **Aseptic Filling**: The sterile solution or suspension is filled into sterile vials, ampoules, or prefilled syringes in an **aseptic environment**. The filling process must ensure that the drug is not contaminated during handling or filling.
- **Lyophilization (Freeze-Drying)**: For certain injectables, especially biologics, **lyophilization** is used to remove water content and stabilize the drug. This involves freezing the formulation, followed by drying under vacuum, which ensures the drug remains stable for extended periods.
- **Sterilization**: After filling, some injectable products require **sterilization** via methods such as **autoclaving** (for heat-stable formulations) or **filtration** (for heat-sensitive formulations).
- **Packaging**: The vials or syringes are sealed in a sterile environment and packaged in **tamper-proof containers**. Packaging must protect the product from contamination and ensure sterility until use.
- **4. Topical Forms: Manufacturing Processes for Creams, Ointments, Gels, and Lotions**

  Topical dosage forms are applied to the skin for localized effects. These formulations require careful selection of excipients to achieve the desired texture, stability, and drug delivery.

  Manufacturing Process:
- **Creams and Ointments:**

  - **Emulsification**: For creams (oil-in-water or water-in-oil), the oil and water phases are emulsified using an emulsifying agent. The API is then dispersed in the emulsion.
  - **Homogenization**: To ensure uniform distribution of the API and excipients, the mixture is homogenized. This process helps achieve the desired consistency and smooth texture.

- **Gels:**

  - **Gel Formation**: Gels are formed by dispersing the gelling agent (such as **carbomer** or **hydroxyethyl cellulose**) in water or alcohol. The gel is then mixed with the API and additional excipients to achieve the desired viscosity and texture.

- **Lotions:**

- ◦ **Mixing and Homogenization**: Lotions are typically oil-in-water emulsions. The API is dispersed in a mixture of water and excipients (emulsifiers), and the lotion is homogenized to achieve a smooth, spreadable consistency.

- **Packaging**: Topical products are filled into **tubes**, **jars**, or **pump dispensers**, ensuring that the packaging maintains the stability and prevents contamination of the product.
- **5. Liquid Dosage Forms: Manufacturing Processes for Solutions, Suspensions, and Emulsions**

  Liquid dosage forms, such as solutions, suspensions, and emulsions, are widely used for patients who have difficulty swallowing tablets or capsules.

  Manufacturing Process:
- **Solutions:**

- ◦ **Dissolution**: The API is dissolved in an appropriate solvent (e.g., water, alcohol) under controlled conditions. The formulation is then filtered to remove any impurities or undissolved particles.

- **Suspensions:**

- ◦ **Dispersion**: In suspensions, the API is dispersed in a liquid medium, often with the help of **suspending agents** (e.g., **xanthan gum** or **carboxymethyl cellulose**) to prevent sedimentation of the drug particles. The suspension is mixed to ensure uniform distribution.

- **Emulsions:**

- ◦ **Emulsification**: Emulsions are formed by mixing immiscible liquids (typically oil and water) with an emulsifying agent (e.g., **lecithin, polysorbates**). The process requires careful mixing and stabilizing to prevent phase separation.

- **Sterilization and Filtration**: Both solutions and suspensions are subjected to **sterilization** (autoclaving or filtration) to ensure they are free of microbial contamination.

- **Packaging**: Liquid dosage forms are packaged in **bottles, vials,** or **blisters,** and special care is taken to ensure that containers are tightly sealed to prevent contamination.
- **6. Controlled-Release Dosage Forms: Techniques for Formulating Sustained-Release, Extended-Release, and Targeted Delivery Systems**
  Controlled-release formulations are designed to release the API over an extended period, maintaining therapeutic drug levels without the need for frequent dosing.
  Manufacturing Process:
- **Sustained-Release (SR) and Extended-Release (ER):**

  - **Matrix Systems:** Drugs are embedded in a matrix made of **polymers** (e.g., **HPMC, ethylcellulose**) that control the rate at which the drug is released over time.
  - **Coated Systems:** Coating the drug with a polymeric film allows for the delayed release of the API. The thickness and composition of the coating determine the release rate.

- **Targeted Delivery Systems:**

  - **Nanoparticles** and **liposomes** are used to encapsulate the API and direct it to specific sites in the body, such as cancer cells or inflamed tissues. These systems often use surface modifications to improve targeting and drug absorption.

- **Packaging and Dosing**: Controlled-release formulations are often packaged in special blister packs or bottles, with clear instructions on dosage schedules to ensure that the drug is taken as intended.
- **Key Quality Control Tests and Standards**
  Quality control (QC) plays a critical role in the pharmaceutical manufacturing process. It ensures that the final product is safe, effective, and of high quality. QC tests are performed at various stages of production to verify that the drug product complies with the required specifications for identity, purity, content uniformity, dissolution, physical and chemical characteristics, microbiological safety, and packaging integrity. Below is an overview of the key quality control tests and standards used in pharmaceutical manufacturing.

1. Identity and Purity Tests: Ensuring the Drug Substance is Pure and Correctly Identified

- **Identity Testing**: This test ensures that the drug substance is what it is supposed to be. It verifies the correct drug is present in the formulation. Techniques like **chromatography** (e.g., **HPLC** or **TLC**), **spectroscopy** (e.g., **UV-Vis, IR**), and **mass spectrometry** are commonly used to confirm the identity of the API.

- **Purity Testing**: Purity testing determines the presence of any impurities or contaminants in the drug substance. High levels of impurities can compromise the safety and efficacy of the drug. **Chromatographic methods** are often used to separate and quantify impurities, while **specific tests** may be conducted for residual solvents, heavy metals, or microbial contamination.

- **2. Content Uniformity: Ensuring Consistent Distribution of the Active Ingredient in Each Dose**

  Content uniformity is a critical quality control parameter, ensuring that each dosage unit (e.g., tablet or capsule) contains the correct amount of the active pharmaceutical ingredient (API). Variations in content can lead to either underdosing (which may result in therapeutic failure) or overdosing (which may result in toxicity).

- **Testing Method**: The content uniformity test is typically performed using **HPLC** or **UV spectrophotometry** to measure the API concentration in each dosage unit. A uniform distribution is crucial for tablets, capsules, and powders for oral suspension, and each unit must meet a **specified range of variation** (usually within ±10% of the labeled dose).

- **3. Dissolution Testing: Evaluating the Rate and Extent of Drug Release from the Dosage Form**

  Dissolution testing evaluates how quickly and completely the drug is released from the dosage form (e.g., tablet, capsule) into the dissolution medium. This test simulates the conditions of the gastrointestinal tract, where the drug will dissolve and be absorbed.

- **Purpose**: The rate and extent of dissolution are critical for understanding how the drug will be absorbed in the body. Drugs that dissolve too slowly may have delayed onset, while those that dissolve too quickly may cause side effects or require frequent dosing.

- **Testing Method: Dissolution testers** (e.g., **USP Apparatus 1 or 2**) are commonly used to evaluate the dissolution profile. The test is performed by placing the dosage form in a specific volume of dissolution medium and rotating it at a standard speed and temperature. Samples are taken at set intervals and analyzed for API concentration.

- **4. Physical and Chemical Testing: Tests for Hardness, Friability, Disintegration, Viscosity, and pH**

  Various physical and chemical tests are conducted to ensure the physical integrity and stability of the drug product.

- **Hardness Testing**: This measures the strength of tablets and assesses whether they can withstand mechanical stress during packaging, transport, and storage. Tablets must be strong enough to avoid breaking but also not too hard that they cannot be easily disintegrated in the gastrointestinal tract. The **Pfizer hardness tester** or **Vernier caliper** is used to test the hardness of tablets.

- **Friability Testing**: Friability refers to the tendency of tablets to break apart or crumble. Tablets are subjected to a rotating drum, and the percentage weight loss is measured. The **USP standards** typically set a friability limit of ≤1% for most tablets.

- **Disintegration Testing**: Disintegration testing evaluates how quickly tablets or capsules break apart when exposed to a specific fluid at a set temperature. This is important for ensuring that the drug is released effectively in the gastrointestinal tract.

- **Viscosity Testing**: For liquid formulations like suspensions, emulsions, or gels, viscosity is tested to ensure the appropriate thickness and flow. **Brookfield viscometers** or similar instruments are used to measure the viscosity of liquids.

- **pH Testing**: The pH of liquid formulations is critical as it can affect the stability, solubility, and bioavailability of the API. The pH is measured using a **pH meter**, and the formulation is adjusted if necessary to ensure it is within the desired range for stability and efficacy.

- **5. Microbial Testing: Ensuring Sterility and Absence of Harmful Microorganisms in the Product**

  Microbial testing ensures that the drug product is free from harmful microorganisms such as bacteria, fungi, or yeast that could compromise safety and efficacy.

- **Sterility Testing**: Sterility is a critical concern for **injectables, ophthalmic formulations**, and **topical products** that are applied to broken skin or mucous membranes. The **USP** provides guidelines for sterility testing, including **direct inoculation** or **membrane filtration** methods.

- **Microbial Limits Testing**: For non-sterile products (e.g., tablets, creams), microbial limits tests are conducted to determine the acceptable levels of microbial contamination. **Total bacterial count** and **yeast and mold count** are assessed using **plate count** methods or **most probable number (MPN)** tests.
- **Endotoxin Testing**: For injectables, particularly parenterals, **endotoxin testing** (using the **Limulus Amebocyte Lysate (LAL) test**) is required to ensure that the product does not contain harmful levels of endotoxins from bacteria.
- **6. Packaging Integrity: Tests to Ensure Packaging Protects the Drug from Degradation and Contamination**

  The integrity of the packaging is essential for protecting the drug from environmental factors such as light, moisture, and air. Packaging must ensure the stability and sterility of the product until it is used by the patient.
- **Leak Testing**: For injectable products and other sealed containers, **leak tests** ensure that there are no breaches in the packaging that could lead to contamination. The most common method is the **vacuum decay test**, where the sealed container is subjected to a vacuum, and any leaks are detected by a drop in pressure.
- **Seal Strength Testing**: For blister packs and other sealed packaging, tests are conducted to ensure that the seals are secure and will not open unintentionally during handling or transportation.
- **Moisture Resistance**: Packaging must protect the drug from moisture, particularly for hygroscopic drugs. **Water vapor transmission rate (WVTR)** testing is used to assess the ability of packaging materials to prevent moisture ingress.
- **Light Protection**: For drugs that are sensitive to light, packaging must be designed to block UV rays. **UV permeability tests** can be conducted to ensure the packaging offers adequate protection from light.
- **Good Manufacturing Practices (GMP)**

  Good Manufacturing Practices (GMP) are a set of guidelines and regulations designed to ensure that pharmaceutical products are consistently produced and controlled according to quality standards. GMP covers all aspects of production, from the raw materials used to the final product, ensuring that drugs are safe, effective, and of high quality. Adherence to GMP ensures that pharmaceutical manufacturers meet regulatory requirements and maintain the trust of patients, healthcare professionals, and regulatory agencies.

1. GMP Overview: Importance of GMP in Ensuring Consistent Quality and Safety of Drug Products

GMP is crucial in the pharmaceutical industry to ensure that drugs are produced with consistent quality, safety, and efficacy. The guidelines are designed to minimize the risks associated with drug production, such as contamination, mix-ups, and errors. Compliance with GMP guarantees that pharmaceutical products are safe for consumption and meet the required standards of quality.

- **Ensures Product Quality**: GMP ensures that the drug is manufactured to meet the required specifications, including potency, safety, and consistency across different batches.

- **Prevents Contamination**: Proper practices and controls are in place to prevent contamination by bacteria, viruses, or chemicals during the production process, ensuring that the drug product remains sterile and uncontaminated.

- **Reduces Risk of Errors**: By establishing standardized processes, GMP minimizes human error, equipment failure, and other risks that may lead to product defects or inconsistency.

2. Regulatory Compliance: Adhering to GMP Guidelines Set by Regulatory Agencies like the FDA and EMA

Pharmaceutical companies must comply with GMP regulations to obtain approval for marketing their products. Regulatory agencies, such as the **FDA (U.S.), EMA (European Union)**, and **CDSCO (India)**, set specific GMP guidelines that must be followed during the manufacturing process.

- **FDA Guidelines**: The **FDA** enforces **21 CFR Part 210 and 211**, which detail the GMP regulations for the manufacture of drugs. These guidelines cover all aspects of production, from the receipt of raw materials to final product release.

- **EMA Guidelines**: The **European Medicines Agency (EMA)** provides detailed GMP guidelines that ensure the quality of medicinal products in the European Union. These guidelines include requirements for quality control, validation, and documentation.

- **International Harmonization**: Agencies like the **World Health Organization (WHO)** and the **International Council for**

Harmonisation (ICH) work to harmonize GMP standards across regions, which helps ensure consistent product quality worldwide.

3. Facility Design and Equipment: Standards for Cleanroom Design, Equipment Validation, and Maintenance

The design and maintenance of manufacturing facilities and equipment are central to GMP compliance. Pharmaceutical production areas must meet stringent standards to minimize contamination and ensure proper functioning.

- **Cleanroom Design**: Cleanrooms are controlled environments that minimize airborne particles and microbial contamination. These rooms must meet specific requirements for airflow, temperature, humidity, and cleanliness. The **ISO 14644** standard defines the cleanliness level of the air in cleanrooms.
- **Equipment Validation**: All equipment used in the manufacturing process must be validated to ensure that it operates according to its intended function and does not interfere with the quality of the drug product. Validation includes ensuring that equipment is calibrated, properly maintained, and functioning at optimal performance.
- **Equipment Maintenance**: Regular maintenance and calibration are essential for equipment reliability. Preventive maintenance schedules are established to ensure that equipment does not fail during production and that any potential issues are addressed before they affect the drug product.

4. Personnel Training and Hygiene: Ensuring Proper Training, Hygiene, and Safety Protocols for Manufacturing Staff

Personnel are a critical part of maintaining GMP compliance. Training, hygiene, and safety protocols help prevent contamination and ensure that employees follow the required standards during manufacturing.

- **Training**: All employees involved in drug production must be trained in GMP principles, the specific manufacturing processes they are involved in, and the risks associated with non-compliance. Continuous training ensures that personnel stay updated with changes in regulations and best practices.

- **Hygiene**: Manufacturing staff must follow strict hygiene protocols to prevent contamination. This includes wearing protective clothing (e.g., gloves, masks, gowns) and practicing hand washing, especially when handling active ingredients or finished products.
- **Safety Protocols**: Personnel must follow safety protocols to protect themselves and the drug product from contamination. This includes using cleanroom-specific procedures and avoiding unnecessary movement in critical production areas.
- **5. Documentation and Traceability: Requirements for Proper Documentation of Manufacturing Processes, Batch Records, and Product Traceability**

  Documentation and traceability are essential components of GMP. They ensure that every step of the manufacturing process is carefully documented, monitored, and can be traced back in the event of a quality issue.
- **Batch Records**: A **batch record** is a detailed log of the entire production process for each batch of drug product. It includes information on raw materials used, equipment used, production steps, in-process testing results, and final product testing. Batch records provide a comprehensive trail for quality assurance and regulatory compliance.
- **Traceability**: Traceability ensures that the origin of all materials used in the manufacturing process can be tracked. This includes raw materials, excipients, and packaging materials. If a defect is discovered, traceability allows the manufacturer to identify the source of the issue, whether it's a particular batch of raw material or a step in the manufacturing process.
- **Document Control**: Proper document control ensures that all records are accurate, complete, and up-to-date. This includes the management of manufacturing logs, testing results, equipment calibration reports, and deviations from standard operating procedures (SOPs). Any changes to documentation or processes must be properly reviewed and approved to ensure compliance with GMP.

In-Process and Final Product Testing

In the pharmaceutical manufacturing process, both **in-process testing** and **final product testing** are essential to ensure that the drug meets all required specifications for safety, efficacy, and quality. These tests help monitor the product at various stages of production and validate that the final product is consistent and compliant with regulatory requirements.

1. In-Process Testing: Ongoing Testing During the Manufacturing Process to Monitor Critical Parameters

In-process testing involves continuous or periodic testing during the production process to monitor critical parameters and ensure that the manufacturing process is under control. These tests help identify and correct any potential issues before the final product is completed, preventing batch failures or deviations.

- **Purpose**: The goal of in-process testing is to monitor parameters that can affect the quality of the final product, such as the consistency of mixing, temperature control, and the weight variation of individual units.
- **Critical Parameters Monitored:**

  - **Temperature**: Ensuring that equipment such as mixers, granulators, and dryers operate within the required temperature ranges. For example, improper temperatures during **granulation** or **drying** can lead to poor particle size distribution or drug degradation.
  - **Mixing Speed**: Consistency in mixing speed is essential for uniform distribution of the API and excipients in solid dosage forms. Variations in mixing speed can lead to **poor content uniformity** or **inconsistent drug release**.
  - **Weight Variation**: Monitoring the weight of tablets or capsules ensures that each unit contains the correct amount of the API. This is particularly important for maintaining **content uniformity**.
  - **pH and Viscosity**: For liquid formulations, parameters like pH and viscosity are continuously monitored during production to ensure that the drug remains within the required specifications.

- **Methods**: The testing is performed using various methods, including **spectrophotometry**, **chromatography**, **viscometry**, and other instrumental techniques to monitor quality-critical parameters throughout the manufacturing process.

2. Final Product Testing: Final Testing of the Product Before Release to Ensure Compliance with All Specifications

Final product testing is performed once the drug product is completed, but before it is released for distribution. The purpose of final testing is to ensure that the drug product meets all required specifications for identity, potency, purity, dissolution, and stability, confirming that it is safe and effective for patient use.

Key Tests:

- **Identity Testing**: Verifying that the correct drug is present in the final formulation and that it matches the approved specifications.
- **Potency**: Testing the **API content** to ensure that the drug contains the correct amount of active ingredient as specified. Potency is commonly tested using techniques like **HPLC** or **UV-Vis spectrophotometry**.
- **Dissolution Testing**: Ensuring that the drug releases the active ingredient at the correct rate and extent to ensure proper absorption.
- **Microbial Testing**: Ensuring the absence of harmful microorganisms in non-sterile products.
- **Stability**: The final product is tested for stability to confirm that it maintains its efficacy and safety over the shelf life and under storage conditions.
- **Compliance with Specifications**: The product must meet all **pharmacopoeial** and **internal company specifications** for release, including standards set by regulatory agencies such as the **FDA, EMA,** or **CDSCO**.

3. Release Criteria: Criteria for Releasing the Product to the Market Based on Testing Results, Including Potency, Safety, and Stability

Before a batch is released to the market, it must meet strict **release criteria** based on the results from final product testing. These criteria ensure that the drug is safe, effective, and meets the expected quality standards.

- **Potency**: The drug must have the correct potency, ensuring that it will produce the desired therapeutic effect in patients.
- **Safety**: The product must be free from any harmful impurities, contaminants, or microbial contamination that could pose a risk to patients.
- **Stability**: The drug must meet the required stability standards, ensuring that it maintains its quality and efficacy throughout its shelf life. This is particularly important for determining the **expiration date** of the product.

- **Compliance with Regulatory Standards**: The final product must comply with all regulatory guidelines, including those established by agencies such as the **FDA** or **EMA**, to be released for sale.
- The **release criteria** ensure that only products that have passed all required quality control tests and meet the established specifications are distributed to patients.

4. Handling Non-Conformances: Procedures for Dealing with Batch Failures, Deviations, and Corrective Actions

During the manufacturing process, there may be instances where batches do not meet the required quality standards or where deviations from the established process occur. **Non-conformances** must be addressed promptly to ensure that the final product is safe and effective. A clear and structured approach to managing non-conformances helps identify the root cause and ensures that corrective actions are taken to prevent recurrence.

- **Non-Conformance Events:**

  - **Batch Failures**: If a batch fails a critical quality control test, such as content uniformity or dissolution, it must be evaluated to determine if the entire batch is unsuitable for release. The batch may be discarded, reworked, or held for further investigation.
  - **Deviations**: Deviations refer to instances where the manufacturing process or testing procedures do not conform to the established **Standard Operating Procedures (SOPs)** or **Good Manufacturing Practices (GMP)**. Deviations may occur due to equipment malfunctions, human error, or environmental factors.

- **Corrective Actions:**

  - **Root Cause Analysis**: When a batch fails or a deviation occurs, a thorough investigation is conducted to determine the root cause. This can involve analyzing the manufacturing process, reviewing batch records, and identifying any procedural or equipment issues.
  - **Corrective and Preventive Actions (CAPA)**: Based on the investigation, corrective actions are implemented to address the immediate issue (e.g., adjusting the process or repairing equipment). Preventive actions are also put in place to ensure that similar issues do not arise in future batches (e.g., revising SOPs, retraining

personnel, or upgrading equipment).

- **Documentation of Non-Conformances**: All non-conformances, deviations, and corrective actions must be thoroughly documented as part of the **quality management system (QMS)**. This documentation provides a clear record for regulatory compliance and internal audits.
- **Regulatory Reporting**: In some cases, manufacturers are required to report non-conformances, deviations, or recalls to regulatory authorities. This ensures transparency and helps maintain product safety standards.

CHAPTER FOUR

Pharmaceutical Excipients in Product Development

This chapter delves into the essential excipients used in pharmaceutical formulations. Excipients serve multiple purposes, including enhancing the stability, solubility, bioavailability, and overall effectiveness of the drug. Understanding their roles is crucial for developing formulations that meet the required standards for safety, efficacy, and patient compliance.

Solvents and solubilizers are used in pharmaceutical formulations to dissolve or disperse the Active Pharmaceutical Ingredient (API), ensuring it is in an appropriate form for delivery to the target site of action. The selection of the right solvent or solubilizer is crucial in enhancing the solubility and bioavailability of poorly soluble drugs.

4.1 Types of Solvents:

1. **Water:**

   - **Role:** Water is the most commonly used solvent in pharmaceutical formulations, especially for **oral liquid formulations** such as **solutions, syrups,** and **suspensions.** It is often preferred due to its **biocompatibility, non-toxicity,** and ability to dissolve a wide range of hydrophilic APIs.
   - **Applications:**

     - Used in the preparation of **aqueous solutions** (e.g., intravenous solutions, oral solutions).
     - Key component in **oral suspensions** where the drug particles are dispersed in water.

- Commonly used in **reconstitutable formulations**, such as **powder for oral suspension**.

- Advantages:

  - Safe, inexpensive, and easily available.
  - The most effective solvent for hydrophilic drugs.

2. **Alcohol:**

   - **Role:** Alcohol is frequently used as a solvent in **oral liquid formulations** (e.g., **tinctures, spirits**) and in some **injectable products**. Alcohol helps dissolve hydrophobic drugs that cannot be dissolved in water.
   - **Applications:**

     - **Oral Liquid Formulations:** Alcohol is used in the preparation of **tinctures** (which are alcoholic solutions of medicinal substances) and **elixirs** (which are solutions of both alcohol and water containing flavoring agents).
     - **Injectables:** Certain **intravenous (IV) drugs** are formulated in alcohol to help dissolve the drug and prevent crystallization.

   - **Advantages:**

     - Alcohol can dissolve both hydrophilic and lipophilic (fat-soluble) drugs.
     - It has antimicrobial properties, which are beneficial for injectable solutions.

3. **Organic Solvents:**

   - **Role:** Organic solvents are used when a drug is poorly soluble in water but can be dissolved in organic solvents. These solvents include **ethanol, propylene glycol,** and **glycerin.** These solvents are particularly useful when water-based solutions are not feasible for certain drugs.
   - **Applications:**

- **Hydrophobic Drug Formulations**: Organic solvents are used for dissolving hydrophobic (lipophilic) drugs in **oral liquid formulations, injectables**, and **topical formulations**.
- **Cosmetic and Topical Products**: For creams, ointments, and gels, these solvents can solubilize the drug for effective delivery across the skin.

○ **Examples:**

- **Ethanol**: Often used in **oral solutions** for both hydrophilic and lipophilic drugs.
- **Propylene Glycol**: Commonly used in **oral**, **parenteral**, and **topical** formulations as a solvent for drugs that require low toxicity.
- **Glycerin**: Used in **oral syrups** and **topical formulations**, acting as both a solvent and humectant (moisture-retaining agent).

○ **Advantages:**

- Can dissolve a wide range of hydrophobic drugs, which are difficult to dissolve in water.
- Many organic solvents (like glycerin) are non-toxic and compatible with the human body.

Solubilizers:

Solubilizers are excipients that enhance the solubility of poorly soluble APIs, improving the **bioavailability** of the drug. Poorly soluble drugs often have limited absorption in the gastrointestinal tract, reducing their therapeutic efficacy.

- **Types of Solubilizers:**

○ **Surfactants**: These molecules have hydrophilic and hydrophobic ends, allowing them to solubilize drugs by forming **micelles** in aqueous solutions. Common surfactants include **Polysorbates (e.g., Tween 80)** and **Sodium Lauryl Sulfate (SLS)**.
○ **Co-Solvents**: Co-solvents such as **ethanol, propylene glycol**, and **glycerin** are often used in combination with water to improve the

solubility of poorly soluble drugs.

- ◦ **Cyclodextrins:** These are cyclic oligosaccharides that can form inclusion complexes with hydrophobic drugs, enhancing their solubility and stability in aqueous solutions. Cyclodextrins are commonly used in **oral solutions** and **injectables**.

- **Applications:**

  - ◦ **Oral Formulations:** Solubilizers are used to improve the solubility and bioavailability of **poorly soluble drugs**, making them suitable for oral administration. Solubilizers can enhance the drug's ability to dissolve in the gastrointestinal fluid, improving absorption.
  - ◦ **Injectables:** Solubilizers are essential in formulating injectable products, especially when the drug is poorly soluble in water. For example, **polyethylene glycol (PEG)** can be used to solubilize drugs for intravenous formulations.
  - ◦ **Topical and Ophthalmic Formulations:** Solubilizers can also be used in topical creams, gels, and ophthalmic solutions to enhance drug solubility and ensure effective delivery.

Applications in Pharmaceutical Formulations

Solvents are critical in the formulation of pharmaceutical products, particularly for **oral, injectable,** and **topical** dosage forms. They are used to dissolve or disperse the **Active Pharmaceutical Ingredient (API)**, ensuring that the drug is in a suitable form for absorption and therapeutic effect. Below are the key applications of solvents in different pharmaceutical formulations:

1. Oral Solutions and Suspensions: Solvents Used to Dissolve or Suspend the API in Liquid Dosage Forms

Oral solutions and **suspensions** are common dosage forms, particularly for patients who have difficulty swallowing solid tablets or capsules. Solvents play a crucial role in ensuring that the API is delivered effectively.

- **Oral Solutions:**

  - ◦ **Solvents** such as **water, ethanol,** and **propylene glycol** are used to dissolve the API. In this case, the drug is dissolved in a solvent to form a **clear, homogeneous solution.**

- ◦ **Applications:**

  - ▪ Drugs that are highly soluble or designed to be rapidly absorbed in the digestive tract are often formulated as oral solutions.
  - ▪ Common examples include **liquid antibiotics (e.g., amoxicillin), antipyretics (e.g., paracetamol)**, and **antacids.**

- **Oral Suspensions:**

  - ◦ **Solvents** like **water** or **glycerin** are used in **suspensions** to disperse the API in an aqueous base. In suspensions, the drug is not completely dissolved but rather exists as small solid particles suspended in the solvent.
  - ◦ **Applications:**

    - ▪ For drugs that are poorly soluble in water, **suspending agents** such as **xanthan gum** or **carboxymethyl cellulose** are used to ensure that the drug particles remain uniformly dispersed in the liquid.
    - ▪ Common examples include **liquid formulations for pediatric use** or drugs like **ibuprofen suspension** and **antifungal suspensions.**

2. Injectables: Solvents Used to Dissolve or Dilute the Drug for Intravenous, Intramuscular, or Subcutaneous Administration

Injectables are essential in delivering drugs that need to be rapidly absorbed into the bloodstream, especially in critical care situations. The choice of solvent for injectable formulations is crucial to ensure the **solubility, stability,** and **biocompatibility** of the drug.

- **Intravenous (IV) Injectables:**

  - ◦ **Water** is the most commonly used solvent for **IV formulations** due to its ability to dissolve a wide range of drugs and its biocompatibility with the human body.
  - ◦ **Co-solvents** like **propylene glycol** or **ethanol** are sometimes used when the API is poorly soluble in water. These co-solvents help dissolve the drug and ensure that it remains stable in the solution until administration.
  - ◦ **Applications:**

- **Chemotherapy drugs**, **antibiotics**, and **parenteral nutrition** solutions often require specific solvents to dissolve the drug and maintain its efficacy.
- **Sterile filtration** and **aseptic conditions** are essential to prevent microbial contamination.

- **Intramuscular (IM) and Subcutaneous (SC) Injectables:**

  - **Oil-based solvents** (e.g., **sesame oil, castor oil**) are used for **IM and SC injectables** to ensure **slow and sustained release** of the drug. Oil-based solvents help to reduce the irritation that water-based formulations might cause when injected into muscles or subcutaneous tissue.
  - **Water** and **glycerin** may also be used depending on the formulation, ensuring the drug is safely delivered without the need for complex administration techniques.
  - **Applications:**

    - **Hormones, vaccines**, and **long-acting antibiotics** are commonly formulated as oil-based injectables to control the drug release over time.

3. Topical Formulations: Solvents Help in the Dispersion of the Drug for Creams, Gels, and Lotions

Topical formulations are designed for local delivery of the drug to the skin or mucous membranes. The use of solvents in these formulations is essential for ensuring that the drug is properly dissolved or dispersed and that it can penetrate the skin barrier efficiently.

- **Creams, Ointments, and Gels:**

  - **Solvents** like **water, propylene glycol, glycerin**, and **ethanol** are used in **topical formulations** to dissolve or disperse the API. Water is often used in **emulsion-based** creams (oil-in-water or water-in-oil) where the solvent helps to dissolve the drug and ensure uniform distribution.
  - **Oil-based solvents** such as **mineral oil** or **petrolatum** are used in **ointments** to provide a protective barrier and improve drug retention

on the skin.

- **Applications:**

    ◦ **Topical corticosteroids** (e.g., **hydrocortisone cream**), **antifungal creams**, and **local anesthetics** (e.g., **lidocaine gel**) are formulated using solvents to ensure the active ingredient is effectively delivered to the target site.
    ◦ **Gels** often contain solvents such as **ethanol** or **water** combined with gelling agents like **carbomers**. These gels help deliver drugs for **skin conditions**, providing **localized pain relief** or **anti-inflammatory effects**.

- **Lotions:**

    ◦ **Lotions** are thin, liquid formulations used for large skin areas. **Water** or **ethanol** is commonly used as the solvent, along with **emulsifying agents** to help dissolve or disperse the drug throughout the formulation.
    ◦ **Applications:**

        ▪ **Moisturizing lotions, antiseptic lotions,** and **sunscreens** often rely on solvents to solubilize the active ingredients, ensuring they are evenly distributed and effective upon application.

Solubilizers

Solubilizers are excipients used in pharmaceutical formulations to enhance the solubility of poorly water-soluble drugs. Many drugs, particularly those with low solubility, face challenges in achieving adequate bioavailability because they do not dissolve well in the body's aqueous environment. Solubilizers help overcome this issue by improving the dissolution rate and ensuring that more of the active pharmaceutical ingredient (API) is available for absorption, thus improving the drug's **bioavailability** and **therapeutic efficacy**.

Types of Solubilizers:

1. **Surfactants:**

- **Structure**: Surfactants are amphiphilic molecules, meaning they have both hydrophilic (water-loving) and hydrophobic (oil-loving) parts. This unique structure allows surfactants to reduce the surface tension between the drug and the solvent, facilitating the solubilization process.
- **Mechanism**: Surfactants work by forming **micelles** in aqueous solutions, where the hydrophobic part of the molecule encapsulates the poorly soluble drug, allowing it to dissolve in water. Micelles create an environment where the lipophilic drug is solubilized, increasing its availability in the aqueous medium.
- **Examples**:

  - **Polysorbates (e.g., Tween 80, Tween 20)**: These non-ionic surfactants are widely used in pharmaceutical formulations to solubilize hydrophobic drugs.
  - **Sodium Lauryl Sulfate (SLS)**: A commonly used surfactant that can solubilize hydrophobic compounds in oral and injectable formulations.

2. **Co-solvents**:

   - **Structure**: Co-solvents are organic solvents that, when combined with water, improve the solubility of poorly water-soluble drugs. By reducing the polarity of the solvent system, co-solvents help dissolve hydrophobic drugs.
   - **Mechanism**: Co-solvents work by interacting with the API to create a more favorable environment for solubility. They are typically used in **oral liquid formulations** or **injectables** where water alone is insufficient to dissolve the API.
   - **Examples**:

     - **Ethanol**: Used in many oral formulations (e.g., **tinctures, elixirs**) and injectables to solubilize hydrophobic drugs.
     - **Propylene Glycol**: Often used in **topical, oral**, and **parenteral** formulations to dissolve poorly soluble drugs.
     - **Glycerin**: A commonly used co-solvent for oral suspensions and topical formulations.

3. **Complexing Agents (e.g., Cyclodextrins):**

- **Structure:** Cyclodextrins are cyclic oligosaccharides made of glucose molecules arranged in a ring structure. They have a hydrophilic outer surface and a hydrophobic central cavity.
- **Mechanism:** Cyclodextrins solubilize poorly water-soluble drugs by forming inclusion complexes, where the hydrophobic drug is encapsulated in the cavity of the cyclodextrin molecule. This protects the drug from degradation and improves its solubility in water.
- **Types of Cyclodextrins:**

  - **Alpha-cyclodextrin:** Composed of six glucose units, often used for drugs with moderate hydrophobicity.
  - **Beta-cyclodextrin:** Composed of seven glucose units, commonly used for enhancing the solubility of moderately lipophilic drugs.
  - **Gamma-cyclodextrin:** Composed of eight glucose units, effective for larger, more hydrophobic drug molecules.

- **Applications:** Cyclodextrins are widely used in **oral**, **injectable**, and **topical formulations** to improve the solubility and stability of poorly soluble drugs, as well as to enhance their bioavailability.
- **Examples:**

  - **Hydroxypropyl-beta-cyclodextrin (HPβCD):** Commonly used in formulations to improve the solubility and stability of drugs like **itraconazole, ketoconazole,** and **paclitaxel.**

Applications of Solubilizers:

1. **Oral Solutions and Suspensions:**

- **Surfactants** and **co-solvents** are frequently used in **oral liquid formulations** to improve the solubility of poorly water-soluble drugs. These formulations can help ensure that the drug is absorbed effectively when ingested.
- **Cyclodextrins** are used in **oral formulations** to solubilize hydrophobic drugs and enhance their absorption in the gastrointestinal tract, improving bioavailability.

2. **Injectables:**

   - **Co-solvents** like **propylene glycol** and **ethanol** are commonly used in injectable formulations, particularly for drugs that are poorly soluble in water. By using these solvents, manufacturers can prepare solutions that ensure the drug remains dissolved and is available for injection without causing irritation or precipitation.
   - **Cyclodextrins** are used in **parenteral formulations** to improve solubility and reduce the need for large volumes of solvents, which can improve the drug's ease of administration and reduce the risk of toxicity from excess excipient.

3. **Topical and Ophthalmic Formulations:**

   - Solubilizers are used in **topical creams, gels,** and **ointments** to improve the solubility of lipophilic drugs, allowing them to penetrate the skin barrier more effectively. For example, **propylene glycol** and **glycerin** are used to improve the solubility and absorption of drugs in **topical formulations.**
   - **Cyclodextrins** can also be used in **ophthalmic solutions** to enhance the solubility of drugs and improve their ability to be absorbed through the cornea.

4. **Enhanced Bioavailability:**

   - Solubilizers play a key role in improving the **bioavailability** of poorly soluble drugs by ensuring that a sufficient concentration of the drug is available for absorption after administration. This is especially important for drugs that have **low aqueous solubility**, which may otherwise have poor or inconsistent absorption profiles.

5. **Sustained or Controlled-Release Formulations:**

   - Solubilizers can be used in **sustained-release** or **controlled-release** formulations to modulate the release rate of poorly soluble drugs. This can improve the therapeutic outcome by maintaining drug levels within the therapeutic window over an extended period, reducing the frequency of dosing.

4.2 Cyclodextrins and Their Applications

Cyclodextrins are a class of cyclic oligosaccharides made up of glucose units linked by α-(1,4)-glycosidic bonds. These molecules have a unique structure with a **hydrophilic exterior** and a **hydrophobic cavity** that allows them to form inclusion complexes with a variety of hydrophobic drugs. Cyclodextrins play a significant role in enhancing the solubility, stability, and bioavailability of poorly water-soluble drugs.

Structure of Cyclodextrins

Cyclodextrins are **cyclic** structures composed of **glucose** molecules arranged in a ring shape. The number of glucose units can vary, and different types of cyclodextrins are classified based on their ring size.

- **Alpha-Cyclodextrin (α-CD)**: Composed of **six glucose units**.
- **Beta-Cyclodextrin (β-CD)**: Composed of **seven glucose units**. This is the most commonly used cyclodextrin in pharmaceutical formulations.
- **Gamma-Cyclodextrin (γ-CD)**: Composed of **eight glucose units**.

These cyclodextrins are characterized by a **hydrophilic exterior** (due to the hydroxyl groups on the glucose units) and a **hydrophobic cavity** in the center of the ring. The hydrophobic cavity allows cyclodextrins to **encapsulate** hydrophobic molecules, forming inclusion complexes.

- **Hydrophilic Exterior**: The exterior of the cyclodextrin is water-soluble, which makes it suitable for inclusion in aqueous drug formulations.
- **Hydrophobic Cavity**: The interior cavity of the cyclodextrin is hydrophobic and capable of trapping lipophilic (fat-soluble) molecules. This enables the cyclodextrin to solubilize poorly water-soluble drugs.

Applications of Cyclodextrins

Cyclodextrins have widespread use in **pharmaceutical formulations** due to their ability to enhance the solubility, stability, and bioavailability of poorly soluble drugs. They are particularly valuable for drugs that are hydrophobic and have limited solubility in water. Some of the key applications include:

1. Role in Solubility and Stability

Cyclodextrins significantly enhance the **solubility** and **stability** of poorly soluble drugs by forming inclusion complexes. By encapsulating the hydrophobic part of the drug molecule, cyclodextrins prevent degradation caused by light, oxygen, or moisture, thus improving the overall stability of the drug.

- **Improved Solubility**: Cyclodextrins can increase the solubility of poorly water-soluble drugs by forming **water-soluble inclusion complexes**, allowing drugs to dissolve better in the aqueous environment of the gastrointestinal tract.
- **Stability Enhancement**: Cyclodextrins can stabilize drugs that are prone to **oxidation**, **hydrolysis**, or **photo-degradation** by **shielding** them within the hydrophobic cavity, reducing their exposure to degrading factors.

2. Controlled Release of Drugs

Cyclodextrins are used in the formulation of **controlled-release** systems, where they can modulate the release of the drug over time. The encapsulation of the drug within the cyclodextrin complex allows for **gradual drug release** as the complex slowly dissociates in the body.

- **Sustained Release**: Cyclodextrins provide a controlled release profile, reducing fluctuations in drug plasma levels and improving patient compliance by allowing for less frequent dosing.
- **Targeted Release**: Cyclodextrins can be engineered to release drugs at specific sites in the gastrointestinal tract or in particular tissues, enhancing the drug's therapeutic efficacy and minimizing side effects.

3. Oral Formulations

Cyclodextrins are widely used in **oral formulations** to enhance the **bioavailability** of drugs, particularly those with poor solubility.

- **Improved Bioavailability**: Many drugs that have limited water solubility, such as **itraconazole** (an antifungal), **paclitaxel** (an anticancer agent), and **griseofulvin** (an antifungal), benefit from cyclodextrin inclusion complexes, which improve their absorption in the gastrointestinal tract.
- **Drug Delivery Systems**: Cyclodextrins are used in **solid dosage forms** (e.g., tablets, powders) and **liquid formulations** (e.g., oral suspensions,

solutions) to enhance solubility and ensure consistent drug absorption.

4. Injectable Formulations

Cyclodextrins are also used in **injectable formulations**, particularly for drugs that are poorly soluble in water. By forming inclusion complexes with the API, cyclodextrins allow drugs to be solubilized without the need for toxic organic solvents.

- **Parenteral Formulations**: Cyclodextrins are useful in **injectable products** where they help solubilize hydrophobic drugs such as **diazepam, phenytoin**, and **ketoconazole**, enabling their safe and effective administration via injection.
- **Reduced Solvent Toxicity**: Cyclodextrins reduce the need for organic solvents, which can be harmful to the patient, making these formulations safer.

5. Topical and Ophthalmic Formulations

Cyclodextrins are used in **topical** and **ophthalmic formulations** to enhance the solubility and skin penetration of drugs, especially those that are lipophilic.

- **Topical Delivery**: Cyclodextrins can be used in **creams, gels,** and **lotions** to solubilize drugs and improve their **dermal absorption**, which is particularly useful for drugs like **anti-inflammatory agents, analgesics,** and **antibiotics** that are poorly soluble in water.
- **Ophthalmic Solutions**: Cyclodextrins are used in **eye drops** to increase the solubility of drugs like **pilocarpine** and **timolol**, improving the **ocular bioavailability** and therapeutic outcomes for eye diseases.

Role in Solubility and Stability of Cyclodextrins

Cyclodextrins play a significant role in improving the **solubility** and stability of poorly water-soluble drugs, making them crucial excipients in pharmaceutical formulations. Their unique structure—comprising a hydrophilic outer surface and a hydrophobic inner cavity—enables them to form inclusion complexes with hydrophobic drugs, improving their dissolution and bioavailability. Additionally, cyclodextrins protect sensitive drugs from degradation, ensuring they remain stable throughout the formulation process and during storage.

1. Cyclodextrins Form Inclusion Complexes with Poorly Soluble Drugs

Inclusion Complex Formation: Cyclodextrins can encapsulate the hydrophobic portions of poorly soluble drugs in their hydrophobic cavity, forming **inclusion complexes**. This process improves the drug's solubility by effectively "solubilizing" the API in an aqueous solution, thus making it more bioavailable when administered orally or via other routes.

- **Mechanism**: The hydrophobic part of the drug molecule is housed within the cyclodextrin's cavity, while the hydrophilic exterior interacts favorably with the aqueous environment. This interaction helps solvate the drug and keeps it in solution, reducing the tendency for the drug to precipitate out.
- **Impact on Solubility**:

  - **Improved Drug Dissolution**: Drugs that are poorly soluble in water benefit from cyclodextrins, which allow for better dispersion in the gastrointestinal tract, leading to enhanced dissolution and absorption.
  - **Enhanced Bioavailability**: By improving the solubility of poorly soluble drugs, cyclodextrins increase the amount of API available for absorption, thereby improving the **bioavailability** of the drug. This is particularly useful for **lipophilic drugs** like **paclitaxel**, **griseofulvin**, and **itraconazole**, which are typically difficult to dissolve in water.

2. Cyclodextrins Stabilize Unstable Drugs by Protecting Them from Degradation

Cyclodextrins not only improve solubility but also play a vital role in **stabilizing** drugs that are sensitive to environmental factors such as **light**, **oxygen**, **moisture**, and **heat**. By encapsulating the API in the hydrophobic cavity, cyclodextrins prevent exposure to these degradation factors, helping maintain the chemical integrity of the drug.

- **Protection from Light**: Many drugs, especially those with aromatic rings or conjugated double bonds, can undergo **photodegradation** when exposed to light. Cyclodextrins shield these drugs from light exposure by encapsulating them, thus reducing the risk of photo-induced degradation.

- **Protection from Moisture**: Drugs that are **hygroscopic** or prone to **hydrolytic degradation** (e.g., **aspirin, penicillin**) can be stabilized by cyclodextrins, which act as a protective barrier to moisture. This is especially important in **oral tablets, capsules,** and **injectable formulations**, where moisture can cause the drug to degrade or lose potency.
- **Prevention of Oxidation**: Drugs that are susceptible to **oxidative degradation** (e.g., **vitamin A, adrenaline**) benefit from the inclusion of cyclodextrins, which reduce their exposure to oxygen. The encapsulation process limits the amount of oxygen in contact with the drug, preventing the formation of harmful **oxidative by-products** and maintaining the drug's stability over time.
- **Thermal Stability**: Cyclodextrins can also help stabilize drugs that are sensitive to heat. By encapsulating the drug, they reduce its exposure to thermal degradation during the manufacturing process, especially in heat-sensitive formulations like **biologics** or **protein-based drugs**.

Controlled Release:

Cyclodextrins play an important role in **controlled-release formulations**, where the Active Pharmaceutical Ingredient (API) is gradually released over an extended period. This controlled release ensures that the drug maintains therapeutic levels in the bloodstream for a longer duration, improving the therapeutic effect and reducing the frequency of dosing. Additionally, controlled release helps to minimize the occurrence of **peak-trough fluctuations**, which are often associated with side effects.

1. Cyclodextrins in Controlled-Release Formulations

Cyclodextrins can be incorporated into controlled-release systems to modulate the release rate of the drug, providing **sustained** or **extended-release** over time. By forming **inclusion complexes** with the drug, cyclodextrins control the rate at which the API is released from the formulation.

- **Mechanism**: The API is encapsulated in the hydrophobic cavity of the cyclodextrin, which restricts its release in a controlled manner. The complex dissociates gradually over time, releasing the drug slowly into the surrounding environment (e.g., the gastrointestinal tract), depending on the drug's solubility and the cyclodextrin's characteristics.

- **Extended or Sustained Release**: Cyclodextrins can help achieve both **extended-release (ER)** and **sustained-release (SR)** profiles, allowing for the **gradual liberation** of the API over hours or even days. This improves the therapeutic effect by maintaining **consistent drug levels** and reducing the need for multiple doses throughout the day.

2. Benefits of Controlled Release Using Cyclodextrins

- **Improved Therapeutic Effect**: By releasing the drug slowly over time, controlled-release formulations ensure that the drug remains effective for a longer period, maintaining the therapeutic effect without the need for frequent administration. This is particularly beneficial for drugs that have a **short half-life** or for patients who may have difficulty adhering to a dosing schedule.
- **Reduced Side Effects**: With conventional immediate-release formulations, the drug can rapidly reach high concentrations in the bloodstream, potentially causing side effects. By slowing down the release of the drug, cyclodextrins help to **maintain steady plasma levels**, reducing the occurrence of **peak plasma concentrations** that may lead to adverse effects.
- **Minimized Dosing Frequency**: Controlled-release formulations can be designed to provide drug release over 12, 24, or even 48 hours. This reduces the need for frequent dosing, improving **patient compliance** and convenience, especially for drugs that need to be taken multiple times per day.
- **Enhanced Bioavailability**: For poorly soluble drugs, controlled-release formulations with cyclodextrins can enhance bioavailability by ensuring more consistent and efficient absorption throughout the gastrointestinal tract. Cyclodextrins help solubilize hydrophobic drugs, improving their dissolution and absorption at different sites along the GI tract.

3. Applications of Cyclodextrins in Controlled Release

- **Oral Dosage Forms**: Cyclodextrins are commonly used in **oral tablets** and **capsules** for controlled-release formulations. The inclusion complex formed with the drug allows for **slow and sustained drug release** in the digestive tract, improving patient compliance and therapeutic outcomes.

- **Injectable Formulations**: In injectable formulations, cyclodextrins can be used to create **slow-release** systems, where the drug is gradually released from the injectable depot. This is particularly useful for **biologics** or drugs that need to be administered **less frequently**.
- **Topical Formulations**: Cyclodextrins are also employed in **topical gels, creams, and ointments** for controlled release, where the API is slowly delivered through the skin. This can be useful for drugs targeting localized action, such as **anti-inflammatory** or **analgesic** agents.

Applications of Cyclodextrins

Cyclodextrins are widely used in pharmaceutical formulations to improve the **solubility, stability,** and **bioavailability** of poorly soluble drugs. Their unique ability to form inclusion complexes with hydrophobic drugs makes them a valuable tool across various dosage forms, including **oral, injectable**, and **topical formulations**. Below are the key applications of cyclodextrins in these formulations.

1. Oral Drug Formulations:

Cyclodextrins are often used in **oral formulations** to improve the solubility and bioavailability of poorly soluble drugs. Poor solubility is a common challenge for many drugs, especially those with lipophilic (fat-soluble) properties. By forming inclusion complexes with cyclodextrins, these drugs can dissolve more readily in the aqueous environment of the gastrointestinal tract, leading to better absorption and therapeutic efficacy.

- **Mechanism**: Cyclodextrins increase the solubility of poorly soluble drugs by forming a stable complex, where the hydrophobic part of the drug is encapsulated inside the cyclodextrin's cavity, while the hydrophilic exterior interacts with the surrounding aqueous environment. This process helps the drug dissolve and reach the bloodstream more efficiently.
- **Applications:**

  - **Anticancer Drugs**: Many **anticancer agents**, such as **paclitaxel**, are poorly soluble in water. Cyclodextrins can enhance their solubility, allowing for better absorption and effectiveness.
  - **Antibiotics: Griseofulvin**, an antifungal agent, is another example of a poorly soluble drug that benefits from the inclusion complex with cyclodextrins to improve its oral bioavailability.

- **Steroids: Prednisolone** and other steroids that have low solubility in water can be formulated with cyclodextrins to improve their solubility and absorption.

- **Benefits:**

  - Enhanced **bioavailability** for poorly soluble drugs.
  - Reduced **dose variability** and improved **therapeutic response**.

2. Injectables:

Cyclodextrins are also used to formulate **injectable products**, particularly for drugs that are poorly soluble in water. Many **intravenous (IV) drugs** or **injectables** require solvents or solubilizers to ensure that the active ingredient can be delivered in a stable, dissolvable form. Cyclodextrins serve as effective solubilizers for **hydrophobic** drugs, ensuring that they remain in solution until administered.

- **Mechanism:** By encapsulating the hydrophobic drug molecules inside the cyclodextrin's hydrophobic cavity, the drug is protected from crystallization and remains dissolved in the solution. This enables the drug to be administered intravenously or intramuscularly without the need for toxic solvents.
- **Applications:**

  - **Diazepam:** A drug used for treating anxiety and seizures, diazepam is poorly soluble in water, and cyclodextrins are used to solubilize it for IV administration.
  - **Phenytoin:** Another drug commonly administered intravenously to control seizures, which is also poorly soluble in water. Cyclodextrins enhance its solubility and stability in IV formulations.
  - **Ketoconazole:** This antifungal agent is used intravenously for systemic infections, and cyclodextrins help solubilize the drug for parenteral use.

- **Benefits:**

  - Ensures the solubility of poorly water-soluble drugs in **aqueous injectable formulations**.

○ Reduces the need for **harmful solvents**, ensuring safer administration.

3. Topical Formulations:

Cyclodextrins are also widely used in **topical formulations** to enhance the delivery and stability of drugs with poor solubility. In topical products such as **creams, gels, ointments**, and **lotions**, cyclodextrins help improve the **penetration** of the drug through the skin and increase its stability.

- **Mechanism**: Cyclodextrins enhance the **skin penetration** of drugs by forming complexes with poorly soluble drugs, making it easier for the drug to be absorbed through the stratum corneum (the outermost layer of the skin). The drug encapsulated within the cyclodextrin is protected from environmental factors like **light** and **moisture**, increasing its stability on the skin.

Applications:

○ **Anti-inflammatory drugs**: Drugs like **diclofenac** and **hydrocortisone**, which are used topically to treat conditions like arthritis or eczema, can be enhanced with cyclodextrins to improve skin absorption and stability.
○ **Antifungal Agents**: **Clotrimazole** and **ketoconazole**, used in topical antifungal treatments, benefit from the enhanced solubility and skin penetration provided by cyclodextrins.
○ **Analgesics**: Topical analgesics such as **lidocaine** are often formulated with cyclodextrins to increase their solubility, leading to improved local drug delivery for pain relief.
○ **Benefits**:

  ○ Enhanced **drug penetration** through the skin, improving the effectiveness of topical treatments.
  ○ **Increased stability** of drugs in the formulation, reducing degradation due to environmental exposure.
  ○ Reduced **irritation** or side effects by providing controlled, localized delivery.

4.3 Non-Ionic Surfactants

Non-ionic surfactants are a class of surfactants that do not carry a charge, making them highly versatile in pharmaceutical formulations. These surfactants are commonly used to stabilize **emulsions**, which are mixtures of **oil** and **water** phases that do not naturally mix. Non-ionic surfactants, such as **polysorbates** (e.g., **Tween 80**), are particularly effective because they can reduce the **interfacial tension** between the oil and water phases, allowing the two substances to remain stable when mixed. Below is an overview of how non-ionic surfactants are applied in **emulsions** and their specific benefits.

Applications in Emulsions

Emulsions are commonly used in pharmaceutical formulations to deliver drugs in both **oral** and **topical** forms. These formulations can be oil-in-water (O/W) or water-in-oil (W/O) emulsions, and non-ionic surfactants are crucial for stabilizing these emulsions.

1. Stabilizing Oil-in-Water (O/W) Emulsions

In an **oil-in-water emulsion**, oil droplets are dispersed in a continuous water phase. Non-ionic surfactants are particularly effective in stabilizing O/W emulsions by reducing the **interfacial tension** between the oil and water phases, allowing the oil to remain evenly dispersed in the aqueous medium.

- **Role of Non-Ionic Surfactants:**

  - **Reduce Surface Tension**: Non-ionic surfactants like **polysorbates (Tween 80)** are used to lower the surface tension between the hydrophilic (water-loving) and hydrophobic (oil-loving) molecules, allowing the emulsion to form and remain stable.
  - **Improved Stability**: The surfactants help create a stable interface around the oil droplets, preventing the oil from separating from the water phase. This ensures that the emulsion remains homogeneous and effective for extended periods.
  - **Applications:**

- **Injectable formulations**: Non-ionic surfactants like **Tween 80** are used to stabilize oil-in-water injectable emulsions, ensuring that the drug remains solubilized for intravenous administration.
- **Oral formulations**: Certain **oral suspensions** and **liquid formulations** also benefit from O/W emulsions stabilized by non-ionic surfactants. For example, **creams** and **liquids** containing **lipophilic APIs** (such as certain vitamins or hormones) are formulated to improve solubility and absorption.

2. Stabilizing Water-in-Oil (W/O) Emulsions

In a **water-in-oil emulsion**, water droplets are dispersed in an oil phase. Non-ionic surfactants are also effective in stabilizing W/O emulsions by reducing interfacial tension, but they are typically chosen based on their ability to interact with the oil phase to form a stable barrier around the water droplets.

- **Role of Non-Ionic Surfactants:**

  - **Water Protection**: Non-ionic surfactants help to keep water droplets uniformly dispersed within the oil, which is crucial for creating a stable W/O emulsion. This is particularly useful for formulations designed to provide prolonged release or moisturization.
  - **Viscosity and Texture**: The use of non-ionic surfactants in W/O emulsions also influences the **viscosity** and **texture** of the formulation, which is essential for creating **topical formulations** such as ointments and creams that require a rich, emollient feel.
  - **Applications:**

    - **Topical Formulations**: W/O emulsions are often used in **creams, lotions,** and **ointments** for **dermatological** or **cosmetic** products. These formulations are designed to provide a **moisturizing effect,** where the oil phase provides an occlusive barrier and the water phase offers hydration to the skin.
    - **Transdermal Delivery**: Non-ionic surfactants in W/O emulsions can also be used in **transdermal drug delivery systems** to enhance the absorption of lipophilic drugs through the skin.

3. Types of Non-Ionic Surfactants Used in Emulsions

- **Polysorbates (e.g., Tween 80, Tween 20):**

  - **Polysorbates** are among the most commonly used non-ionic surfactants in pharmaceutical emulsions. **Tween 80**, in particular, is widely used due to its ability to form stable O/W emulsions and its excellent solubilizing properties for both **hydrophilic** and **lipophilic drugs**.
  - Applications:

    - **Injectable formulations:** Tween 80 is used to stabilize **parenteral emulsions**, especially in the formulation of **lipid emulsions** for intravenous nutrition or drug delivery.
    - **Topical formulations:** It is also used in the preparation of **creams, lotions,** and **gels**, where it helps to solubilize and stabilize the active ingredient.

- **Poloxamers:**

  - **Poloxamers** are another class of non-ionic surfactants that are used to stabilize emulsions, particularly in **topical formulations** and **injectables.** They are block copolymers of ethylene oxide and propylene oxide and are known for their ability to form both O/W and W/O emulsions.
  - Applications:

    - **Ophthalmic solutions:** Poloxamers are used to formulate eye drops, where they help in solubilizing hydrophobic drugs and stabilizing emulsions for ocular delivery.

- **Sucrose Esters:**

  - **Sucrose esters** are non-ionic surfactants derived from sugar and fatty acids, used to create highly stable emulsions, particularly in **food, cosmetic,** and **pharmaceutical formulations.**
  - Applications:

    - **Cosmetic products:** Sucrose esters are used in **creams** and **lotions** to stabilize emulsions and improve texture. In pharmaceuticals, they are used in topical formulations to provide moisturizing properties.

Applications in Suspensions:

Surfactants play a key role in the formulation of **suspensions**, which are liquid dosage forms containing solid drug particles dispersed in a liquid medium. The primary challenge with suspensions is ensuring that the solid drug particles do not **settle** or **aggregate** over time, which can lead to inconsistent dosing and reduced efficacy. Surfactants, particularly **non-ionic surfactants**, help to **suspend** these solid particles in the liquid phase and prevent separation or clumping, thereby improving the **uniformity**, **stability**, and **consistency** of the suspension.

1. Role of Surfactants in Suspensions

Surfactants are used in suspensions for their ability to reduce **surface tension** between the solid particles and the liquid medium, promoting a uniform and stable dispersion. By lowering the interfacial tension, surfactants help to disperse the solid drug particles more evenly, ensuring that they stay suspended and do not form aggregates or clumps.

- **Prevent Settling**: Surfactants help to keep the solid drug particles suspended in the liquid, preventing them from settling at the bottom of the container. This ensures that the drug remains evenly distributed throughout the formulation, providing consistent dosing with every use.
- **Prevent Aggregation**: Surfactants can also prevent the **aggregation** (clumping) of solid particles. This is particularly important for **fine powders** that are prone to sticking together. By reducing the particle-particle interaction, surfactants ensure that the drug particles remain separate and uniformly dispersed in the liquid.
- **Enhance Stability**: Surfactants improve the **long-term stability** of the suspension by preventing the particles from flocculating (forming loose clusters) or coalescing (joining together into larger clumps). This leads to a **stable suspension** with a prolonged shelf-life, ensuring that the drug remains effective and safe over time.

2. Types of Surfactants Used in Suspensions

- **Non-Ionic Surfactants:**

- **Polysorbates (e.g., Tween 80, Tween 20)**: These surfactants are commonly used in suspensions to stabilize and solubilize poorly soluble drugs. They are favored for their mild properties, which are less likely to irritate the skin or mucous membranes.
- **Sorbitan esters**: These surfactants are used in suspensions to improve the **stability** and **uniformity** of the drug particles.

- **Anionic Surfactants**:

  - **Sodium Lauryl Sulfate (SLS)**: SLS is an **anionic surfactant** commonly used to reduce the surface tension between the solid drug and the liquid medium, improving the suspension's ability to prevent particle settling.

- **Cationic Surfactants**:

  - **Cetyltrimethylammonium bromide (CTAB)**: Though less commonly used, cationic surfactants like **CTAB** are sometimes employed in suspensions to modify the surface charge of the drug particles, which can enhance stability by preventing aggregation.

3. Applications in Pharmaceutical Suspensions

- **Oral Suspensions**:

  - In **oral suspensions**, surfactants help maintain the drug particles in suspension, ensuring accurate and consistent dosing. For example, **antibiotic suspensions** often contain surfactants to keep the active ingredient evenly distributed, as the particles can easily settle without proper stabilization.

- **Injectable Suspensions**:

  - Surfactants are used in **injectable suspensions** (e.g., for **long-acting formulations**) to keep the solid particles uniformly suspended in the solvent, ensuring the drug can be injected smoothly without clogging the needle or creating inconsistent doses.

- **Topical Suspensions:**

  - **Topical suspensions** (such as **calamine lotion** for skin conditions) also benefit from surfactants to ensure that the solid drug particles are evenly distributed in the liquid base, improving the consistency and effectiveness of the product.

4. Benefits of Using Surfactants in Suspensions

- **Improved Uniformity**: By stabilizing the suspension and preventing particle settlement or aggregation, surfactants ensure that each dose contains the same amount of the active ingredient. This leads to **consistent dosing** and predictable therapeutic outcomes.
- **Enhanced Stability**: Surfactants reduce the tendency of drug particles to clump together or settle, thus improving the **physical stability** of the suspension and extending its shelf-life. This is particularly important for **antibiotics, antifungals,** and **vitamins,** which are often poorly soluble and prone to degradation.
- **Better Patient Compliance**: Consistent and uniform drug delivery improves patient outcomes and ensures the proper administration of the prescribed dose, making it easier for patients to adhere to their medication regimen.

Solubilization:

Non-ionic surfactants are widely used in pharmaceutical formulations to enhance the solubility of **poorly soluble drugs**, especially in **liquid dosage forms**. Many drugs have limited solubility in water, which can significantly affect their **bioavailability** and **therapeutic efficacy**. Surfactants, particularly **non-ionic surfactants**, can address this issue by improving the solubility of these hydrophobic drugs, facilitating their absorption and ensuring consistent therapeutic outcomes.

Role of Non-Ionic Surfactants in Solubilization

Non-ionic surfactants are amphiphilic molecules, meaning they contain both hydrophilic (water-loving) and hydrophobic (lipid-loving) regions in their structure. This unique property allows them to interact with both aqueous and lipophilic substances, making them ideal for solubilizing **hydrophobic drugs.**

- **Micelle Formation**: When non-ionic surfactants are added to a solution, they self-assemble into structures called **micelles**. A micelle is a spherical arrangement of surfactant molecules, where the hydrophobic tails face inward, creating a hydrophobic core, and the hydrophilic heads face outward, interacting with the surrounding aqueous environment.
- **Encapsulation of the Drug**: The hydrophobic drug molecules can be solubilized by being encapsulated within the hydrophobic core of the micelle. This prevents the drug from crystallizing or precipitating out of solution and increases its solubility in the aqueous medium.
- **Enhanced Solubility**: By forming micelles, surfactants increase the **available surface area** of the drug in solution, allowing a larger amount of the drug to dissolve. This is especially important for poorly soluble compounds that would otherwise have limited absorption in the gastrointestinal tract.

Applications in Pharmaceutical Formulations

1. **Oral Drug Formulations:**

   - In **oral liquid formulations**, non-ionic surfactants are used to enhance the solubility of **poorly water-soluble drugs**. By forming micelles, surfactants help the drug dissolve in the aqueous environment of the gastrointestinal tract, improving **absorption** and **bioavailability**.
   - **Examples**: Drugs like **griseofulvin** (an antifungal) and **diazepam** (used for anxiety and seizures) have poor water solubility and benefit from solubilization by non-ionic surfactants in their oral suspension formulations.

2. **Injectables:**

   - In injectable formulations, non-ionic surfactants such as **polysorbates (Tween 80)** are used to solubilize drugs that are otherwise insoluble in water, ensuring that the drug remains in solution for intravenous or intramuscular administration.
   - **Examples: Phenytoin** (used to treat seizures) and **diazepam** are formulated with surfactants to improve their solubility in intravenous preparations.

3. **Topical Formulations:**

- For **topical formulations** such as **creams, ointments,** and **gels,** non-ionic surfactants enhance the solubility and penetration of hydrophobic drugs through the skin. They help dissolve the drug in the formulation and facilitate its absorption through the skin barrier.
- **Examples: Hydrocortisone** and **lidocaine** (local anesthetic) are formulated with surfactants in topical preparations to improve their solubility and effectiveness.

4. **Ophthalmic Formulations:**

- **Ophthalmic solutions** require solubilizers to improve the solubility of lipophilic drugs, allowing them to be effectively delivered to the eye.
- **Examples: Pilocarpine** (used in glaucoma treatment) is often solubilized using non-ionic surfactants in **eye drops** to ensure it remains in solution for better ocular bioavailability.

Benefits of Solubilization with Non-Ionic Surfactants

- **Improved Bioavailability:** By increasing the solubility of poorly soluble drugs, non-ionic surfactants enhance **absorption** and **bioavailability,** especially for drugs that have limited solubility in water. This leads to more effective therapeutic outcomes with lower doses.
- **Reduced Side Effects:** Surfactants help to maintain the drug in solution, preventing precipitation or crystallization that could lead to **local irritation** or **dose variability.**
- **Improved Formulation Stability:** Surfactants stabilize drugs in solution, preventing crystallization and ensuring that the drug remains uniformly distributed throughout the formulation, which enhances the stability of the product over time.
- **Enhanced Patient Compliance:** By improving the solubility of poorly soluble drugs, surfactants help to create formulations that are easier to administer and more effective, contributing to better patient compliance, especially in the case of oral and topical products.

Examples of Non-Ionic Surfactants:

Non-ionic surfactants are widely used in pharmaceutical formulations due to their versatility, mild nature, and effectiveness in solubilizing poorly soluble drugs. Some of the most commonly used non-ionic surfactants include **Polysorbates** (e.g., **Tween 20, Tween 80**). These surfactants are particularly useful in **oral liquid formulations, injectable emulsions**, and **ophthalmic solutions.**

Polysorbates (e.g., Tween 20, Tween 80)

Polysorbates are a class of **non-ionic surfactants** that are commonly used in pharmaceutical formulations. They are **ester derivatives** of **polyoxyethylene sorbitan** and are known for their **excellent emulsifying, solubilizing**, and **stabilizing** properties. Polysorbates are often used to improve the solubility and stability of poorly soluble drugs and to help in the formation and stabilization of emulsions.

Applications of Polysorbates:

1. **Oral Liquid Formulations:**

    ◦ **Polysorbates**, particularly **Tween 20** and **Tween 80**, are widely used in **oral suspensions** and **solutions** to solubilize hydrophobic drugs, improving their bioavailability and therapeutic effect.
    ◦ **Example:**

        ▪ **Griseofulvin** (an antifungal agent) is often formulated with **Tween 80** in oral liquid suspensions to enhance its solubility and ensure more efficient absorption.
        ▪ **Diazepam**, an anxiolytic drug, is solubilized using **Tween 20** in **oral solutions**, allowing for consistent dosing and improved patient compliance.

2. **Injectable Emulsions:**

    ◦ **Polysorbates** are used in **injectable emulsions** to stabilize the oil-in-water or water-in-oil emulsions, preventing phase separation and ensuring uniform distribution of the drug in the solution.
    ◦ **Example:**

        ▪ **Propofol**, an intravenous anesthetic, is often formulated with **Tween 80** in injectable emulsions to solubilize the lipophilic drug and provide smooth, stable administration.

- **Diazepam** (for seizure control) is another example of a drug that benefits from the use of **Polysorbates** in **parenteral formulations** to ensure stability and solubility.

3. **Ophthalmic Solutions:**

    - In **ophthalmic formulations, Polysorbates** help to improve the solubility and stability of drugs, allowing for effective delivery to the eye. These surfactants are also used to stabilize the emulsion or solution, preventing drug crystallization and ensuring consistent release.
    - **Example:**

        - **Pilocarpine** (used in the treatment of glaucoma) and **timolol** (a beta-blocker used for intraocular pressure reduction) are commonly formulated with **Polysorbates** to ensure the drugs remain solubilized in the eye drop solution, enhancing **ocular bioavailability** and therapeutic effects.

Advantages of Using Polysorbates in Pharmaceutical Formulations:

- **Solubilizing Properties**: Polysorbates help to solubilize lipophilic (fat-soluble) drugs, which are difficult to dissolve in water-based solutions.
- **Stabilization of Emulsions**: By reducing surface tension, **Polysorbates** help stabilize emulsions, ensuring the oil and water phases remain well mixed and preventing separation during storage.
- **Mild Nature**: Polysorbates are **non-ionic**, meaning they are generally less irritating to the skin, eyes, and mucous membranes, making them suitable for **topical** and **ophthalmic** applications.
- **Improved Drug Delivery**: By improving solubility and ensuring uniform dispersion in the formulation, **Polysorbates** enhance the **bioavailability and therapeutic efficacy** of drugs, especially those that are poorly soluble.

4.4 Polyethylene Glycols (PEG) and Sorbitols

Polyethylene Glycols (PEG) and **Sorbitols** are important excipients in pharmaceutical formulations, contributing to the **solubility, stability, and bioavailability** of drugs. **PEG** is a versatile polymer with a wide range of applications across **oral, topical,** and **parenteral** products, while **Sorbitol** serves as a humectant, sweetener, and stabilizing agent in various formulations.

Polyethylene Glycols (PEG)

Structure and Properties:

Polyethylene Glycol (PEG) is a **water-soluble polymer** made up of repeating ethylene glycol units ($-CH_2CH_2O-$). PEG can vary in molecular weight, which affects its **physical properties** such as **viscosity, melting point**, and **solubility**. PEG is a **non-toxic, biocompatible,** and **versatile excipient** that is used in multiple pharmaceutical applications. Its solubility in water and compatibility with a wide range of substances make it a valuable component in many formulations.

- **Molecular Weight Variability**: PEG can be synthesized with various molecular weights, ranging from low molecular weight PEG (e.g., **PEG 400**) to high molecular weight PEG (e.g., **PEG 6000**). The molecular weight of PEG determines its physical properties, including its ability to act as a **solvent, plasticizer,** or **carrier** in drug formulations.

Applications of Polyethylene Glycol (PEG)

- **Oral Products:**

  - **Binder in Tablet Formulations**: PEG is commonly used as a **binder** in **tablet formulations** to hold the ingredients together and improve the tablet's mechanical strength. It ensures that the tablet remains intact during storage and handling but also helps in **rapid dissolution** once ingested.

  - **Solvent for Liquid Preparations**: PEG is used as a **solvent** in **oral liquid formulations.** Its ability to dissolve hydrophobic and poorly soluble drugs enhances their **bioavailability.** PEG is commonly used in **liquid suspensions** and **syrups**, where it helps solubilize active ingredients, making them easier for the body to absorb.

- **Osmotic Agent in Controlled-Release Systems**: PEG is used in **controlled-release formulations** as an **osmotic agent**. In these systems, PEG helps regulate the **release rate** of the active ingredient, providing a sustained and consistent release of the drug over time, which is particularly beneficial for drugs requiring prolonged therapeutic effects.

- **Topical Products**:

  - **Creams, Ointments, and Gels**: PEG is commonly used in **topical formulations** such as **creams, ointments**, and **gels**. It serves as both a **solvent** and **emulsifier**, helping to dissolve or suspend the active ingredient in the formulation and ensuring uniform distribution. PEG also improves the **texture** of the formulation, making it smoother and more pleasant to apply.
  - **Hydrating and Moisturizing Agent**: PEG is often used in **moisturizing lotions** and **gels** for its **humectant properties**, which help retain moisture in the skin. It provides a **smooth, non-greasy feel**, enhancing the sensory attributes of the formulation.
  - **Topical Drug Delivery**: PEG helps enhance the **penetration** of drugs through the skin by **increasing solubility** and facilitating the drug's absorption, making it effective for transdermal drug delivery systems.

- **Parenteral Products**:

  - **Injectable Formulations**: PEG is used in injectable formulations due to its **biocompatibility** and ability to **stabilize sensitive biologics**. For biologic drugs like **proteins, antibodies**, and **vaccines**, PEG acts as a **stabilizer**, preventing degradation or aggregation of the active pharmaceutical ingredient.
  - **Nanoparticle Drug Delivery**: PEGylated nanoparticles (PEG-bound particles) are used in **targeted drug delivery** systems, where the drug is encapsulated within PEG-coated particles. This helps to improve the **circulation time** of the drug in the body and directs the drug to the targeted site of action, reducing side effects.

- **Enhancing Solubility of Hydrophobic Drugs**: PEG is used to solubilize hydrophobic drugs, which are often difficult to administer intravenously. It helps improve the **solubility**, ensuring that the drug can be delivered effectively to the bloodstream.

Sorbitols

Sorbitol is a sugar alcohol used as a **humectant, sweetener**, and **stabilizing agent** in pharmaceutical formulations. It is often used in both **oral** and **topical** formulations due to its ability to attract and retain moisture.

- **Oral Formulations:**

  - **Sweetener**: Sorbitol is commonly used as a **sweetener** in **liquid preparations** such as **syrups, suspensions**, and **chewable tablets**. It provides sweetness without causing a significant rise in blood sugar levels, making it suitable for diabetic formulations.
  - **Humectant**: In **oral syrups** and **gels**, sorbitol is used to retain moisture, ensuring the formulation does not dry out or become overly thick.

- **Topical Formulations:**

  - **Humectant in Lotions and Creams**: Sorbitol is used in **cosmetic** and **pharmaceutical creams** and **lotions** to maintain moisture and improve the texture of the product. It helps prevent the skin from drying out and retains water, providing prolonged hydration.
  - **Ointments**: Sorbitol serves as a stabilizing agent in **topical ointments**, providing a smooth consistency and improving the spreadability of the product.

- **Stabilizer for Biologics:**

  - **Injectable Products**: Sorbitol is used in **parenteral formulations** as a **stabilizer** for biologics and vaccines. It helps maintain the stability of proteins and other sensitive biologic molecules during storage and administration.

Structure and Properties

- **Chemical Structure**: Sorbitol, also known as **D-sorbitol**, is a **sugar alcohol** composed of a six-carbon structure with hydroxyl groups (-OH) on each carbon atom except for the carbonyl group. It is derived from the reduction of **glucose**.
- **Water Solubility**: Sorbitol is highly soluble in water and has a sweet taste, making it an ideal **sugar substitute** in pharmaceutical products, especially for **diabetic formulations** where traditional sugars may not be suitable.
- **Viscosity and Moisture Retention**: Sorbitol has **viscous** properties and is often used to increase the **viscosity** of liquid formulations. It is also a **humectant**, which means it helps retain moisture, preventing the formulation from drying out or becoming too thick over time.

Applications of Sorbitol
Oral Products:

- Sorbitol is commonly used in **oral pharmaceutical formulations**, where it acts as a **sweetener, humectant,** and **viscosity enhancer**.

  - **Syrups and Liquid Formulations**: Sorbitol is used in **oral syrups** and **liquid formulations** as a sweetener and to **improve palatability**. It is particularly useful in formulations for pediatric or geriatric populations who may have difficulty swallowing pills or tablets.
  - **Chewable Tablets**: In **chewable tablets**, sorbitol helps to provide a pleasant taste and texture. It also serves as a **binder**, helping to hold the tablet together while improving the **mouthfeel**.
  - **Diabetic Formulations**: Because sorbitol does not raise blood sugar levels significantly, it is commonly used in **sugar-free** formulations for **diabetic patients** or for those who need to control their sugar intake.

- **Example**: Sorbitol is often used in **liquid analgesics, antacids, antihistamines,** and other oral preparations to make them more palatable without increasing blood sugar levels.

Topical Formulations:

- Sorbitol is also used extensively in **topical formulations**, where its **hydrating** and **moisture-retaining** properties help maintain the integrity of the skin.

  - **Gels**: In **gels**, sorbitol helps enhance the **hydration** and **spreadability** of the formulation. It acts as a **humectant**, ensuring that the gel maintains moisture in the skin, preventing it from drying out or becoming too thick.
  - **Lotions and Creams**: Sorbitol is added to **creams** and **lotions** to help retain moisture, ensuring that the skin stays hydrated and soft. It also improves the **texture** of these products, making them easier to apply and absorb.
  - **Moisturizing Effect**: Sorbitol prevents the loss of moisture from the skin by forming a barrier, which is especially useful in **dry skin treatments** or **moisturizing products.**

- **Example**: Sorbitol is commonly used in **skin care products** like **moisturizing lotions**, **sunblock creams**, and **hand creams**, where it helps in hydrating the skin and improving the overall **skin feel**.

Parenteral Products:

- Sorbitol is also used in **injectable formulations**, particularly in **parenteral products** where its ability to **adjust osmolarity** and **stabilize drugs** plays a crucial role in the safety and effectiveness of the drug.

  - **Adjusting Osmolarity**: Sorbitol is used to adjust the **osmolarity** of parenteral solutions, especially when the API is poorly soluble in water. This ensures that the injectable formulation is compatible with the **physiological environment** of the body, preventing irritation or damage to tissues.
  - **Stabilizing Biologics**: Sorbitol is commonly used in **injectable biologics** (e.g., **insulin**, **vaccines**) to stabilize the proteins and prevent **denaturation** or **aggregation**. It helps to **maintain the structural integrity** of the drug during storage and administration.
  - **Formulating Injectables**: Sorbitol is used in certain **intravenous** or **subcutaneous** solutions, where it improves the solubility of the active ingredient, ensuring the formulation can be effectively administered

without the risk of **precipitation** or **clogging** the needle.

- **Example**: Sorbitol is used in the formulation of **intravenous fluids, insulin injections**, and **vaccines**, where it stabilizes the formulation and helps with **drug solubilization**.

Benefits of Using Sorbitol in Pharmaceutical Formulations

- **Non-Toxic and Biocompatible**: Sorbitol is safe for use in pharmaceutical formulations, both for **oral** and **parenteral** applications. It has a low toxicity profile, making it suitable for long-term use in various drug formulations.

- **Moisture Retention**: As a **humectant**, sorbitol helps prevent the **drying out** of formulations, maintaining the stability and texture of the product.

- **Taste Masking**: Sorbitol is often used as a **sweetener** in liquid formulations to mask the unpleasant taste of certain drugs, improving the overall patient experience.

- **Viscosity Control**: Sorbitol helps in controlling the **viscosity** of liquids, making them easier to swallow or apply topically.

4.5 Suspending and Emulsifying Agents

Suspending and **emulsifying agents** are critical excipients in pharmaceutical formulations, particularly for liquid dosage forms such as **suspensions, emulsions,** and **creams.** These agents help improve the stability, uniformity, and effectiveness of the final product by ensuring that solid particles or immiscible liquids remain properly dispersed and do not separate over time.

Importance in Formulations

- **Suspending Agents:**

  - **Role:** Suspensions are liquid formulations in which solid drug particles are dispersed in a liquid phase. These drug particles have a tendency to settle due to gravity, which can result in an **inconsistent dose** and affect the stability of the formulation. **Suspending agents** help to **prevent sedimentation** and ensure **uniform distribution** of the solid particles throughout the liquid.
  - **Mechanism:** Suspending agents work by **increasing the viscosity** of the liquid phase. This thickening of the liquid reduces the rate at which the solid particles settle and helps maintain a uniform suspension over time. Additionally, they can interact with the drug particles to prevent **aggregation** or **clumping,** ensuring that the particles remain evenly dispersed.
  - **Applications:**

    - **Oral Suspensions:** Suspensions for pediatric use often require suspending agents to ensure that the drug is evenly distributed in the liquid and that the child receives the correct dose with each administration.
    - **Injectable Suspensions:** Certain **injectables,** such as **long-acting formulations** (e.g., **depot injections**), use suspending agents to ensure the drug remains evenly distributed and can be administered smoothly without clogging the needle.

  - **Examples of Suspending Agents:**

- **Xanthan Gum**: A natural polysaccharide used to increase the viscosity of suspensions.
- **Carboxymethylcellulose (CMC)**: A cellulose derivative used as a **viscosity enhancer** in liquid formulations.
- **Hydroxyethylcellulose (HEC)**: A polymer used in suspensions and topical formulations for its thickening properties.
- **Tragacanth**: A natural gum used to maintain stability and prevent sedimentation in suspensions.

- **Emulsifying Agents**:

  - **Role: Emulsions** are formulations where two immiscible liquids (e.g., oil and water) are mixed to form a stable dispersion. Since oil and water do not naturally combine, emulsifying agents are required to stabilize the mixture by reducing the **interfacial tension** between the two phases, preventing phase separation and ensuring the emulsion remains stable over time.
  - **Mechanism**: Emulsifying agents are typically surfactants that have both **hydrophobic** (oil-loving) and **hydrophilic** (water-loving) regions. These agents position themselves at the **interface** between the oil and water phases, lowering the energy required to mix the two phases. This results in a **stable emulsion** where the droplets of one phase are dispersed in the other.
  - **Applications**:

    - **Oral Emulsions**: Emulsions are used for delivering lipophilic drugs that are poorly soluble in water. Emulsifying agents help ensure that the drug is effectively delivered and absorbed.
    - **Topical Emulsions: Creams, lotions,** and **ointments** are often emulsions, with emulsifying agents helping to stabilize the oil and water phases. These products are widely used in dermatology to deliver drugs to the skin.
    - **Injectable Emulsions: Oil-in-water** emulsions are used for intravenous nutrition and drug delivery, where the emulsifying agent ensures the stability of the emulsion and prevents phase separation during storage and administration.

  - **Examples of Emulsifying Agents:**

- **Polysorbates (e.g., Tween 80)**: Commonly used in both **oil-in-water** and **water-in-oil** emulsions, polysorbates are effective in stabilizing emulsions, especially in injectable and topical formulations.
- **Lecithin**: A phospholipid used in both **oral** and **injectable emulsions**, lecithin is particularly useful in **lipid-based formulations** and is widely used in **parenteral nutrition**.
- **Sorbitan esters** (e.g., **Span 80**): These are used in **water-in-oil emulsions**, particularly in **topical formulations** and some injectable emulsions.
- **Cetyl Alcohol**: A fatty alcohol that serves as an emulsifier in **creams** and **lotions**, providing both emulsifying and stabilizing properties.

Benefits of Suspending and Emulsifying Agents in Pharmaceutical Formulations

- **Enhanced Stability**: By preventing phase separation in emulsions and sedimentation in suspensions, **suspending** and **emulsifying agents** ensure that the formulation remains stable over time, providing consistent therapeutic effects.
- **Improved Uniformity**: These agents ensure that the active pharmaceutical ingredient (API) is evenly distributed throughout the formulation, guaranteeing consistent dosing in each administration.
- **Increased Patient Compliance**: Formulations with appropriate suspending and emulsifying agents are easier to administer and have better texture, improving **patient acceptability** and **compliance**, especially for pediatric and geriatric patients.
- **Versatility in Drug Delivery**: These agents enable the delivery of poorly soluble drugs in a variety of formulations (oral, injectable, and topical), expanding the therapeutic options for drugs that would otherwise be difficult to formulate.

Application in Liquid Dosage Forms

Both **suspensions** and **emulsions** are important liquid dosage forms in pharmaceutical products, especially for drugs that are poorly soluble in water. The use of appropriate **suspending** and **emulsifying agents** is critical to ensure the stability, uniformity, and therapeutic effectiveness of these formulations. Below is an overview of their applications in

liquid dosage forms.

1. Suspensions:

A **suspension** is a liquid dosage form in which solid drug particles are dispersed in a liquid medium. These particles have a tendency to settle over time due to gravity, which can lead to an inconsistent dose if not properly stabilized. **Suspending agents** are added to the formulation to help maintain the uniform distribution of the solid particles, ensuring that they do not settle or aggregate.

- **Role of Suspending Agents:**

  - Suspending agents increase the **viscosity** of the suspension, which reduces the rate of settling of the solid drug particles and helps to maintain **uniform dispersion.**
  - These agents also help to **prevent aggregation** of drug particles, ensuring that the suspension remains homogeneous over time.

- **Common Suspending Agents:**

  - **Xanthan Gum:** A **polysaccharide** used as a thickening agent in suspensions. It is effective at maintaining the uniformity of suspensions and improving their **viscosity.** Xanthan gum is widely used in **oral suspensions,** especially for **pediatric formulations.**
  - **Carboxymethyl Cellulose (CMC):** A **cellulose derivative** that is commonly used in **oral** and **topical** suspensions. It enhances the stability of suspensions by increasing their viscosity and preventing the particles from settling.
  - **Tragacanth:** A **natural gum** that helps to thicken liquid formulations and stabilize suspensions. It is used in suspensions for **pediatric** and **geriatric patients,** where the ease of swallowing and uniformity is crucial.

- **Applications:**

  - **Oral Suspensions:** Used for **antibiotics, antipyretics,** and other drugs that are poorly soluble in water. Suspending agents ensure that the active ingredient remains evenly distributed, ensuring accurate dosing.

- ◦ **Injectable Suspensions**: Used in **long-acting injectable formulations** (e.g., **depot injections**), where the drug needs to be slowly released over time. The suspending agent helps to prevent sedimentation and ensures a **consistent dose** with each administration.

2. Emulsions:

An **emulsion** is a system consisting of two immiscible liquids, typically **oil** and **water**, where one phase (either oil or water) is dispersed as droplets in the other. Emulsions are commonly used in pharmaceutical products like **topical creams, lotions**, and **parenteral emulsions**. The key challenge in emulsions is to stabilize the mixture and prevent the two phases from separating. **Emulsifying agents** play a crucial role in reducing the **interfacial tension** between the oil and water phases, stabilizing the emulsion.

- **Role of Emulsifying Agents:**

  - ◦ Emulsifying agents act by reducing the surface tension between the oil and water phases, allowing them to mix and form a stable emulsion. These agents also prevent the **coalescence** of droplets, maintaining a **stable dispersion** over time.
  - ◦ Depending on the type of emulsion (oil-in-water or water-in-oil), different emulsifying agents are chosen to ensure proper stabilization.

- **Common Emulsifying Agents:**

  - ◦ **Lecithin**: A **phospholipid** used to stabilize both **oil-in-water** (O/W) and **water-in-oil** (W/O) emulsions. Lecithin is commonly used in **topical** and **parenteral formulations** to improve the solubility of lipophilic drugs and enhance stability.
  - ◦ **Polyethylene Glycol (PEG)**: PEG is a widely used emulsifier in **injectable emulsions**, where it helps to stabilize the oil droplets and reduce **phase separation**. PEG is particularly beneficial in formulating lipid-based intravenous emulsions.
  - ◦ **Polysorbates (e.g., Tween 80)**: Polysorbates are versatile emulsifiers commonly used in **oil-in-water emulsions**, especially in **injectable emulsions** and **oral formulations**. They help in stabilizing emulsions

and ensuring the uniform distribution of the drug in the formulation.

- **Applications:**

  - **Topical Creams and Lotions**: Oil-in-water emulsions are commonly used in **creams** and **lotions** for **dermatological** applications. The **water phase** hydrates the skin, while the **oil phase** helps to form a protective barrier, enhancing the therapeutic effect of the drug.
  - **Injectable Emulsions**: **Oil-in-water emulsions** are often used in **intravenous nutrition** and **lipid-based drug delivery** systems. The emulsifying agents help to solubilize the drug and prevent phase separation during storage and injection.
  - **Ophthalmic Emulsions**: Emulsions are also used in **eye drops** where emulsifying agents ensure that the active ingredient is properly solubilized in the emulsion, facilitating delivery to the eye.

Applications of Suspending and Emulsifying Agents

Suspending and **emulsifying agents** play crucial roles in maintaining the stability, uniformity, and effectiveness of pharmaceutical formulations. These agents ensure that the drug is properly dispersed or solubilized in the formulation, which is essential for achieving consistent dosing and enhancing therapeutic efficacy. Below are the key applications of **suspending agents** in **oral suspensions, emulsifying agents** in **topical emulsions,** and the use of emulsifying agents in **injectable formulations.**

1. Oral Suspensions: Ensuring Even Dispersion of Drug Particles in a Liquid Form

In **oral suspensions**, solid drug particles are dispersed in a liquid phase. However, these particles have a natural tendency to settle over time due to gravity, leading to uneven distribution and inconsistent dosing. **Suspending agents** are used to **prevent settling** and ensure that the drug particles remain evenly distributed throughout the liquid.

- **Role of Suspending Agents:**

  - **Increase Viscosity**: By increasing the **viscosity** of the liquid, suspending agents slow down the settling of the drug particles, ensuring that the drug remains uniformly dispersed.

- **Prevent Aggregation**: Suspending agents help prevent the particles from **aggregating** or clumping together, which could lead to inconsistent dosing.
- **Ensure Accurate Dosing**: Suspended particles in a liquid are more easily measured for each dose, ensuring that the correct amount of the drug is administered with every use.

- **Common Suspending Agents:**

  - **Xanthan Gum**: A natural polysaccharide that increases the viscosity of the suspension, keeping drug particles uniformly dispersed.
  - **Carboxymethylcellulose (CMC)**: A cellulose derivative that is widely used as a suspending agent in oral suspensions.
  - **Hydroxyethylcellulose (HEC)**: A polymer that enhances the stability of suspensions and prevents sedimentation.

- **Applications:**

  - **Antibiotic Suspensions**: For **antibiotics** like **amoxicillin** or **ampicillin**, suspending agents ensure uniform distribution of the drug, making it easier for patients (especially children) to consume the medication.
  - **Antipyretics and Analgesics**: For drugs like **paracetamol** and **ibuprofen**, suspending agents ensure the proper suspension of the drug and effective pain or fever relief.

2. Topical Emulsions: Ensuring the Stability of Creams and Lotions that Combine Water and Oil Phases

Emulsions are systems where two immiscible liquids—**oil** and **water**—are mixed together, forming a stable dispersion. These emulsions are commonly used in **topical formulations** like **creams, lotions,** and **ointments. Emulsifying agents** are essential for stabilizing the mixture, ensuring that the oil and water phases do not separate over time.

- **Role of Emulsifying Agents:**

  - **Reduce Interfacial Tension**: Emulsifying agents reduce the **interfacial tension** between the oil and water phases, allowing them to mix and form a stable emulsion.

- ○ **Prevent Phase Separation**: By stabilizing the oil-water interface, emulsifying agents prevent the two phases from separating, ensuring the formulation remains uniform and stable.
- ○ **Improve Drug Delivery**: In topical formulations, emulsions help to deliver the drug effectively to the skin, improving absorption and ensuring the therapeutic effect.

- **Common Emulsifying Agents:**

  - ○ **Lecithin**: A phospholipid that is used to stabilize both **oil-in-water** and **water-in-oil** emulsions. Lecithin is often used in **creams** and **lotions** for its ability to improve skin hydration and deliver active ingredients.
  - ○ **Polysorbates (e.g., Tween 80)**: Widely used in **oil-in-water emulsions**, polysorbates help stabilize emulsions in **topical creams** and **injectable emulsions**.
  - ○ **Cetyl Alcohol**: A fatty alcohol that acts as an emulsifying agent and helps in the stabilization of **topical emulsions** like **moisturizing creams**.

- **Applications:**

  - ○ **Skin Care Products: Moisturizing creams, anti-aging lotions**, and **sunblock creams** are often emulsions that rely on emulsifying agents to stabilize the formulation and deliver active ingredients effectively.
  - ○ **Cosmetics**: Emulsifying agents are used in **cosmetic products** such as **foundations** and **makeup removers** to ensure a smooth texture and uniform dispersion of ingredients.
  - ○ **Dermatological Treatments: Topical steroids** or **anti-fungal creams** use emulsions to enhance drug penetration and improve the stability of the formulation.

3. Injectables: Some Injectable Formulations, such as Emulsions for Parenteral Nutrition, Require Emulsifying Agents for Proper Drug Delivery

In **injectable formulations**, emulsifying agents are crucial for stabilizing **emulsions** in parenteral products, such as **intravenous (IV) nutrition**

solutions, lipid-based drug delivery systems, and certain **injectable drugs** that are poorly soluble in water.

- **Role of Emulsifying Agents:**

  - **Stabilize Lipid Emulsions:** Emulsifying agents are used to stabilize **lipid emulsions** in injectable formulations, ensuring that the oil droplets remain uniformly dispersed and do not aggregate, which could cause adverse effects or interfere with the drug delivery process.
  - **Prevent Phase Separation:** Emulsifying agents help to maintain the **uniform distribution** of the oil and aqueous phases, preventing separation and ensuring consistent dosing and drug absorption.
  - **Improve Drug Delivery:** Emulsions provide a **controlled release** of lipophilic drugs, which is especially useful in parenteral nutrition, where patients may require lipid-based formulations for long-term drug delivery.

- **Common Emulsifying Agents:**

  - **Lecithin:** Commonly used in **parenteral nutrition solutions** and **lipid emulsions** to solubilize fats and vitamins, ensuring the stability and proper delivery of essential nutrients.
  - **Polysorbates (e.g., Tween 80):** Used in **injectable emulsions** for **lipophilic drugs** like **propofol** to stabilize the emulsion and prevent phase separation during storage and administration.
  - **Polyethylene Glycol (PEG):** Used in **lipid emulsions** to enhance solubility and stabilize the formulation, particularly in **intravenous formulations.**

- **Applications:**

  - **Parenteral Nutrition: Intravenous lipid emulsions** used for patients requiring **nutritional support** rely on emulsifying agents to maintain the stability and efficacy of the product.
  - **Injectable Anesthetics: Propofol,** used for sedation and anesthesia, is commonly formulated as an **injectable emulsion,** stabilized by emulsifying agents like **polysorbates.**

- **Biologics**: Certain **protein-based drugs** are formulated in **lipid emulsions** or **micellar systems**, where emulsifying agents help ensure their stability and efficient drug delivery.

CHAPTER FIVE

Excipients for Oral, Parenteral, and Aerosol Dosage Forms

5.1 Tablet and Capsule Excipients

In **tablet** and **capsule** formulations, excipients are essential for maintaining the physical integrity, stability, and effectiveness of the drug. These excipients serve a variety of functions, from **binding** the drug particles together to improving **dissolution** and **bioavailability**.

Function of Tablet and Capsule Excipients

Excipients in tablets and capsules serve multiple roles, including ensuring the drug's stability, facilitating manufacturing, and enabling effective drug delivery. They are necessary to maintain the physical properties of the dosage form, support the pharmacological activity of the API, and improve patient compliance.

- **Binder:** Binders help hold the tablet ingredients together by providing cohesion to the powder blend, allowing it to form a solid tablet. This ensures that the tablet stays intact during storage and handling but will disintegrate when ingested for drug release.
- **Diluent (Filler):** Diluent excipients are used to provide bulk to the formulation and ensure that an appropriate dose of the active ingredient is delivered. They also help maintain the **mechanical properties** of tablets.
- **Disintegrant:** Disintegrants ensure that the tablet or capsule breaks apart at the site of action (e.g., in the stomach) to allow the drug to be released for absorption. Disintegrants facilitate the breakdown of the dosage form

after ingestion.

- **Lubricant**: Lubricants are used to reduce friction during the tablet compression process, preventing the tablet ingredients from sticking to the machine. They also improve the **flowability** of powders during the manufacturing process.
- **Glidant**: Glidants are excipients that improve the flow properties of powders during tablet compression, ensuring uniformity and consistency in tablet weight and drug content.

Types of Excipients for Tablets and Capsules

1. **Binders:**

   - **Function**: Bind the powder ingredients together to form a cohesive mass, ensuring tablet integrity.
   - **Examples:**

     - **Povidone (Polyvinylpyrrolidone)**: A commonly used binder in tablet formulations that dissolves easily in water and provides excellent binding strength.
     - **Hydroxypropyl methylcellulose (HPMC)**: A versatile binder used in both immediate-release and controlled-release tablets.
     - **Starch**: A natural binder used in a variety of formulations, often for granulation processes.

2. **Diluent (Filler):**

   - **Function**: Adds bulk to the formulation to ensure the correct dosage of the active ingredient.
   - **Examples:**

     - **Lactose**: One of the most commonly used fillers, lactose is ideal for tablet formulations due to its **low cost** and **excellent compressibility**.
     - **Microcrystalline cellulose (MCC)**: Used as a filler and binder in tablet formulations, it also improves **disintegration** and **dissolution**.

- **Dicalcium phosphate**: A commonly used diluent, especially in formulations requiring good **flow properties**.

3. **Disintegrants**:

   - **Function**: Facilitate the breakdown of tablets or capsules in the digestive tract, enabling drug release.
   - **Examples**:

     - **Croscarmellose sodium**: A super disintegrant that swells rapidly upon contact with water, helping tablets break apart quickly.
     - **Sodium starch glycolate**: Another disintegrant used to enhance the disintegration of tablets and capsules.
     - **Cross-linked polyvinylpyrrolidone (PVP)**: A disintegrant commonly used in **oral dosage forms**, especially when a fast release rate is desired.

4. **Lubricants**:

   - **Function**: Reduce friction during the manufacturing process and prevent ingredients from sticking to the equipment.
   - **Examples**:

     - **Magnesium stearate**: The most common lubricant in tablet formulations, helping improve the flow of powders during compression and ensuring ease of tablet ejection.
     - **Stearic acid**: A fatty acid used in combination with magnesium stearate in tablet formulations to improve lubrication.
     - **Talc**: Often used as a lubricant and glidant in tablet and capsule formulations.

5. **Glidants**:

   - **Function**: Improve powder flow during tablet manufacturing, ensuring uniformity in dosing.
   - **Examples**:

- **Colloidal silica**: A glidant that enhances powder flow and aids in reducing friction during the tablet compression process.
- **Talc**: Also acts as a glidant, improving the **flowability** of powders and granules in tablet manufacturing.

Selection Criteria for Tablet and Capsule Excipients

Choosing the appropriate excipients for tablet and capsule formulations requires consideration of several factors to ensure that the dosage form is stable, effective, and patient-friendly.

- Compatibility with the API: The excipient should not interact negatively with the API, potentially altering its stability or therapeutic efficacy.
- Regulatory Approval: Excipients used in pharmaceutical formulations must meet regulatory standards for safety and efficacy, as defined by organizations such as the FDA, EMA, and WHO.
- Physical Properties: Excipients should have desirable flowability, compressibility, and meltability for efficient manufacturing processes.
- Cost-effectiveness: The excipients should be cost-effective and readily available to ensure affordability in large-scale production.
- Desired Release Profile: The choice of excipients may depend on the desired **release rate** of the drug (e.g., immediate-release, extended-release, controlled-release).

Types of Excipients in Tablets and Capsules

Excipients are vital components in the formulation of **tablets** and **capsules**, ensuring the product's stability, performance, and ease of manufacture. Each type of excipient serves a specific function to improve the overall characteristics of the dosage form, such as its mechanical integrity, dissolution profile, and manufacturability. Below is a detailed look at the key types of excipients used in **oral dosage forms** such as tablets and capsules:

1. Binders:

- Function: Binders are used to hold the ingredients together and ensure that the tablet remains intact during storage and handling. They provide cohesive properties to the powder blend, allowing it to be compressed into a solid tablet. Binders are essential for maintaining the physical integrity of the tablet, ensuring it does not crumble or break easily.

- Common Examples:

  - Povidone: A water-soluble binder that dissolves easily, providing excellent binding properties and is widely used in wet granulation processes.
  - Cellulose derivatives (e.g., Hydroxypropyl methylcellulose - HPMC): Used for both binders and controlled-release formulations, cellulose derivatives are effective in improving tablet integrity and drug release profiles.
  - Starch: A natural binder often used in tablet formulations due to its effectiveness and availability.

- Role in Tablet Formulation:

  - Ensuring tablet cohesion.
  - Improving the tablet's mechanical strength for handling and transport.
  - Allowing for easy disintegration during the release of the drug in the body.

2. Diluent (Filler):

- Function: Diluent or fillers are excipients used to add bulk to the formulation, especially when the dose of the active pharmaceutical ingredient (API) is too small to form a tablet by itself. Fillers help in achieving accurate dosage and ensure uniformity in the formulation. They are often inert and do not interact with the drug, serving only as a vehicle to deliver the API.
- Common Examples:

  - Lactose: A commonly used diluent in tablet formulations, especially for oral tablets. It is highly compressible and helps to form a uniform mixture.
  - Microcrystalline Cellulose (MCC): A versatile filler and binder that enhances the compressibility and flowability of the formulation.
  - Dicalcium Phosphate: Often used in formulations requiring excellent flow properties and cost-effectiveness.

- Role in Tablet Formulation:

  - Provides bulk to small quantities of the drug.
  - Ensures accurate dosing by contributing to the required tablet size and weight.
  - Improves the consistency of tablet manufacturing and helps with compression.

3. Disintegrants:

- **Function**: Disintegrants facilitate the breakdown of the tablet once it is ingested. Their primary role is to ensure that the tablet disintegrates into smaller particles, allowing for the **release** and **absorption** of the drug. This is crucial for ensuring that the active ingredient is **rapidly released** and can exert its pharmacological effect.
- **Common Examples:**

  - **Starch**: A natural disintegrant that absorbs water, swells, and breaks the tablet into smaller particles for faster drug release.
  - **Croscarmellose Sodium**: A **super disintegrant** that swells quickly in the presence of water and is often used in rapid-release tablets.
  - **Sodium Starch Glycolate**: Another **super disintegrant** that promotes quick disintegration, commonly used in both **immediate-release** and **extended-release** formulations.

- **Role in Tablet Formulation:**

  - **Promotes quick disintegration** in the stomach, ensuring fast drug release.
  - **Reduces the time to onset of action** by improving the dissolution rate of the drug.
  - **Enhances bioavailability** by allowing the API to be rapidly absorbed into the bloodstream.

4. Lubricants:

- **Function**: Lubricants are used to **reduce friction** during tablet compression and prevent the formulation from sticking to the equipment, such as the die and punches during tableting. They ensure that tablets are easily ejected from the press and reduce wear and tear on the manufacturing equipment. Lubricants also help improve the **flowability** of the powder blend during tablet production.

- **Common Examples:**

  - **Magnesium Stearate:** One of the most commonly used lubricants. It is used to reduce friction during tablet compression and prevent sticking.
  - **Stearic Acid:** A fatty acid that serves as a lubricant, particularly useful in fatty formulations.
  - **Talc:** Used as a lubricant in tablet manufacturing, though less commonly than magnesium stearate.

- **Role in Tablet Formulation:**

  - **Prevents sticking** of the formulation to the tablet compression machinery.
  - **Enhances the ease of ejection** of the tablets from the die, ensuring uniform tablet size.
  - **Improves the consistency** and quality of tablet production.

5. Glidants:

- **Function:** Glidants are excipients used to improve the **flowability** of the powder blend during the tableting process. They ensure that the powder moves smoothly through the tablet press, improving uniformity in tablet weight and active ingredient content. Glidants reduce friction between particles, enhancing the efficiency of the manufacturing process.
- **Common Examples:**

  - **Talc:** A commonly used glidant that improves the flowability of the powder and reduces friction during compression.
  - **Colloidal Silica (e.g., Aerosil):** A fine powder that acts as a glidant and helps improve the flow properties of powders.
  - **Magnesium Stearate:** While primarily used as a lubricant, magnesium stearate also exhibits **glidant properties**, aiding in the smooth flow of powder during compression.

- **Role in Tablet Formulation:**

  - **Improves powder flow** during tablet manufacturing, leading to more consistent tablet weight and content.
  - **Reduces friction** between particles during compression, allowing for more efficient manufacturing and reduced wear on machinery.
  - **Ensures uniform distribution** of the API in each tablet, contributing to accurate dosing.

Selection Criteria for Tablet and Capsule Excipients

When formulating tablets and capsules, the selection of excipients is a critical step in ensuring that the dosage form is safe, effective, and manufacturable. The right excipient not only helps in achieving the desired therapeutic effect but also ensures stability, bioavailability, and patient compliance. Below are the key selection criteria for excipients used in oral dosage forms such as tablets and capsules:

1. Compatibility with the API and Other Excipients

- Purpose: The excipients must be chemically and physically compatible with the active pharmaceutical ingredient (API) and other excipients in the formulation. Incompatible excipients may lead to undesirable reactions such as degradation of the drug, precipitation, or loss of efficacy.
- Considerations:

  - Chemical Compatibility: Excipients should not cause chemical interactions with the API that could alter its stability, potency, or safety.
  - Physical Compatibility: The excipients should not affect the physical properties of the API, such as crystallinity, solubility, or dissolution profile.
  - Interaction with Other Excipients: The excipients used in the formulation should not interfere with the function of other excipients. For example, a lubricant should not hinder the disintegration of a tablet, and a binders should not negatively affect the flowability of the powder blend.

2. Regulatory Approval for Use in Pharmaceuticals

- Purpose: All excipients used in pharmaceutical formulations must be approved by relevant regulatory agencies, such as the FDA, EMA, or WHO, to ensure that they meet safety and quality standards.
- Considerations:

  - Monographs: Excipients should have official monographs in recognized pharmacopoeias (e.g., USP, EP, or IP), which specify their quality standards and acceptable limits for use in pharmaceuticals.
  - Safety Profile: The excipient must have a known safety profile and should not cause adverse effects when used in therapeutic doses.
  - Approval for Use in Specific Dosage Forms: Regulatory bodies may have specific guidelines regarding which excipients are suitable for use in certain dosage forms (e.g., oral, injectable, or topical).

3. Cost-Effectiveness and Availability

- Purpose: The excipient must be readily available and cost-effective to ensure that the drug product can be manufactured at a competitive price while maintaining its quality.
- Considerations:

  - Availability: The excipient should be widely available from reliable suppliers to prevent supply chain disruptions during manufacturing.
  - Cost-Effectiveness: Excipients should be cost-efficient, especially for large-scale manufacturing. The cost of excipients must be balanced against their functionality to ensure the product remains affordable for patients without compromising on quality or effectiveness.
  - Bulk Purchasing: For large-scale manufacturing, excipients should be available in bulk and at competitive prices to optimize the overall cost of production.

4. Desired Functionality (e.g., Controlled Release, Immediate Release, etc.)

- Purpose: The choice of excipients should be guided by the desired release profile of the drug, whether it is immediate release, controlled release, or extended release. The excipients must support the intended drug delivery system to achieve the desired therapeutic outcomes.

- Considerations:

  - Release Profile: Excipients such as binders, fillers, disintegrants, and coating agents are selected based on their ability to influence the drug's release rate. For example, controlled-release excipients (like hydroxypropyl methylcellulose (HPMC)) are used to ensure a gradual release of the drug, whereas immediate-release excipients (such as lactose and starch) are used to release the drug quickly.
  - Targeted Delivery: If the formulation requires targeted drug delivery (e.g., for oral, parenteral, or topical use), the excipients must be compatible with drug release mechanisms like enteric coatings or nanoparticle systems.
  - Bioavailability: Excipients can also influence bioavailability, ensuring that a sufficient amount of the drug reaches the bloodstream, especially for poorly soluble drugs. Solubilizers, such as cyclodextrins, are often included for this purpose.
  - Stability of Release: For formulations with extended-release or sustained-release characteristics, excipients need to help maintain the consistency of drug release over a prolonged period.

5.2 Directly Compressible Vehicles

Directly compressible vehicles are a category of excipients used in tablet manufacturing that allow for the direct compression of powdered drug ingredients into tablets without the need for additional processing steps, such as **wet granulation** or **dry granulation**. These excipients are specifically selected based on their ability to form stable, cohesive tablets under pressure, offering significant advantages in the manufacturing process.

Role of Directly Compressible Vehicles

Directly compressible vehicles are used to create **tablets** without requiring **granulation** (a process where powders are agglomerated into larger particles before compression). These vehicles have the **physical properties** necessary to withstand the compression force in the tablet press, facilitating the formation of a **solid, stable tablet**.

- **Compression Ability**: Directly compressible excipients are designed to **compact** under pressure without the need for **additional binder solutions** or granulation steps. This ability is essential for the smooth operation of high-speed tablet presses.
- **Function**: These excipients form the bulk of the tablet and help the active pharmaceutical ingredient (API) to be evenly distributed throughout the formulation. In addition to their **compaction** properties, they may also contribute to **dissolution** and **bioavailability**.

Advantages of Directly Compressible Vehicles

1. **Reduced Manufacturing Time:**

   - Direct compression eliminates the need for complex steps such as **wet granulation** or **dry granulation**. This not only **speeds up the tablet manufacturing process** but also reduces the time spent on drying, milling, and blending.
   - **Faster Production**: With fewer processing steps, **tablet production** can proceed more quickly, allowing for higher throughput and **faster time to market**.

2. Cost-Effective:

- **Fewer Processing Steps**: Directly compressible vehicles reduce the number of steps in the manufacturing process, which translates into lower **operational costs**. There is no need for expensive equipment or extra labor for granulation or drying.
- **Energy Savings**: Since there is no need for heating or drying (as in the case of wet granulation), **energy consumption** is significantly reduced, contributing to **lower production costs**.
- **Lower Capital Investment**: Manufacturers do not need to invest in granulation equipment, making it more cost-effective, especially for large-scale production.

3. Improved Stability:

- **Reduced Exposure to Moisture and Heat**: One of the significant advantages of directly compressible vehicles is that the excipients are not exposed to **moisture** or **high temperatures** during manufacturing (as in wet granulation), which helps in **preserving the stability** of the active ingredient.
- **Minimized Degradation**: Heat-sensitive APIs are better preserved because there is no need for drying or high-temperature processing, which could otherwise degrade sensitive compounds.
- **Preserved API Integrity**: The lack of harsh processing conditions helps to maintain the **chemical stability** of the drug, ensuring its **potency** and **efficacy**.

Examples of Directly Compressible Vehicles

1. Microcrystalline Cellulose (MCC):

- **MCC** is one of the most commonly used excipients in direct compression. It is highly **compressible**, providing good **tablet hardness** and **disintegration properties**. MCC is widely used in **immediate-release** formulations due to its excellent ability to compress under pressure.

2. Dicalcium Phosphate:

○ **Dicalcium phosphate** is often used as a filler and a directly compressible vehicle. It has excellent **flowability** and can form stable tablets under compression without the need for granulation.

3. **Lactose:**

○ **Lactose** is another widely used excipient in direct compression tablets, providing bulk to the formulation. It is particularly useful in formulations where low or moderate compression is required.

4. **Starch (Pre-gelatinized):**

○ **Pre-gelatinized starch** is often used in direct compression because it is **stable** and helps provide the necessary mechanical strength to the tablet. It can also contribute to **drug dissolution** once the tablet reaches the stomach.

5. **Sodium Bicarbonate:**

○ **Sodium bicarbonate** can also be used in direct compression tablets, particularly in effervescent tablets. It helps to provide a **controlled release** of the API through the generation of gas when the tablet is dissolved in water.

Limitations of Directly Compressible Vehicles

While **directly compressible vehicles** offer significant advantages in the tablet manufacturing process, there are also some limitations associated with their use in certain formulations. These limitations can affect the quality, performance, and feasibility of directly compressing tablets, particularly when the **active pharmaceutical ingredient (API)** is not compatible or when the excipient properties do not meet the formulation's requirements.

1. Limited Availability of Suitable Excipients

• **Compatibility with APIs:** Not all **active pharmaceutical ingredients (APIs)** are compatible with directly compressible vehicles. Some drugs may not **flow well** during the compression process or may have incompatible **chemical properties** that affect their stability or bioavailability.

- ○ **Issue**: Certain APIs may **degrade** or **lose efficacy** when exposed to the excipients, particularly in **moisture-sensitive** or **heat-sensitive** drugs.
- ○ **Solution**: A suitable excipient must be chosen based on the API's **physical and chemical properties**. However, the number of **directly compressible excipients** available that can work with a wide variety of APIs is limited.
- ○ **Example**: Certain **biologic drugs** or **highly potent drugs** may require specialized excipients, often requiring **wet or dry granulation** to ensure proper formulation.

2. Risk of Poor Flow Properties

- **Flowability**: Some directly compressible vehicles may have **poor flow properties**, which can affect the **uniformity** of the powder blend and, consequently, the **uniformity of dosing**.

  - ○ **Issue**: Poor flow characteristics can lead to inconsistent **tablet weight** and **active ingredient distribution**, resulting in **dose variability** or defects such as **capping, lamination**, or **tablet breakage** during compression.
  - ○ **Solution**: **Glidants** or **flow enhancers** can be used in combination with the excipients to improve flowability, but this may add complexity to the formulation.

- **Compression Issues**: Some excipients may not compress easily under the applied pressure, leading to **soft tablets**, poor **hardness**, or **friability**. This is especially problematic for drugs that require high **tablet strength** for stability during transportation and storage.

Examples of Directly Compressible Vehicles

1. **Microcrystalline Cellulose (MCC):**

   - ○ **Role**: MCC is one of the most widely used **directly compressible vehicles** due to its **excellent flowability** and **compressibility**. It is often used as a **filler** and **binder** in tablet formulations. MCC also enhances the **disintegration** of tablets, ensuring that the drug is released effectively upon ingestion.

- **Applications:** MCC is compatible with a wide range of APIs and is commonly used in **immediate-release** tablet formulations.

2. **Dicalcium Phosphate:**

- **Role:** Dicalcium phosphate is commonly used as a **filler** or **diluent** in **directly compressible tablet formulations**. It provides bulk to the tablet and ensures the consistency of the final dosage form. It has **good compressibility** and **flow properties**, making it a popular excipient in tablet manufacturing.
- **Applications:** It is often used in **non-sterile** tablets and is particularly suitable for use in **direct compression** processes where large-scale production is required.

5.3 Coating Materials

Coating materials are essential excipients used in the formulation of tablets and capsules to provide various functional benefits such as **taste masking, stability enhancement, controlled drug release,** and **targeted delivery.** Coatings can improve the **patient experience** and ensure the proper **bioavailability** of the drug. There are several types of coating materials used, including **sugar coating, film coating,** and **enteric coating,** each with specific purposes and advantages.

Types of Coating Materials

1. Sugar Coating

- **Purpose:** Sugar coating involves the application of a **sugar-based solution** over the tablet surface, creating a **protective layer** that enhances the appearance, **taste masking,** and **physical integrity** of the tablet.
- **Function:**

  - **Taste Masking:** One of the most significant benefits of sugar coating is its ability to mask the **unpleasant taste** of certain **bitter** or **pungent** drugs, making them more palatable for patients, especially children.
  - **Aesthetic Improvement:** Sugar-coated tablets have a shiny, smooth, and colorful appearance, which can improve **patient acceptance** and make the tablet more appealing.
  - **Protection:** The sugar coating helps to **protect** the API from environmental factors like moisture, oxygen, and light, improving the **stability** of the drug.

- **Applications:**

  - **Chewable Tablets:** Sugar coating is often used for **chewable tablets,** especially in pediatric formulations, where **taste masking** is essential.
  - **Over-the-Counter (OTC)** Tablets: Commonly used for **consumer-friendly** products like **vitamins** and **antacids** to enhance their appearance and ease of consumption.

- **Limitations**: Sugar coating is more time-consuming and less cost-effective compared to **film coating**, as it requires multiple coating layers and drying time. It can also result in a larger tablet size.

2. Film Coating

- **Purpose**: Film coating involves applying a **thin polymer layer** over the tablet, which is typically **clear** and **smooth**. This coating provides a variety of benefits, including the ability to control **drug release**, enhance **stability**, and make tablets easier to swallow.
- **Function**:

  - **Controlled Release**: Film coatings can be formulated to control the release of the drug, either by **extended-release** or **sustained-release** mechanisms. The coating may dissolve slowly, allowing the drug to be released gradually over time.
  - **Improved Stability**: Film coatings protect the API from exposure to moisture, air, or light, enhancing the stability of the drug and prolonging its shelf life.
  - **Ease of Swallowing**: The smooth, sleek finish of film-coated tablets makes them easier to swallow compared to uncoated tablets, improving patient compliance.

- **Common Film Coating Materials**:

  - **Hydroxypropyl Methylcellulose (HPMC)**: A widely used polymer in film coatings, particularly for **extended-release** formulations.
  - **Polyvinyl Alcohol (PVA)**: A water-soluble polymer used to create a thin, flexible film. PVA coatings are often used in immediate-release and controlled-release formulations.
  - **Ethylcellulose**: A commonly used polymer for **sustained-release** coatings, especially in **tablet matrix systems**.

- **Applications**:

  - **Controlled-Release Tablets**: Film coatings are essential in **controlled-release tablets**, where they help to regulate the **drug release rate**, ensuring that the drug is released slowly over time.

- ○ **Improved Aesthetics**: Film coatings are also used for aesthetic purposes, giving tablets a glossy, smooth appearance that enhances their **market appeal**.
- ○ **Functional Coatings**: Some film coatings provide additional functionality, such as **water-resistant coatings** for formulations that are sensitive to moisture.

3. Enteric Coating

- **Purpose**: **Enteric coatings** are designed to prevent the release of the drug in the **acidic environment** of the stomach and ensure the drug dissolves in the **more alkaline** environment of the intestines. This type of coating is especially important for drugs that are either **irritating to the stomach** or **unstable** in acidic conditions.
- **Function**:

  - ○ **Targeted Release**: Enteric coatings protect drugs from gastric acid, ensuring that the drug is released only in the **small intestine**, where the pH is higher and the drug is more likely to be absorbed.
  - ○ **Protection of Sensitive Drugs**: Certain drugs, such as **protein-based drugs** or **proton pump inhibitors (PPIs)**, are sensitive to stomach acid. Enteric coatings protect the drug from **degradation** in the stomach and allow it to be absorbed at the **site of action** in the intestines.
  - ○ **Reduced Gastric Irritation**: Drugs like **NSAIDs** (Non-Steroidal Anti-Inflammatory Drugs) can irritate the stomach lining. An enteric coating prevents the drug from coming into contact with the stomach, reducing the risk of gastric ulcers or other issues.

- **Common Enteric Coating Materials**:

  - ○ **Shellac**: A natural polymer used for enteric coatings, which is stable in acidic environments and dissolves in alkaline conditions.
  - ○ **Methacrylic Acid Copolymers**: These are synthetic polymers that are often used to create coatings that are resistant to stomach acid and dissolve at higher pH levels found in the intestines. **Eudragit L and S** are examples of methacrylic acid copolymers used in enteric coatings.

- **Applications:**

  ○ **Acid-Sensitive Drugs:** Enteric coatings are commonly used for drugs such as **omeprazole** (a proton pump inhibitor), **aspirin,** and **antibiotics** that need to be protected from stomach acid.
  ○ **Biologics:** Protein-based drugs, including **insulin** and **peptides,** are often encapsulated in enteric-coated tablets to prevent their breakdown in the stomach and to ensure they are delivered to the small intestine.

Applications in Controlled Release and Stability

Coating materials are not only important for improving the **aesthetic appeal** and **patient compliance** of pharmaceutical formulations but also play critical roles in controlling the **drug release,** enhancing the **stability** of the active pharmaceutical ingredient (API), and enabling **targeted delivery.** These functional coatings are widely used in **controlled-release, stability-enhancing,** and **targeted drug delivery** systems, ensuring that the drug reaches its therapeutic effect more efficiently and with minimal side effects.

1. Controlled Release

- **Purpose:** Coating materials are often used in **controlled-release** and **sustained-release** formulations to regulate the release rate of the drug, allowing for a prolonged therapeutic effect with fewer doses over time.
- **Function:**

  ○ **Extended Release:** Coatings can be designed to **slow the release** of the API over an extended period, which reduces the frequency of dosing and provides a more consistent therapeutic effect throughout the day.
  ○ **Sustained Release:** This type of release ensures a **steady-state concentration** of the drug in the bloodstream, which helps maintain efficacy and minimizes fluctuations in drug levels that could cause side effects.
  ○ **Mechanism:** The coating materials are engineered to dissolve gradually or to be **permeable to water** or **acid,** controlling the rate at which the drug is released.

- **Applications:**

- ○ **Tablets and Capsules: Film coatings** and **enteric coatings** are used in sustained-release and extended-release tablets to provide a **prolonged drug effect.** For example, **hydroxypropyl methylcellulose (HPMC)** is often used for sustained-release formulations due to its ability to form a gel layer upon contact with water, slowly releasing the drug.
- ○ **Oral Dosage Forms:** Many **oral dosage forms,** such as **pain relievers** or **antidepressants,** benefit from controlled-release coatings that allow the drug to be absorbed gradually over a longer period.

2. Improved Stability

- **Purpose:** Coating materials can help **protect sensitive APIs** from degradation caused by environmental factors such as **moisture, light,** and **oxygen.** By providing a protective barrier, coatings can improve the **shelf-life** of the drug and ensure its potency and effectiveness for longer durations.
- **Function:**

  - ○ **Protection from Moisture:** Some drugs, especially **hydrophobic** or **hygroscopic** compounds, are sensitive to **moisture** and can degrade or lose efficacy when exposed to humidity. Coatings act as barriers that protect these drugs from moisture, ensuring that they remain stable.
  - ○ **Protection from Light and Oxygen:** Coatings can shield the drug from **light** and **oxygen,** two major factors that can cause oxidative degradation of sensitive compounds. **Film coatings** are particularly effective in providing **light protection.**
  - ○ **Enhanced Shelf Life:** By minimizing exposure to these environmental factors, the **overall stability** of the drug is improved, leading to a **longer shelf-life** and greater **therapeutic effectiveness** over time.

- **Applications:**

  - ○ **Sensitive APIs:** Drugs like **vitamins, hormones,** and **biologics** are often coated to prevent degradation due to **exposure to light** or **oxidation.**

- ○ **Pharmaceutical Tablets and Capsules**: Coated tablets and capsules are often used for **moisture-sensitive** APIs, providing **physical protection** from **external environmental factors** that could cause the drug to deteriorate.

3. Targeted Delivery

- **Purpose**: Coating materials are designed to ensure that the drug is released at a specific site within the **gastrointestinal (GI) tract** or **body**. This is especially important for drugs that are sensitive to **stomach acid** or require release in a specific area for optimal absorption.
- **Function**:

  - ○ **Enteric Coating: Enteric coatings** are designed to prevent drug release in the acidic environment of the stomach and allow it to dissolve in the more alkaline environment of the **small intestine**. This is particularly useful for drugs that may irritate the stomach or degrade in an acidic medium.
  - ○ **Targeted Drug Release**: Coatings can be designed to ensure that the drug is released only at specific areas in the body, providing **targeted delivery** to improve therapeutic outcomes and reduce side effects.
  - ○ **Precision in Release**: Coating materials can be engineered to release the drug in response to specific physiological conditions, such as changes in **pH**, **temperature**, or **enzymatic activity**.

- **Applications**:

  - ○ **Acid-Sensitive Drugs**: Drugs like **omeprazole** (a proton pump inhibitor) or **enteric-coated aspirin** benefit from **enteric coatings**, which protect them from the stomach's acidic environment and ensure release in the small intestine.
  - ○ **Site-Specific Delivery: Targeted delivery** systems are used for drugs that need to act at specific sites, such as **anti-cancer drugs** (delivered directly to tumors) or **anti-inflammatory drugs** (targeted at inflamed areas in the gastrointestinal tract).
  - ○ **Peptides and Biologics: Peptides** and **protein-based drugs** that are susceptible to degradation in the stomach can be coated to ensure that they are released in the **small intestine** where they can be

DR. M. RAMAKRISHNA, M. SANTHOSH ARUNA, G. LAKSHMI DEVI, DR. G.
RAGHAVENDRA

absorbed.

5.4 Types of Excipients for Parenteral Products

In **parenteral formulations**, excipients play an essential role in ensuring the stability, safety, and effectiveness of injectable drugs. These excipients help maintain the **sterility, bioavailability**, and **appropriate pH** of the drug while preventing microbial contamination and degradation. Below is an overview of the key types of excipients used in **parenteral products:**

1. Solvents

Solvents are used to dissolve the **active pharmaceutical ingredient (API)** to form a solution for injection, ensuring the drug is in a suitable form for delivery.

- **Function:**

  - Solvents help dissolve the API into a solution that is stable, **sterile**, and suitable for parenteral administration.
  - They assist in **adjusting the volume** of the injectable product to deliver the correct dose.

- **Common Examples:**

  - **Water:** The most commonly used solvent for injectable formulations. **Water for Injection (WFI)** is highly purified and sterilized water used in parenteral preparations to dissolve the API.
  - **Saline (0.9% Sodium Chloride):** Used as a solvent and also to adjust the osmolarity of the formulation to match the body's natural fluid composition, ensuring safe injection.
  - **Aqueous Solvents:** Other aqueous solvents, such as **Ringer's solution** or **lactated Ringer's**, may be used in specific formulations to mimic bodily fluids and improve biocompatibility.

- **Applications:**

  - **Injectables:** Water and saline are used in the preparation of intravenous (IV), intramuscular (IM), and subcutaneous (SC) injectable formulations.

- **Nutritional Formulations**: Solvents are used in **parenteral nutrition solutions**, where the drug or nutrients are dissolved and delivered intravenously.

2. Preservatives

Preservatives are essential in preventing microbial growth in injectable products, especially for multi-dose vials or ampoules. Parenteral formulations are at a higher risk for contamination due to the need for **sterility** during manufacturing and handling.

- **Function**:

  - Preservatives inhibit microbial growth, ensuring the drug remains **safe** for use throughout its shelf life, especially when the container is opened multiple times.
  - They help maintain **sterility** by preventing the growth of bacteria, fungi, or other microorganisms that could compromise the product.

- **Common Examples**:

  - **Benzyl Alcohol**: A commonly used preservative in parenteral formulations, particularly for multi-dose vials, due to its **antimicrobial** properties.
  - **Phenol**: Often used in vaccines and other injectable products to prevent microbial contamination.
  - **Thimerosal**: A **mercury-containing compound** sometimes used in vaccines and multi-dose vials to preserve sterility.

- **Applications**:

  - **Vaccines**: Preservatives like **Thimerosal** are used to preserve **multi-dose** vials of vaccines.
  - **Antibiotics**: Some injectable antibiotics contain preservatives like **benzyl alcohol** to prevent microbial contamination during use.

3. Stabilizers

Stabilizers are used to prevent the degradation of sensitive drugs, particularly **biologics** and **protein-based therapies**. These excipients maintain the **structural integrity** of the drug and extend its shelf life.

- **Function:**

  - Stabilizers help protect the **API** from **oxidation, hydrolysis,** or **thermal degradation**, ensuring that the drug remains effective over time.
  - They can also help maintain the **physical** and **chemical stability** of proteins, peptides, and other biologics that are sensitive to environmental conditions.

- **Common Examples:**

  - **Sodium Chloride:** Used as a stabilizer in injectable formulations, **sodium chloride** helps maintain **osmotic pressure** and **pH stability.**
  - **Tromethamine:** A **buffer** and stabilizer used in parenteral products, particularly in biologics, to prevent degradation due to pH fluctuations.
  - **Disodium Edetate (EDTA):** A chelating agent that can stabilize formulations by binding metal ions that may catalyze degradation reactions.

- **Applications:**

  - **Biologics:** Stabilizers are used in biologic formulations (e.g., **monoclonal antibodies**) to preserve their **efficacy** and **longevity.**
  - **Vaccines and Enzyme Inhibitors:** Stabilizers help maintain the potency and **shelf-life** of vaccines and biologics that are sensitive to environmental conditions.

4. Buffers

Buffers are used to maintain a stable **pH** environment in parenteral products, which is essential for the solubility, stability, and **bioavailability** of the drug. **pH control** ensures the drug is in the **correct ionization state** and remains effective after administration.

- **Function:**

- Buffers help maintain a constant **pH** in the formulation, ensuring that the drug remains in its most effective form and minimizing the risk of **precipitation** or **degradation**.
- They ensure that the drug does not cause irritation to the site of injection by maintaining the formulation at a physiologically compatible pH.

- **Common Examples:**

  - **Phosphate Buffers:** Widely used in **injectable solutions** to maintain a stable pH range, phosphate buffers are especially useful for biologics and other sensitive compounds.
  - **Citrate Buffers:** Often used in **parenteral formulations** for their ability to maintain a stable pH while also having **stabilizing** properties for certain proteins or biologics.
  - **Acetate Buffers:** Used to maintain a stable pH in formulations that require slightly acidic conditions.

- **Applications:**

  - **Biologic Formulations:** Buffering agents like **phosphate** or **citrate** are commonly used in biologics, such as **insulin** and **monoclonal antibodies**, to preserve the stability of the protein.
  - **Injectable Drugs:** Many **IV fluids** and **injectable medications** use buffers to maintain an appropriate pH for safe and effective administration.

Special Considerations for Parenteral Products

Parenteral formulations, which include **injectables** and **infusions**, require careful consideration during formulation, manufacturing, and packaging to ensure their **safety, efficacy,** and **patient compliance**. These products must adhere to stringent **regulatory standards** and undergo specific processes to meet the needs of **sterility, pyrogenicity,** and **packaging requirements**. Below are the key special considerations for parenteral products.

1. Sterility and Pyrogenicity

- **Sterility:**

- Parenteral products must be **sterile** to ensure that they are free from harmful microorganisms such as bacteria, viruses, or fungi that could cause **infection** when administered directly into the body.
- **Sterilization Methods:**

  - **Heat sterilization** (e.g., **autoclaving**) is commonly used for aqueous solutions and some solid drugs.
  - **Filtration sterilization** is often employed for heat-sensitive products, where the liquid is passed through a **sterilizing filter** to remove microorganisms.
  - **Gamma radiation** is used for sterilizing certain biologics and equipment.

- **Regulatory Compliance**: Regulatory agencies like the **FDA**, **EMA**, and **WHO** have stringent guidelines for the **sterilization** of **parenteral products**. Parenteral formulations must meet these standards to ensure **patient safety**.

- **Pyrogenicity:**

  - **Pyrogens** are substances, typically **endotoxins** produced by bacteria, that can cause **fever** and **inflammation** when introduced into the body.
  - **Endotoxin Testing**: Parenteral products must undergo **pyrogen testing** (e.g., **LAL test (Limulus Amebocyte Lysate)**) to ensure that the formulation is free from pyrogens, particularly for **injectable** products, where even small amounts of endotoxins can cause severe **adverse reactions**.
  - **Packaging Considerations**: The packaging for parenteral products must also be **sterile** to prevent contamination during storage and transport.

2. Packaging for Parenteral Products

The packaging of **parenteral products** is critical to maintaining the **sterility**, **stability**, and **efficacy** of the drug. Special packaging is required to prevent contamination, degradation, and ensure the **safe delivery** of the drug.

- **Sterile Packaging**: The **primary packaging** (e.g., **vials, ampoules, syringes**) must be **sterile** and **tamper-evident** to ensure that the product remains uncontaminated until use. The **secondary packaging** often includes **seals** or **wrapping** to provide an additional layer of protection.
- **Environmental Protection**: Packaging should protect the drug from **moisture, light**, and **oxygen** that could compromise the stability of the API, especially for **biologics** and **sensitive drugs**.

  - **Light Protection**: For light-sensitive drugs (e.g., certain **vitamins, biologics**), **amber-colored** or **opaque** containers are used to shield the drug from **photodegradation**.
  - **Moisture Protection**: **Desiccants** are often included in the packaging to absorb moisture, preventing **hydrolysis** or **degradation** of the drug.
  - **Oxygen Protection**: Some parenteral products require packaging with **oxygen-impermeable** materials to prevent oxidation, especially for **lipid-based** formulations or **protein drugs**.

- **Single vs. Multi-Dose Packaging**:

  - **Single-dose vials** are used for products that are used in one go, ensuring that the entire amount of drug is used immediately, maintaining sterility.
  - **Multi-dose vials** are used for formulations that allow for multiple uses. These require the inclusion of **preservatives** to prevent microbial contamination with each use. Proper **packaging design** and labeling are crucial to ensure that the drug remains sterile and safe for use over multiple administrations.

- **Compatibility with Injection Equipment**: The packaging must also be **compatible with injection devices**, such as **syringes, infusion bags**, and **IV administration sets**. Packaging must allow easy access to the drug, with no risk of leakage or difficulty in withdrawing the drug from the vial.

5.5 *Excipients for Aerosols and Novel Drug Delivery Systems (NDDS)*

Aerosols and **Novel Drug Delivery Systems (NDDS)** are innovative and effective delivery mechanisms for pharmaceuticals, especially for **inhalation** therapies, **topical applications**, and **targeted drug delivery**. Excipients play a pivotal role in **aerosol formulations** and **NDDS**, ensuring that the drug is effectively delivered, remains stable, and achieves the desired therapeutic effect. Below is an overview of the key excipients used in **aerosol** formulations and **novel drug delivery systems**.

Role in Aerosols

Aerosols are commonly used for inhalation therapies (e.g., asthma inhalers) and for **topical drug delivery** (e.g., sprays for wound care). Aerosol formulations typically consist of a **drug** and a **propellant** that helps deliver the drug to the desired site of action, such as the **lungs** or **skin**. The excipients in aerosol formulations are crucial for **drug solubilization, stability**, and the **propulsion mechanism**.

1. Propellants

- **Function**: Propellants are key excipients used in aerosol formulations to drive the drug formulation from the container and into the desired site (e.g., the **lungs, skin**, or **nasal passages**). They help create the necessary pressure within the container, enabling the drug to be **atomized** or **sprayed** effectively.
- **Types of Propellants:**

  - **Hydrofluoroalkanes (HFAs):** HFAs, such as **HFA-134a** and **HFA-227**, are the most commonly used propellants in modern aerosol products, especially in **pressurized metered-dose inhalers (MDIs)**. They are **non-toxic** and have a **lower environmental impact** compared to older propellants like **CFCs** (chlorofluorocarbons), which were phased out due to their negative impact on the **ozone layer**.
  - **Compressed Gases:** Some aerosol formulations use **compressed gases** like **nitrous oxide (N2O)** or **carbon dioxide (CO2)** as propellants. These are used in non-pressurized aerosol products, such as spray-on medications for topical use.

- ○ **Liquefied Gases**: Propellants like **liquid butane** or **isobutane** are also used in some aerosol formulations, where the gas is liquefied under pressure and helps propel the drug once the container is opened.

- **Applications**:

  - ○ **Inhalation Aerosols**: In **MDIs** for respiratory diseases like asthma or COPD, propellants help deliver the drug (e.g., bronchodilators or corticosteroids) directly to the lungs for quick absorption.
  - ○ **Topical Aerosols**: Propellants are used in **topical sprays** to deliver drugs like **antiseptics, analgesics**, and **antifungals** directly onto the skin or other body surfaces.

2. Solubilizers and Stabilizers

- **Function**: Solubilizers and stabilizers are important excipients that help dissolve the active pharmaceutical ingredient (API) and prevent the degradation of sensitive drugs in aerosol formulations. These excipients enhance the **drug's solubility**, **stability**, and ensure its proper delivery over time.
- **Solubilizers**:

  - ○ **Polyethylene Glycol (PEG)**: PEG is used to **solubilize** hydrophobic drugs in aerosol formulations. It helps improve the **solubility** of the API in the propellant or solvent mixture, ensuring that the drug is delivered efficiently and uniformly.
  - ○ **Sorbitan Esters**: Sorbitan esters (e.g., **Sorbitan monolaurate**) are surfactants used as solubilizers to improve the solubility of APIs that are poorly soluble in propellants. These esters help emulsify and dissolve lipophilic compounds, enabling them to be effectively dispersed in aerosol systems.

- **Stabilizers**:

  - ○ **Antioxidants (e.g., Ascorbic Acid, Tocopherol)**: Aerosol formulations, especially those containing biologics or unstable APIs, require stabilizers to prevent **oxidation** and maintain the drug's activity. **Antioxidants** help preserve the integrity of the drug and extend its shelf life.

- ○ **Chelating Agents (e.g., EDTA): Ethylenediaminetetraacetic acid (EDTA)** can be used to chelate metal ions, which could catalyze **oxidation reactions,** and thus help stabilize sensitive drugs in aerosol formulations.

- **Applications:**

  - ○ **Inhalation Drugs:** For inhaled **corticosteroids, bronchodilators,** and **antibiotics,** solubilizers and stabilizers help ensure that the drug is delivered in a **stable** and **effective** form while avoiding degradation during storage.

  - ○ **Topical Aerosols:** In formulations like **skin sprays** or **nasal sprays,** solubilizers and stabilizers help maintain the consistency of the formulation and preserve the **efficacy** of the active ingredient.

Role in Novel Drug Delivery Systems (NDDS)

Novel Drug Delivery Systems (NDDS) are advanced formulations that aim to deliver drugs to specific sites in the body, **improve bioavailability,** and **optimize therapeutic efficacy.** Excipients play a crucial role in the development of **NDDS,** such as **liposomes, microparticles, nanoparticles,** and **microspheres,** by providing **controlled release,** enhancing drug targeting, and improving drug **solubility.**

- **Function:**

  - ○ **Controlled and Targeted Drug Release:** NDDS can use excipients to achieve **sustained release** or **targeted delivery** of the drug. This minimizes side effects and improves the therapeutic response.

  - ○ **Enhancing Drug Solubility and Bioavailability:** Excipients like **cyclodextrins, solubilizers,** and **lipid-based formulations** help to improve the solubility of poorly water-soluble drugs, ensuring better absorption in the body.

  - ○ **Stabilization of Sensitive Drugs:** Excipients can also stabilize sensitive APIs, such as biologics or vaccines, preventing degradation and ensuring the drug's efficacy.

- **Examples of NDDS:**

- **Liposomes**: Liposomes are used to encapsulate hydrophilic or hydrophobic drugs, protecting them from degradation and allowing **targeted delivery** to specific cells or tissues.
- **Nanoparticles and Nanocarriers**: These are used in **cancer treatment** and **gene delivery**, where the drug is delivered directly to the target site, reducing side effects.
- **Microspheres and Microcapsules**: Used for **sustained-release** formulations, these excipients provide controlled release of the drug over a prolonged period, improving patient compliance.

Applications in Novel Drug Delivery Systems (NDDS)

Novel Drug Delivery Systems (NDDS) have revolutionized pharmaceutical formulations by providing **targeted drug delivery**, **controlled release**, and enhanced **bioavailability** of drugs. Excipients play a vital role in the design and effectiveness of these systems, allowing for **precise delivery** to specific areas of the body, ensuring sustained therapeutic effects, and improving the **solubility** and **absorption** of poorly soluble drugs. Below are the key applications of excipients in NDDS and examples of how they are utilized.

1. Targeted Drug Delivery

- **Role of Excipients**: Excipients in **NDDS** are crucial for ensuring that the drug is delivered to specific **sites of action** in the body. By using **biocompatible carriers** such as **liposomes, nanoparticles,** and **microspheres**, excipients help enhance the **selectivity** of the drug delivery system, reducing the **systemic exposure** and **side effects** typically associated with traditional drug delivery methods.
- **Mechanism**:

  - **Targeting** is achieved by modifying the surface properties of delivery systems, such as incorporating **ligands** or **antibodies** that specifically recognize and bind to receptors on target cells or tissues (e.g., tumor **cells, macrophages**, etc.).
  - **Excipients** can also be used to alter the **physicochemical properties** of the drug, facilitating its passage across biological barriers, such as the **blood-brain barrier** or **tumor vasculature**.

- **Applications**:

- **Cancer Treatment: Liposomes** and **nanoparticles** are used to deliver anticancer drugs directly to **tumors**, improving drug concentration at the target site while minimizing damage to surrounding healthy tissues.
- **Infectious Diseases: Antiviral** drugs and other **biologics** are delivered via **liposomes** or **microspheres**, targeting specific cells or tissues to enhance efficacy and reduce systemic side effects.

2. Controlled and Sustained Release

- **Role of Excipients**: NDDS can be designed to provide **controlled release** (CR) or **sustained release** (SR) of drugs, which ensures **steady plasma levels** of the drug over extended periods. This allows for less frequent dosing and maintains **therapeutic effectiveness** while reducing fluctuations in drug concentrations that can lead to side effects.
- **Mechanism:**

  - **Excipients** in **CR** and **SR** formulations control the **rate of release** of the drug by acting as **barriers** or **gels** that gradually allow the drug to diffuse out of the carrier over time.
  - These systems can be engineered to respond to **pH**, **temperature**, or **enzymatic action**, providing a **customized release** profile for the drug.

- **Applications:**

  - **Pain Management: Opioid analgesics** and **anti-inflammatory drugs** benefit from **sustained-release formulations**, which help maintain **consistent pain relief** and reduce the need for frequent dosing.
  - **Hormonal Therapies: Hormone replacement therapy (HRT)** and **contraceptives** use controlled-release systems to provide **steady hormone levels**, improving efficacy and reducing side effects.

3. Improved Bioavailability

- **Role of Excipients**: Many drugs, especially those that are **poorly soluble** in water, face challenges in achieving **adequate bioavailability**. Excipients, such as **cyclodextrins, solubilizers**, and **lipid-based systems,** are used to enhance the **solubility** and **absorption** of such drugs, allowing them to be delivered effectively via NDDS.

- **Mechanism:**

  - **Cyclodextrins** form **inclusion complexes** with lipophilic drugs, enhancing their **solubility** in water and improving their absorption in the gastrointestinal tract.
  - **Lipid-based formulations**, such as **self-emulsifying drug delivery systems (SEDDS)**, increase the solubility of hydrophobic drugs by encapsulating them in **lipid droplets**, facilitating absorption via the intestinal wall.

- **Applications:**

  - **Poorly Soluble Drugs**: **Anticancer drugs**, **antibiotics**, and **antiviral drugs** with low solubility benefit from the use of **cyclodextrins** or **lipid-based carriers** in NDDS to enhance their **bioavailability**.
  - **Oral Formulations**: Drugs like **poorly soluble statins, antifungals, and peptides** can be formulated with **solubilizing excipients** to improve their **bioavailability** and therapeutic effects.

Examples of NDDS Technologies
1. Liposomes

- **Definition: Liposomes** are spherical **vesicles** made from lipid bilayers, which can encapsulate both **hydrophilic** and **lipophilic** drugs. They provide an effective way to deliver drugs to specific target tissues, such as **tumors, inflammatory sites**, or **infected cells**.
- **Applications:**

  - **Cancer Therapy**: Liposomes are used to deliver **anticancer agents** directly to tumors, improving **drug targeting** while reducing systemic toxicity. Drugs like **doxorubicin** are encapsulated in liposomes for **targeted cancer treatment**.
  - **Antiviral Drugs: Liposomal formulations** of antiviral drugs, such as **amantadine**, are used for targeted delivery, improving **bioavailability** and reducing side effects.

2. Nanoparticles

- **Definition: Nanoparticles** are tiny particles (ranging from **1 to 100 nm**) that can carry drugs or biologics. Due to their small size, they can easily penetrate **biological barriers** and be delivered directly to specific tissues or cells, improving therapeutic efficacy and reducing side effects.
- **Applications:**

  - **Oncology: Nanoparticles** are widely used in **cancer therapy** to deliver **chemotherapy drugs** directly to the tumor site, thereby minimizing **systemic exposure** and **toxicity**.
  - **Gene Therapy: Nanoparticles** are also used in **gene delivery systems** for targeted **DNA or RNA** delivery to **specific cells**, enabling the treatment of genetic disorders.
  - **Drug Targeting: Nanoparticles** are designed to target **specific cell receptors**, improving drug delivery to **infected cells** or **immune cells**, such as in the case of **immunotherapy**.

CHAPTER SIX

Optimization Techniques in Pharmaceutical Development

6.1 Overview of Optimization Techniques

Optimization is an essential process in **pharmaceutical development** that focuses on refining and improving the formulation, manufacturing processes, and overall drug product quality. By applying optimization techniques, the development team can ensure that the drug product performs at its best in terms of **efficacy, safety, cost-effectiveness**, and **regulatory compliance**. Below is an overview of the **importance, principles**, and **methods** of optimization in the pharmaceutical industry.

Importance of Optimization Techniques

Optimization techniques are crucial in enhancing pharmaceutical products' overall quality, performance, and economic viability. The primary objectives of using optimization techniques are to achieve **superior drug efficacy, consistent quality, reduced production costs**, and **regulatory adherence**.

1. Enhancing Product Performance

The goal of optimization in pharmaceutical development is to enhance the **performance** of the drug product. Optimization can improve several aspects of a drug's formulation:

- **Bioavailability**: By improving the **solubility** or **dissolution rate** of the active pharmaceutical ingredient (API), optimization ensures better absorption of the drug, leading to higher bioavailability.
- **Solubility**: Drugs that are poorly soluble in water often face challenges in achieving effective therapeutic outcomes. Through **solubility enhancement techniques**, such as the use of **solubilizers** or **cyclodextrins**, optimization helps increase the drug's solubility,

ensuring that a sufficient amount of drug is available for absorption.

- **Stability**: Optimization helps improve the **chemical**, **physical**, and **microbiological stability** of drugs, ensuring that they maintain their potency, appearance, and safety during the shelf life of the product.
- **Release Rate**: Optimization techniques are applied to modify the drug's **release profile**, enabling **controlled release**, **sustained release**, or **targeted release** of the API. This helps maintain therapeutic efficacy over a longer period with fewer doses.

By addressing these factors, optimization improves the overall therapeutic performance of the drug product, ensuring better outcomes for patients.

2. Cost Efficiency

Optimization is essential for enhancing the **cost-effectiveness** of pharmaceutical products, particularly in large-scale production. By refining the formulation and manufacturing process, optimization techniques help identify cost-effective solutions while maintaining the quality and integrity of the product.

- **Reducing Manufacturing Costs**: Optimization allows pharmaceutical companies to **streamline manufacturing processes**, reducing waste, time, and resources. By selecting appropriate **excipients, manufacturing techniques**, and **production equipment**, costs can be minimized without compromising the drug's quality.
- **Cost-Effective Excipients**: The choice of **excipient** (e.g., binders, diluents, stabilizers) plays a significant role in the cost of drug production. Optimization helps select excipients that provide the desired functionality while being **economically viable**.
- **Efficient Process Design**: The use of optimization techniques, such as **design of experiments (DoE)** or **computer modeling**, ensures that the production process is efficient and cost-effective, minimizing the number of steps and reducing the overall cost of goods sold (COGS).

3. Regulatory Compliance

Optimization plays a critical role in ensuring that the product meets **regulatory requirements** set by organizations such as the **FDA, EMA, WHO**, and other national regulatory bodies.

- **Consistency in Quality**: Optimization ensures that the drug product meets **quality standards** across all batches, maintaining consistent **potency, stability,** and **appearance** throughout its shelf life. This consistency is essential for meeting regulatory requirements.
- **Adherence to Guidelines**: Regulatory agencies require that pharmaceutical products meet specific **Good Manufacturing Practices (GMP)** and **Quality by Design (QbD)** principles. Optimization ensures that the product is developed in compliance with these standards, ensuring that all critical attributes (e.g., **drug release, safety, stability**) are consistently met.
- **Data-Driven Decision Making**: Regulatory authorities require comprehensive data to support product claims, such as **bioavailability studies, stability testing,** and **quality control**. Optimization helps generate the necessary data for regulatory submissions, ensuring faster approval and market access.

Principles of Optimization in Pharmaceutical Development

Optimization techniques are guided by several **principles** that help achieve the desired outcomes. These principles ensure that the product development process is efficient, robust, and scientifically grounded.

- **Multivariable Optimization**: The optimization process involves adjusting multiple variables simultaneously, such as **drug concentration, excipient ratios,** and **process conditions**, to identify the most effective formulation.
- **Design of Experiments (DoE)**: A structured approach to conducting experiments that systematically changes multiple factors to determine their effect on the product. This helps identify optimal conditions for formulation and process design.
- **Iterative Process**: Optimization is often an iterative process, where formulations or processes are continuously tested, adjusted, and refined until the desired outcome is achieved.

Methods of Optimization

Several methods are used in pharmaceutical development to optimize both formulations and manufacturing processes. These methods are selected based on the **nature of the product, complexity of the process,** and the desired **outcome**.

1. Classical Methods

- **Trial-and-Error**: Traditional methods where different formulations or processes are tested one at a time to identify the optimal conditions. This method is time-consuming and less efficient but can still be used in some cases.

2. Statistical Methods

- **Factorial Designs**: A statistical approach that involves testing multiple factors simultaneously to assess their influence on the desired outcomes. This method is commonly used to optimize formulation variables (e.g., excipients, concentrations).
- **Response Surface Methodology (RSM)**: A mathematical and statistical technique that explores the relationship between multiple variables and the response, helping to optimize complex processes.
- **Regression Analysis**: Used to understand the relationship between different variables and to predict the outcome based on changes in the factors.

3. Computer Modeling and Simulation

- **Computational Modeling**: Simulation tools help predict the behavior of formulations under various conditions, such as **drug release profiles**, **stability**, and **dissolution rates**. These tools allow for virtual optimization, reducing the need for extensive physical trials.

Practical Examples in Product Design

1. **Formulation Optimization**: In the design of **tablet formulations**, optimization techniques are applied to determine the ideal combination of excipients (e.g., **binders, disintegrants, lubricants**) and the **compression force** to achieve the desired tablet hardness, dissolution rate, and bioavailability.
2. **Process Optimization**: For **granulation processes, mixing time, moisture content,** and **drying conditions** are optimized to achieve the desired particle size, flowability, and compressibility.

3. **Controlled-Release Products**: Optimization techniques are used to fine-tune the release rate of drugs in **extended-release** or **sustained-release formulations**. By adjusting factors like **polymer concentration** and **coating thickness**, the drug release can be extended over several hours or days.

Principles of Optimization in Pharmaceutical Development

Optimization in pharmaceutical development follows a set of principles that guide the process of refining drug formulations and manufacturing processes to achieve the desired **product quality, efficacy**, and **cost-effectiveness**. The following are the core principles that underpin the optimization process:

1. Multivariable Approach

- **Definition**: Optimization often involves adjusting multiple variables at the same time to identify the most effective formulation or process conditions. This approach allows formulators to study the **interactions** between different factors and optimize them simultaneously rather than in isolation.
- **Importance**:

  - **Complexity of Formulations**: In pharmaceutical development, formulations and manufacturing processes are influenced by several factors like **temperature, pressure, pH, concentration of excipients**, and **drug solubility**. Adjusting these variables in isolation may not provide the best solution, as they interact with one another.
  - **Efficiency**: A multivariable approach allows for the **systematic analysis** of all key variables simultaneously, leading to a more comprehensive and efficient optimization process.

- **Example**: In the formulation of an **extended-release tablet**, the **concentration of the polymer, compression force**, and **tablet coating thickness** are all variables that affect the **drug release profile**. Using a multivariable approach, these factors can be optimized together to achieve the desired release rate.

2. Iterative Process

- **Definition**: Optimization is not a one-time event; it is an **ongoing process** in which formulations or processes are **modified, tested**, and **refined** repeatedly until the desired outcome is achieved. This iterative process allows for continuous improvement and **fine-tuning** of the formulation or process.
- **Importance**:

  - **Continuous Improvement**: As new information is gathered from testing, adjustments can be made to **enhance** the formulation or process. This ensures that the final product meets all the **required specifications** for **efficacy, safety**, and **quality**.
  - **Adaptability**: The iterative approach allows for adjustments based on **real-world data** and **feedback** from experiments, ensuring that the product or process is optimized under actual conditions rather than theoretical ones.

- **Example**: In the development of a **sustained-release formulation**, initial formulations might be tested for **drug release** and **stability**. Based on these results, the **excipient concentration** or **manufacturing process** might be adjusted and retested until the desired **release profile** is achieved.

3. Design of Experiments (DoE)

- **Definition**: Design of Experiments (DoE) is a **systematic** approach used to explore the effects of multiple factors on the desired outcome. DoE provides a structured methodology for determining how different variables (factors) interact and influence the results, helping to optimize formulations and processes efficiently.
- **Importance**:

  - **Scientific Approach**: DoE uses **statistical methods** to plan and analyze experiments, ensuring that the results are **reliable** and **accurate**. It helps identify not only the **main effects** of individual factors but also the **interaction effects** between multiple factors.
  - **Optimization Efficiency**: By employing DoE, formulators can optimize a large number of variables in a **shorter amount of time** with fewer experiments. This reduces the need for time-consuming

trial-and-error approaches.

- ○ **Data-Driven Decisions**: DoE provides **quantitative data** that helps in making informed decisions about the best conditions for formulation and process optimization.

- **Example**: In the development of a **tablet formulation**, DoE might be used to study the effects of **binder concentration, disintegrant type,** and **compression force** on the **tablet's hardness, dissolution rate,** and **uniformity**. The results can then guide the selection of the optimal excipient combinations and process parameters.

Methods of Optimization in Pharmaceutical Development

Optimization is a critical part of pharmaceutical development, and there are various methods employed to enhance drug formulations and manufacturing processes. These methods can be broadly categorized into **classical methods** and **statistical methods**, each with distinct approaches for refining formulations and processes. Below is a detailed overview of these two primary optimization methods.

1. Classical Methods

Classical methods in optimization are **traditional approaches** where variables are adjusted one at a time to achieve the desired product attributes or process outcomes. These methods are **simple** and **intuitive** but can be time-consuming and inefficient when dealing with complex formulations or processes involving multiple variables.

Trial-and-Error Approach

- **Definition**: The trial-and-error method involves making **changes** to one variable at a time and testing the results until the optimal outcome is achieved. This is often done without a systematic plan, relying on the experience and intuition of the formulators.
- **Advantages:**

  - ○ **Simplicity**: This method is easy to understand and requires minimal technical expertise, making it suitable for initial stages of development.
  - ○ **Low Cost**: Since this method involves fewer resources and tools, it can be a more **cost-effective** approach for smaller-scale or less complex projects.

- **Disadvantages:**

  - **Time-Consuming**: Adjusting one variable at a time can be very slow, especially when multiple variables need to be optimized.
  - **Inefficiency**: This approach doesn't consider interactions between multiple variables, meaning the optimal result may not be found in fewer trials. Multiple rounds of testing are often needed.
  - **Limited Scope**: It's not suitable for complex formulations with many factors influencing the outcome, as it cannot account for multiple-variable interactions.

Example:

- **Tablet Hardness**: In a **tablet formulation**, a formulary may adjust the **binder concentration** or **compression force** one at a time and test the hardness of the tablet until the desired strength is achieved. While this method may work for simple systems, it's often inefficient for more complex formulations.

2. Statistical Methods

Statistical methods offer a more **systematic** and **data-driven approach** to optimization by considering multiple variables simultaneously. These methods are essential for **complex formulations** or **manufacturing processes** that involve many interacting factors. Statistical techniques allow for efficient experimentation and help identify the most influential variables quickly.

Factorial Designs

- **Definition**: Factorial designs are a statistical approach where the effects of **multiple factors** (e.g., excipient concentration, temperature, compression force) are tested simultaneously in a structured way. This design allows researchers to evaluate not only the **main effects** of each variable but also their **interaction effects**.
- **Advantages:**

  - **Efficiency**: Factorial designs allow for the evaluation of multiple factors at once, reducing the number of experiments needed.

- ◦ **Comprehensive Analysis**: They provide insights into how factors interact with each other, enabling more precise optimization.

- **Example**:

  - ◦ In a **tablet formulation**, factorial designs could be used to test the effects of **binder concentration**, **disintegrant type**, and **compression force** on the tablet's **dissolution rate** and **hardness**.

Response Surface Methodology (RSM)

- **Definition**: RSM is an extension of factorial designs that helps to optimize formulations or processes by modeling and analyzing the relationship between multiple factors and responses. RSM uses **quadratic equations** to describe how various factors interact and influence the response, allowing the formulation of **mathematical models** for optimization.
- **Advantages**:

  - ◦ **Optimization of Multiple Variables**: RSM helps find the optimal settings for a process by analyzing how variables interact and adjusting them accordingly.
  - ◦ **Graphical Analysis**: The results are often presented in **response surface plots**, making it easier to visualize and interpret the effects of different variables.

- **Example**:

  - ◦ **Drug Release Optimization**: RSM can be applied to optimize the release profile of a drug in a **controlled-release tablet**. Variables like **polymer type**, **concentration**, and **tablet compression force** can be tested to identify the best formulation for sustained release.

Regression Analysis

- **Definition**: Regression analysis is a statistical method used to model and analyze the relationship between one or more independent variables and a dependent variable. In optimization, it's used to predict how changes in variables affect the outcome, helping identify the optimal set of conditions.

- **Advantages:**

  - **Quantitative Prediction:** Regression allows for precise predictions of how changes in variables affect the outcome, improving the efficiency of the optimization process.
  - **Data-Driven:** This method relies on experimental data to form mathematical models, providing an objective basis for decision-making.

- **Example:**

  - In the development of a **sustained-release formulation**, regression analysis could be used to predict the **drug release rate** based on factors like **excipient concentration, polymer type**, and **tablet hardness.**

Aspect	Classical Methods	Statistical Methods
Complexity	Simple, intuitive	Advanced, data-driven
Time Efficiency	Time-consuming, trial-and-error	Efficient, evaluates multiple factors at once
Scope	Limited to simple formulations	Suitable for complex formulations and processes
Cost	Low cost but inefficient for large-scale optimization	May require investment in statistical tools, but more cost-effective in the long run
Precision	Lower precision in optimizing multiple variables	Higher precision with the ability to model interactions between variables

Comparison of Classical and Statistical Methods

Practical Examples in Product Design

Optimization techniques are widely used in pharmaceutical product design to improve the **performance, efficacy,** and **quality** of the drug. Through careful optimization, both the **formulation** and **manufacturing process** can be refined to ensure that the final product meets the desired therapeutic outcomes. Below are two practical examples demonstrating the application of optimization in **formulation development** and **manufacturing processes.**

1. Formulation Development

In **formulation development,** optimization techniques are applied to improve the solubility, stability, and overall effectiveness of the drug. One of the primary challenges in pharmaceutical development is enhancing the **bioavailability** of **poorly soluble drugs.** By selecting the right excipients and optimizing their concentration, formulators can improve the dissolution rate and stability of the drug, ensuring that it reaches its target site and is absorbed effectively.

Example: Optimizing the Choice of Excipients for a Poorly Soluble Drug

- **Problem**: Many drugs, especially **hydrophobic compounds,** have poor solubility in water, leading to **low bioavailability.** This is particularly problematic for oral formulations, where the drug must be dissolved in the gastrointestinal tract before it can be absorbed into the bloodstream.
- **Optimization Process:**

  - **Solubilizers:** The choice of excipients such as **cyclodextrins, polyethylene glycol (PEG),** or **surfactants** can significantly improve the solubility of poorly soluble drugs. For example, **cyclodextrins** form inclusion complexes with the drug, increasing its solubility in aqueous media.
  - **Co-solvents: Co-solvents** like **ethanol** or **propylene glycol** can be added to enhance the solubility of lipophilic drugs, particularly in injectable formulations.
  - **Particle Size Reduction:** Techniques like **nanoparticle formation, micronization,** or **solid dispersions** help improve the **surface area** of the drug, allowing it to dissolve more easily in the gastrointestinal tract.

- **Outcome:**

- **Improved Solubility**: By using excipients like **cyclodextrins** or **surfactants**, the solubility of the drug is significantly enhanced, allowing for more efficient absorption.
- **Increased Bioavailability**: With enhanced solubility, the drug's **bioavailability** is improved, meaning that a higher percentage of the drug reaches the bloodstream, increasing its therapeutic effect.

2. Manufacturing Process

In **manufacturing**, optimization is applied to improve the **tablet hardness, dissolution rate**, and **uniformity** of the final product. Factors such as **compression force, granulation method**, and **moisture content** are critical in ensuring that the drug product meets quality standards, such as **content uniformity** and **tablet integrity**.

Example: Optimizing Compression Force and Granulation Process for Tablet Production

- **Problem**: During the production of **tablets**, achieving the desired **tablet hardness** and **dissolution rate** can be challenging. Insufficient compression force can result in **soft tablets** that are prone to breaking, while excessive compression force can lead to **hard, difficult-to-dissolve tablets**. Additionally, the **granulation process**—whether **wet granulation** or **dry granulation**—can significantly impact the final product's characteristics.
- **Optimization Process:**

  - **Compression Force**: By adjusting the **compression force**, formulators can optimize the **tablet hardness** and **disintegration time**. The correct force ensures that the tablet is firm enough for handling and storage but will break apart efficiently in the stomach for drug release.
  - **Granulation Method**: The **granulation method** is chosen based on the properties of the API and excipients. **Wet granulation** is often used for drugs that are difficult to compress, while **dry granulation** is suitable for drugs that are sensitive to moisture or heat.
  - **Moisture Content**: During **granulation**, the moisture content must be optimized to avoid issues like **overdrying** (leading to hard, brittle tablets) or **underdrying** (leading to poor tablet hardness or poor dissolution).

- ○ **Binder Selection**: The use of the right **binder** (e.g., **hydroxypropyl methylcellulose (HPMC)**, **povidone**) helps the granules hold together during compression while also allowing for efficient **disintegration** and **drug release** after ingestion.

- **Outcome:**

  - ○ **Improved Tablet Hardness and Uniformity**: By optimizing the **compression force** and **granulation method**, the tablets are produced with consistent **hardness, uniformity,** and **content uniformity.**
  - ○ **Optimal Dissolution Rate**: Adjusting the granulation process ensures that the **dissolution rate** meets the desired specification for the API. For example, the tablets can be formulated to have an **immediate-release** profile, ensuring rapid absorption of the drug.
  - ○ **Consistency**: The optimized process ensures that **every batch** of tablets meets the same **quality standards**, minimizing **variability** and ensuring patient safety.

6.2 Factorial Designs in Pharmaceutical Development

Factorial designs are widely used statistical experimental approaches in **pharmaceutical development**. These designs enable the simultaneous investigation of multiple factors that influence the outcome of **formulation development** and **manufacturing processes**. By evaluating the **main effects** and **interaction effects** of different variables, factorial designs help optimize product quality and manufacturing efficiency in a systematic and data-driven manner.

Introduction to Factorial Designs

Definition:

A **factorial design** is a structured approach used in experimental research to study the effects of multiple independent variables (factors) on one or more dependent variables (responses). It systematically varies all the factors to determine their **individual effects** and **interaction effects** on the response.

- **Independent Variables (Factors)**: These are the variables that are manipulated in the experiment. In pharmaceutical development, these could be factors like **excipient concentration, compression force, temperature,** or **dissolution medium.**

- **Dependent Variables (Responses)**: These are the outcomes or results that are measured to assess the impact of the independent variables. For example, in tablet formulations, the dependent variables might include **tablet hardness, dissolution rate, drug release,** or **bioavailability.**

Key Features of Factorial Designs:

- **Main Effects**: The primary impact of each factor on the outcome is measured.

- **Interaction Effects**: Factorial designs allow for the assessment of how two or more factors work together to influence the response. This is especially useful in complex systems where the effect of one factor may depend on the levels of other factors.

Factorial designs are extremely useful in optimizing complex processes because they enable researchers to identify not only the main effects of individual variables but also the **interaction effects** between them, providing a more comprehensive understanding of the system.

Full Factorial vs. Fractional Factorial Designs

Factorial designs can be implemented in different ways, depending on the number of factors involved and the need for computational resources. Two common types of factorial designs are **Full Factorial Designs** and **Fractional Factorial Designs**. The choice between them depends on the complexity of the experiment, the number of factors, and the available resources.

1. Full Factorial Designs

- **Definition**: A **Full Factorial Design** tests all possible combinations of the factors at different levels. If there are two levels for each factor, a full factorial design will require testing every combination of all the factors (e.g., 2^n combinations, where n is the number of factors).

- **Advantages**:

  - **Comprehensive Analysis**: A full factorial design provides a complete analysis of the **main effects** and **interaction effects** of each factor. This is especially useful when it is essential to understand all the interactions between factors.
  - **High Accuracy**: Since all possible combinations are tested, this design offers the most accurate and reliable results, minimizing the risk of missing critical interactions.

- **Disadvantages**:

  - **Resource-Intensive**: Full factorial designs require testing a large number of combinations, which can be **time-consuming** and **costly**. The number of experiments increases exponentially with the number of factors and levels.
  - **Not Feasible for Complex Systems**: For complex systems with many factors, the number of experiments required may be impractical.

- **Example**: In a **tablet formulation**, a full factorial design could involve testing three factors: **binder concentration (2 levels), compression** force (2 levels), and **moisture content (2 levels)**. This would result in 2 × 2 × 2 = 8 combinations to test, and the design would evaluate the effects of each factor and the interaction between them on the **tablet hardness, dissolution rate**, and **content uniformity**.

2. Fractional Factorial Designs

- **Definition**: A **Fractional Factorial Design** tests only a **subset** of the possible combinations from a full factorial design. This approach is used when there are too many factors to test all combinations and is typically chosen for **cost-efficiency** or when **time or resources** are limited.
- **Advantages**:

  - **Cost-Effective**: By testing a fraction of the combinations, **fractional factorial designs** reduce the number of experiments required, making the optimization process more cost-effective.
  - **Resource-Efficient**: This design allows researchers to evaluate many factors with fewer experiments, saving time and reducing the amount of material required.

- **Disadvantages**:

  - **Potential Loss of Information**: Fractional factorial designs only estimate the main effects and some interaction effects, potentially overlooking higher-order interactions or subtle effects.
  - **Increased Risk of Confounding**: If the number of factors is too high, there may be **confounding**, where the effects of one factor are **misinterpreted** due to overlapping interactions.

- **Example**: In a **granulation process optimization**, a fractional factorial design could focus on key factors like **binder concentration, granulation speed**, and **moisture content**, testing only a subset of combinations. This would significantly reduce the number of experiments required, while still providing valuable insights into the process optimization.

Applications of Factorial Designs in Pharmaceutical Development

Factorial designs are widely used in pharmaceutical development for **formulation optimization** and **process optimization**. Some key applications include:

- **Formulation Optimization**: Factorial designs help optimize the combination of **excipients** (e.g., **binders, disintegrants, lubricants**) in tablet formulations, balancing **dissolution rate, tablet hardness**, and **bioavailability**.
- **Process Optimization**: In **tablet compression, granulation, coating**, and **drying**, factorial designs help identify the best **process parameters** (e.g., **compression force, temperature, moisture content**) to achieve desired product characteristics.
- **Stability Studies**: Factorial designs can also be used to study the effect of environmental factors (e.g., **temperature, humidity, light exposure**) on the stability of pharmaceutical products, ensuring that products remain effective during their shelf life.

Importance of Factorial Designs in Pharmaceutical Development

Factorial designs are a powerful statistical tool that play a crucial role in **pharmaceutical development**, particularly when it comes to optimizing **formulations** and **manufacturing processes**. By testing multiple variables simultaneously, factorial designs help identify critical factors and their interactions, providing valuable insights that can lead to more efficient and effective drug development. Below are the key reasons why factorial designs are important in pharmaceutical development:

1. Identifying Key Variables

One of the main advantages of factorial designs is the ability to **identify the most influential factors** that impact the performance of the product or process. This is especially important in **formulation development** and **process optimization**, where multiple variables may affect the final outcome.

- **How it Works**: Factorial designs allow for the systematic manipulation of multiple factors at the same time, helping to identify which factors (e.g., **excipient type, concentration, process parameters**) have the most significant impact on product characteristics such as **dissolution rate, tablet hardness**, or **bioavailability**.
- **Practical Example**:

- ○ In the development of **oral tablets**, factorial designs can help determine which combination of **binders, disintegrants,** and **lubricants** influences the **tablet's dissolution rate** and **bioavailability** the most. By testing various combinations and concentrations of these excipients, the most effective ones can be identified to optimize tablet performance.

- **Benefits:**

  - ○ **Focus on Critical Variables**: Factorial designs help **prioritize** the most critical factors that need to be controlled or optimized in the formulation or process.
  - ○ **Resource Optimization**: By identifying the **key variables**, factorial designs help focus experimentation efforts on the most impactful factors, reducing unnecessary trial-and-error and saving both **time** and **resources**.

2. Understanding Interactions Between Factors

Factorial designs are particularly effective at helping researchers understand the **interactions** between different factors and how they influence the response. Many factors in pharmaceutical development do not act independently, and their **interaction effects** can significantly impact the product's performance or the process's efficiency. Factorial designs provide a comprehensive view of how combinations of factors affect the outcome.

- **How it Works**: In a factorial design, all possible combinations of the levels of the factors are tested. This allows for the evaluation of **interaction effects**, where the combined effect of two or more factors is different from the sum of their individual effects. Understanding these interactions can lead to more **efficient formulations** and **optimized processes**.
- **Practical Example:**

  - ○ In the **granulation process**, factors such as **moisture content, granulation speed,** and **binder concentration** can interact in complex ways. A factorial design can reveal whether higher moisture content combined with a specific binder concentration produces better granules, or if there is a significant interaction between

granulation speed and **compression force** that influences **tablet hardness.**

- **Benefits:**

  - **Optimizing Factor Combinations:** By understanding how factors interact, formulators can adjust the levels of factors in a way that maximizes the desired outcome (e.g., **dissolution rate, tablet hardness, drug release**), even if those interactions are counterintuitive.
  - **Improved Process Efficiency:** In manufacturing, factorial designs help identify **process conditions** where factors work synergistically, leading to more **efficient processes** that reduce costs and time.
  - **Better Predictability:** Knowing how factors interact enables formulators to **predict** how changes in one variable will affect the outcome, allowing for **faster decision-making** and reducing the need for further experiments.

Applications of Factorial Designs in Formulation and Process Optimization

Factorial designs are widely used in **pharmaceutical development** to optimize both **formulations** and **manufacturing processes**. These statistical tools enable the study of **multiple factors** and their **interactions,** providing valuable insights into how different variables influence the outcome. By employing factorial designs, formulators and manufacturers can achieve **improved product quality, efficiency,** and **regulatory compliance.**

1. Formulation Optimization

In **formulation optimization,** factorial designs help evaluate the effects of various excipients on the drug's performance, such as **tablet hardness, dissolution rate,** and **bioavailability.** These designs allow researchers to test multiple excipients simultaneously and understand how they interact to influence the final product.

Application Example: Tablet Formulation

- **Problem:** A formulation that optimizes **tablet hardness** and **dissolution** is crucial for ensuring consistent drug release and bioavailability. Tablets must have the right balance of strength to withstand handling and transport, but also release the drug in the correct amount over time.

- **Optimization Process:**

  - **Factors:** In a factorial design, the factors studied might include **binder type, disintegrant concentration, lubricant type,** and **compression force**.
  - **Experiment:** A factorial design could test different levels of **binders** (e.g., **povidone, hydroxypropyl methylcellulose**), **disintegrants** (e.g., **croscarmellose sodium, starch**), and **lubricants** (e.g., **magnesium stearate**) in different concentrations, along with varying **compression forces**.

- **Outcome:**

  - **Tablet Hardness:** The design would help identify the **binder concentration** that provides optimal **tablet strength**.
  - **Dissolution Rate:** By adjusting **disintegrants** and **lubricants**, the formulation could be optimized for an appropriate **dissolution rate**, ensuring the drug is released at the desired time and bioavailability is maximized.
  - **Bioavailability:** The optimized formulation can improve **drug absorption** by enhancing solubility and ensuring uniform distribution in the body.

Benefits of Formulation Optimization Using Factorial Designs:

- **Simultaneous Evaluation:** Multiple excipients can be optimized at once, reducing the time required for experimentation.
- **Identification of Interactions:** Factorial designs help identify interactions between excipients, allowing for more efficient excipient selection and formulation.
- **Consistency:** Optimized formulations lead to consistent drug performance and better **patient outcomes**.

2. Process Optimization

Factorial designs are also highly effective in **optimizing manufacturing processes**, such as **granulation, drying, compression,** and **coating**. By adjusting multiple process parameters simultaneously, factorial designs help improve product consistency, reduce production costs, and enhance process efficiency.

Application Example: Tablet Manufacturing Process

- **Problem**: In the tablet manufacturing process, achieving consistent **tablet weight, disintegration time**, and **content uniformity** is critical for ensuring product quality and therapeutic efficacy.
- **Optimization Process**:

  - **Factors**: In a factorial design, process variables such as **granulation time, moisture content, compression force**, and **drying temperature** can be optimized.
  - **Experiment**: The design would test different combinations of **granulation time** and **moisture content** to determine their effect on **granule size distribution** and **tablet hardness**. The **compression force** would also be varied to study its effect on **tablet weight** and **disintegration time**.

- **Outcome**:

  - **Granulation Process**: The factorial design would help identify the optimal **granulation time** and **moisture content** to produce granules with the right **flowability** and **compressibility**.
  - **Tablet Compression**: By adjusting **compression force**, the process would ensure that the tablets are produced with the desired **tablet weight, content uniformity**, and **hardness**.
  - **Disintegration Time**: The **moisture content** and **granulation time** could also be optimized to ensure that tablets disintegrate properly, facilitating efficient drug release and absorption.

Benefits of Process Optimization Using Factorial Designs:

- **Efficiency in Process Development**: Factorial designs enable the **simultaneous testing** of multiple process parameters, accelerating process development and improving efficiency.
- **Improved Consistency**: By optimizing process conditions, factorial designs ensure that the final product consistently meets **quality standards**, such as **weight uniformity, dissolution**, and **disintegration**

time.

- **Cost Reduction**: By identifying the optimal process parameters, factorial designs help reduce the need for excessive testing and the use of resources, ultimately reducing production costs.

Case Studies of Factorial Design Applications

Factorial designs are widely applied in pharmaceutical development for **formulation optimization** and **process refinement**. These designs allow for the evaluation of multiple factors and their interactions, leading to more efficient product development. Below is an in-depth look at a **real-world case study** of factorial design applications in **tablet formulation optimization**.

Case Study 1: Optimizing Tablet Formulation
Problem: Optimizing Tablet Hardness and Dissolution Rate

In tablet formulation, achieving the right balance between **tablet hardness** and **dissolution rate** is essential for ensuring the product's **bioavailability** and **patient compliance**. Hardness is important to prevent tablets from breaking during storage or handling, while the dissolution rate directly influences how quickly and efficiently the active pharmaceutical ingredient (API) is absorbed in the body.

For this case study, the goal was to determine how the **type** and **concentration** of **binders** and **disintegrants** affect both the tablet's **hardness** and **dissolution rate**. **Binders** are critical for holding the tablet together, and **disintegrants** help the tablet break apart after ingestion, ensuring the API is released.

Optimization Process Using Factorial Design

To optimize the formulation, a **2-level factorial design** was employed, testing two factors at two levels each:

1. **Binder Type**: Different binder types were tested, including **povidone** (a synthetic binder) and **hydroxypropyl methylcellulose (HPMC)** (a cellulose derivative binder).

   - **Level 1**: Povidone (higher solubility, faster disintegration)
   - **Level 2**: HPMC (slower dissolution, enhanced tablet hardness)

2. **Disintegrant Type**: Two types of disintegrants were evaluated, **croscarmellose sodium** (rapid disintegration) and **starch** (slower

disintegration).

- ◦ **Level 1**: Croscarmellose sodium (quick disintegration)
- ◦ **Level 2**: Starch (slower disintegration)

Each combination of binder and disintegrant type was tested with two levels: the standard concentration (for each binder and disintegrant type) and an increased concentration. This design allowed researchers to study both the **main effects** and **interaction effects** of the excipients on the tablet's performance.

Experimental Setup:

- **Tablet Compression**: Tablets were compressed using a standard **tablet press**. Each formulation was subjected to consistent compression force.
- **Dissolution Testing**: Dissolution tests were conducted using a **USP dissolution apparatus**, measuring the time it took for the drug to be released from the tablet.
- **Tablet Hardness**: Tablet hardness was measured using a **tablet hardness tester** to ensure that the tablets were durable enough for handling and storage.

Results and Findings

The factorial design revealed several important findings regarding the interactions between the **binders** and **disintegrants**.

1. **Binder-Disintegrant Interaction**:

   - ◦ The interaction between **povidone** and **croscarmellose sodium** significantly improved the **dissolution rate** without compromising the **tablet hardness**. This combination allowed for a faster drug release while maintaining tablet integrity.
   - ◦ Conversely, **HPMC** combined with **starch** resulted in **slower dissolution** but also led to more **robust tablets** with better handling properties.

2. **Effect of Binder Type:**

- ◦ **Povidone** produced tablets with better **dissolution rates** but slightly lower hardness compared to **HPMC**. This is due to its **faster disintegration** properties, which facilitated quicker API release.
- ◦ **HPMC**, being a slower-release binder, resulted in **harder tablets** with a slower dissolution rate, which might be suitable for **sustained-release formulations**.

3. **Effect of Disintegrant Type:**

- ◦ **Croscarmellose sodium** improved the **dissolution rate** significantly, likely due to its **rapid swelling** properties, which allowed the tablet to break apart more efficiently after ingestion.
- ◦ **Starch**, while providing slower disintegration, helped to maintain the **tablet's integrity** longer, making it suitable for formulations requiring **slow release**.

Conclusion and Implications

This **factorial design** study allowed the researchers to identify the most effective combination of **binders** and **disintegrants** for achieving both **optimal tablet hardness** and **dissolution rate**. Specifically, the interaction between **povidone** and **croscarmellose sodium** showed the best performance in terms of improving the dissolution rate without compromising tablet strength. This combination was deemed ideal for **immediate-release tablets**, providing **rapid drug absorption** while maintaining **physical stability** during storage.

Practical Implications:

- By optimizing **excipients** using factorial designs, pharmaceutical companies can create **formulations** that offer better **bioavailability** and more **consistent therapeutic effects**.
- This approach can also reduce **production costs** by identifying the optimal combination of excipients that do not require excessive or expensive processing steps.
- The study demonstrates how factorial designs can be applied to **fine-tune** product characteristics, leading to **improved patient outcomes** and better **regulatory compliance**.

Factorial designs are a valuable tool in pharmaceutical formulation development, allowing for the **systematic analysis** of multiple factors and their **interactions** to optimize drug products efficiently.

Case Study 2: Optimizing the Granulation Process Using Factorial Design

In the development of pharmaceutical tablets, the **granulation process** plays a crucial role in ensuring **uniformity, consistency**, and **quality** of the final product. Granules need to have **uniform size distribution** for proper **compression, tablet hardness**, and **dissolution rates**. Additionally, **friability** (the tendency of tablets to break or crumble) is an important factor that must be minimized to maintain the **tablet's integrity** during handling, transport, and storage.

This case study focuses on how a **factorial design** was employed to optimize the **granulation process** by analyzing the effects of several variables, including **binder concentration, wet granulation speed**, and **drying time**, on the **granule size distribution** and **tablet friability**.

Optimization Process Using Factorial Design

Problem: Achieving Optimal Granule Size Distribution and Minimizing Friability

- **Granule Size Distribution**: Granules that are too large or too small can cause problems in the **tablet compression** process. **Large granules** may result in **uneven tablet hardness**, while **small granules** may lead to **high friability**.
- **Friability**: Tablets with high friability are prone to breaking or crumbling during handling and storage, which can result in **dosing errors** and **poor patient compliance**.

Experimental Setup Using Factorial Design

In this study, a **2-level factorial design** was employed to investigate the effects of three independent variables (factors) at two levels each. The factors tested were:

1. **Binder Concentration:**

   - **Level 1:** Low binder concentration (e.g., 2% PVP)
   - **Level 2:** High binder concentration (e.g., 4% PVP)

2. **Wet Granulation Speed:**

  ◦ **Level 1**: Low speed (e.g., 100 rpm)
  ◦ **Level 2**: High speed (e.g., 300 rpm)

3. **Drying Time:**

  ◦ **Level 1**: Short drying time (e.g., 1 hour)
  ◦ **Level 2**: Long drying time (e.g., 3 hours)

The design involved testing all **eight combinations** of these variables, allowing researchers to examine the **main effects** of each factor and the **interaction effects** between the binder concentration, granulation speed, and drying time.

Measured Responses (Dependent Variables):

- **Granule Size Distribution**: The particle size distribution of the granules was measured using **sieve analysis** and **laser diffraction** techniques to ensure uniformity and optimal size for tablet formation.
- **Tablet Friability**: The **friability** of the tablets was measured by subjecting them to mechanical stress in a **friabilator** and calculating the percentage weight loss after a set number of rotations.

Results and Findings

The factorial design study revealed several important insights into the interactions between the factors and their effects on granule size distribution and tablet friability.

1. Effect of Binder Concentration

- **Main Effect**: Increasing the binder concentration led to **larger granules**. Higher binder levels caused the granules to form more cohesive structures, resulting in a more uniform size distribution.
- **Friability**: The **higher binder concentration** reduced friability, as the **stronger granules** were less likely to break during compression or handling.

2. Effect of Wet Granulation Speed

- **Main Effect**: Increasing the wet granulation speed resulted in smaller granules with a more **uniform size distribution**. This is because higher speeds facilitate better mixing and formation of uniform granules.
- **Friability**: **Higher granulation speed** also contributed to **reduced friability**, as the increased shear force during mixing led to **more compact granules** that were less likely to crumble.

3. Effect of Drying Time

- **Main Effect**: Longer drying times resulted in **drier granules**, which were more **brittle** and more likely to break during compression. The optimal drying time was found to be a balance: too short resulted in **moist granules**, and too long made the granules **too dry**, leading to higher friability.
- **Granule Size Distribution**: Longer drying times did not significantly affect the **granule size distribution**, but it did impact the **hardness** of the granules, making them **more uniform**.

Interaction Effects:

- The interaction between **binder concentration** and **wet granulation speed** was found to have the most significant impact on **granule size distribution**. When both factors were optimized, the resulting granules had the **ideal size distribution** with **low friability**.
- **Binder concentration** and **drying time** also showed interaction effects, where the combination of higher binder concentration and moderate drying time produced granules that were both **uniform in size** and had **reduced friability**.

Conclusion and Implications

This **factorial design** study helped identify the optimal conditions for producing **granules** with the desired **uniform size distribution** and **minimal friability**. The optimal conditions included:

- **High binder concentration (4%)**
- **High wet granulation speed (300 rpm)**
- **Moderate drying time (2 hours)**

These conditions resulted in granules that were well-sized and had **low friability**, leading to **stronger tablets** that were less likely to break or crumble during handling and transport. This approach not only ensured consistent **tablet hardness** and **dissolution rates** but also minimized the **risk of product failure** due to friability.

Practical Implications:

- The use of **factorial design** in **granulation** allows manufacturers to optimize multiple process parameters simultaneously, saving both time and resources.
- By understanding the **interaction effects** between binder concentration, granulation speed, and drying time, manufacturers can make informed decisions to optimize **tablet production processes**, improving both product quality and **process efficiency**.

Factorial designs provide a valuable tool for optimizing complex manufacturing processes in pharmaceutical development, ensuring the production of high-quality drug products that meet regulatory standards and deliver the desired therapeutic outcomes for patients.

6.3 Quality by Design (QbD) in Pharmaceutical Development

Quality by Design (QbD) is an advanced and systematic approach in **pharmaceutical development** that ensures the consistent quality of drug products from the very beginning of their design. By focusing on **understanding** the entire process, identifying **critical quality attributes (CQAs)**, and designing robust and scalable manufacturing processes, QbD helps to deliver products that meet regulatory requirements and consistently achieve desired therapeutic outcomes. Below is an overview of the core **principles** of **QbD** and how they are applied in pharmaceutical development.

Overview of QbD Principles

1. Design for Quality

- **Definition**: The primary principle of QbD is to **design** products and processes in a way that **inherently** meets **quality standards**. This is achieved by understanding the **critical quality attributes (CQAs)** and **process parameters** and designing the formulation and manufacturing processes to ensure these attributes are consistently met.
- **Importance:**

  - By integrating **quality** into the design phase, QbD eliminates the need for excessive post-production testing and adjustments. Quality is **built into** the product and process, rather than being tested for after the fact.
  - Understanding the **CQAs** (such as **solubility, stability, dissolution rate**, and **bioavailability**) allows formulators to develop products with consistent performance, reducing variability and improving therapeutic outcomes.

- **Application:**

  - **Formulation Design**: During the development of a **tablet formulation**, formulators will study the **critical attributes** like **dissolution rate** and **tablet hardness**. By designing the formulation with excipients that are best suited for the desired outcome, consistent **product quality** is ensured.

- ○ **Process Design**: For **tablet compression**, parameters like **compression force, granulation time,** and **moisture content** will be controlled to ensure **uniformity** and **content uniformity** in every batch.

2. Risk Management

- **Definition**: **Risk management** in QbD involves identifying potential risks early in the development process that could affect product quality. These risks can be related to the **raw materials, formulation, process conditions,** or even **environmental factors**. Once risks are identified, strategies are developed to mitigate or manage these risks.
- **Importance:**

  - ○ QbD encourages the identification of potential risks at every stage of development. By understanding these risks, pharmaceutical developers can take proactive steps to ensure **consistent quality** and minimize the chance of **failures** in the final product.
  - ○ **Risk management** ensures that the development process is not only **effective** but also **predictable**, with fewer surprises during production or when regulatory authorities assess the product.

- **Application:**

  - ○ **Formulation Risk**: In **biologic drugs**, for instance, risks related to **protein aggregation** or **degradation** may be identified early. Formulators can then choose excipients or adjust the pH to **stabilize the biologic** and reduce risk.
  - ○ **Process Risk**: During manufacturing, the **granulation process** might present risks related to **moisture content** or **granule size distribution**. By identifying these risks in advance, formulations can be optimized to mitigate variations.

- **Risk Assessment Tools**: Tools like **Failure Mode and Effect Analysis (FMEA)** and **Risk Priority Number (RPN)** are often used to systematically assess and prioritize risks in both formulation and manufacturing.

3. Continuous Improvement

- **Definition**: QbD encourages **continuous monitoring** and **improvement** of the product and process throughout its lifecycle. This means that once the product reaches the market, the development team remains involved, continuously evaluating data and performance to ensure that the product maintains its quality and efficacy over time.
- **Importance**:

  - By **monitoring** the process after commercialization, pharmaceutical companies can quickly identify issues such as **manufacturing variations** or **degradation of the drug**, and take corrective actions before the product fails.
  - Continuous improvement helps adapt to changing conditions and **feedback** from customers, healthcare providers, and regulators. This ensures the drug stays effective and remains aligned with **regulatory standards**.

- **Application**:

  - **Post-Launch Monitoring**: For **biologics** or **injectable formulations**, continuous monitoring can detect early signs of **batch variability**, such as differences in **drug stability**. This allows manufacturers to make **adjustments** in the process or formulation to address any challenges before they affect product performance.
  - **Regulatory Updates**: As new guidelines or standards are introduced by regulatory bodies like the **FDA** or **EMA**, companies practicing QbD will ensure that they remain in compliance by continuously adapting their processes based on the most up-to-date regulations.

- **Tools for Continuous Improvement**:

  - **Statistical Process Control (SPC)**: This method uses statistical techniques to monitor and control the manufacturing process, ensuring that the product remains within the desired quality specifications.
  - **Real-Time Release Testing (RTRT)**: This process allows for the continuous monitoring of critical process parameters and quality

attributes during manufacturing, enabling real-time decisions on product release.

Applications of Quality by Design (QbD) in Product Development and Manufacturing

Quality by Design (QbD) is an essential approach that focuses on designing products and processes to meet predefined quality criteria from the outset. It integrates a deeper understanding of the drug's Critical Quality Attributes (CQAs) and Critical Material Attributes (CMAs) to optimize formulations, processes, and manufacturing. Below are detailed applications of QbD in product development and manufacturing.

1. Formulation Development

QbD can be applied to formulation development by considering the Critical Material Attributes (CMAs) and Critical Quality Attributes (CQAs) of the drug. The goal is to ensure that the final product meets all the necessary specifications for safety, efficacy, and quality, while minimizing variations in product performance.

Optimizing Drug Solubility and Dissolution Profiles

- Role of QbD: In formulation development, QbD helps optimize the solubility and dissolution rate of the active pharmaceutical ingredient (API) by carefully understanding the interactions between the API and the excipient(s). This ensures that the final product will have adequate bioavailability and therapeutic efficacy.

- **Process:**

  - Critical Material Attributes (CMAs): These include the physical and chemical properties of the API, such as particle size, polymorphism, solubility, and stability.
  - Critical Quality Attributes (CQAs): These include attributes like dissolution rate, content uniformity, and drug release.
  - Excipients: The choice of excipients (e.g., binders, disintegrants, solubilizers) significantly influences the formulation. QbD helps in selecting the appropriate excipients that enhance the drug's solubility, optimize dissolution profiles, and ensure uniformity and stability.

- **Example:**

- **Optimization of Solubility**: For a poorly soluble drug, QbD can be used to explore the interaction between the drug and **cyclodextrins**, which help improve **solubility** and **bioavailability**. The formulation can be optimized by adjusting the **concentration** of the excipients to achieve the **desired dissolution rate** and therapeutic effect.

Benefits of QbD in Formulation Development:

- **Improved Bioavailability**: Optimizing solubility and dissolution profiles ensures that the drug is absorbed effectively in the body.
- **Regulatory Compliance**: By understanding the key attributes (CMAs and CQAs) and optimizing them early, the final product is more likely to meet regulatory standards, ensuring smoother approval.
- **Consistency**: QbD ensures that the formulation is robust and reproducible, maintaining product quality across different batches.

2. Process Design and Control

QbD plays a crucial role in **process design** and **control** by ensuring that manufacturing processes are **well-defined**, **robust**, and capable of producing **consistent high-quality products**.

Optimizing Manufacturing Processes

- Role of QbD: In the manufacturing process development, QbD focuses on designing processes that are capable of delivering the desired product quality consistently. This includes defining optimal process parameters like mixing times, temperature control, compression force, and granulation time in solid dosage forms.
- **Process Design:**

  - QbD emphasizes the importance of **understanding** how **process variables** affect **CQAs**. For instance, the mixing time in **granulation** can affect the **granule size distribution** and, ultimately, the **tablet's dissolution**.
  - **Critical Process Parameters (CPPs)**, such as **temperature**, **humidity, pH**, and **speed** (for mixing or granulation), are identified and optimized to ensure that the process consistently delivers the desired outcome.

- **Example:**

  - **Tablet Manufacturing:** In tablet production, QbD helps optimize **compression force** to ensure that the tablets are neither too hard (which could affect dissolution) nor too soft (which could lead to friability). Similarly, **granulation speed** and **drying time** are optimized to achieve consistent **granule size** and prevent issues with dissolution or uniformity.

Benefits of QbD in Process Design and Control:

- **Consistency in Manufacturing:** Optimizing process variables ensures that each batch produced has consistent **quality, dissolution,** and **bioavailability.**
- **Efficiency:** By defining and controlling the critical parameters, QbD helps eliminate variations in the process and leads to a more efficient manufacturing setup.
- **Reduced Variability:** The process remains stable and reliable, even with changes in raw material sources or environmental conditions.

3. Control Strategy

A key aspect of QbD is the **development of a control strategy** that ensures consistent product quality throughout the lifecycle of the drug. This involves continuous monitoring and real-time adjustments to ensure that the product consistently meets **specifications** and **regulatory standards.**

Defining a Control Strategy

- **Role of QbD:** QbD provides the framework for establishing a **control strategy,** which outlines the **critical parameters** that must be monitored and controlled during both **formulation** and **manufacturing.** This includes **in-process testing, critical process parameters (CPPs),** and **monitoring** techniques that allow for real-time assessment of product quality.
- **Process:**

  - **In-Process Testing:** QbD emphasizes **continuous monitoring** during manufacturing to ensure that each batch meets the desired quality attributes (e.g., **tablet weight, content uniformity, dissolution rate).**

- ◦ **Critical Process Parameters (CPPs)**: Factors such as **mixing speed, granulation moisture**, and **drying time** are controlled in real-time, allowing adjustments to be made during the manufacturing process.
- ◦ **Real-Time Release Testing (RTRT)**: This involves using **in-line testing** and **process analytical technology (PAT)** to determine the quality of the product during production, eliminating the need for extensive end-product testing.

- **Example:**

- ◦ **Granulation Process**: During the granulation process, real-time measurements of **moisture content** and **granule size distribution** could be taken to adjust **mixing speed** or **binder concentration** as needed, ensuring that the granules are of the desired quality before they proceed to the next stage.
- ◦ **Tablet Compression**: A **tablet compression process** can be continuously monitored using sensors to ensure that the tablets meet weight, hardness, and **dissolution** requirements in real time, making it possible to adjust the **compression force** on the fly.

Benefits of QbD in Control Strategy:

- **Consistency**: Continuous monitoring ensures that products consistently meet **quality standards** during both the formulation and manufacturing stages.
- **Efficiency and Cost Savings**: Real-time adjustments during the manufacturing process help reduce waste and improve overall **production efficiency**.
- **Regulatory Compliance**: A robust control strategy ensures that the product is manufactured according to **Good Manufacturing Practices (GMP)** and complies with **regulatory guidelines** from agencies like the FDA, EMA, and ICII.

Regulatory Guidelines for Implementing Quality by Design (QbD)

The implementation of Quality by Design (QbD) in pharmaceutical development and manufacturing is increasingly supported by regulatory agencies such as the FDA, EMA, and ICH. These organizations recognize the importance of designing quality into the product and process from the very beginning, ensuring that drug products consistently meet quality standards. Below is an overview of the regulatory guidelines that support QbD and its application in the pharmaceutical industry.

1. FDA Guidelines for QbD Implementation

The **U.S. Food and Drug Administration (FDA)** has embraced the principles of QbD as part of its **Pharmaceutical Quality for the 21st Century** initiative, aiming to modernize pharmaceutical manufacturing processes and improve drug product quality.

FDA's QbD Guidelines:

- Guidance for Industry: Q8 (R2) Pharmaceutical Development:

  - The FDA Q8 (R2) guideline emphasizes the importance of understanding the critical quality attributes (CQAs) and critical process parameters (CPPs) in formulation and manufacturing processes. It encourages drug developers to design the formulation and process with the goal of ensuring the product's quality.
  - Key Elements:

    - Design of Experiments (DoE): The FDA encourages the use of DoE and other statistical approaches to explore and optimize the relationships between product and process parameters.
    - Risk-Based Approach: The guideline stresses the importance of using a risk-based approach to identify and manage risks throughout the product development lifecycle.

- **Key Focus**: QbD under FDA guidelines promotes the idea that **quality** should be an **integrated aspect** of the product development process, rather than a result of testing and correcting post-manufacturing. It ensures **consistent product quality** and minimizes variability.

2. EMA Guidelines for QbD Implementation

The **European Medicines Agency (EMA)** also supports QbD principles through its guidelines and works in alignment with the **ICH guidelines** to ensure a **robust and scalable manufacturing process** for pharmaceutical products.

EMA's QbD Framework:

- **Guideline on the Manufacture of the Finished Dosage Form (CHMP/ QWP/486/95):**

  - This guideline aligns with QbD principles by focusing on the development of a robust manufacturing process that consistently meets product specifications.
  - It emphasizes the importance of understanding product characteristics, such as dissolution rate, and defining the critical process parameters that impact product performance.

- **ICH E6 Good Clinical Practice (GCP) and QbD:**

  - The EMA encourages the integration of QbD principles within the context of **clinical development**, stressing the need for continuous **risk assessment** and **data collection** to inform product development decisions.

- **Key Focus: EMA's approach encourages pharmaceutical companies to design products with quality built in from the early stages of development. It encourages manufacturers to establish control strategies and perform in-process testing to maintain consistency across different production batches.**

3. ICH Guidelines for QbD Implementation

The International Council for Harmonisation (ICH) plays a leading role in promoting global harmonization in pharmaceutical regulation and supports the integration of QbD in pharmaceutical development and manufacturing. The ICH guidelines for QbD are designed to align pharmaceutical practices worldwide, ensuring consistent quality and regulatory compliance across markets.

ICH Q8 (Pharmaceutical Development):

- Definition: ICH Q8 focuses on pharmaceutical development and emphasizes the importance of designing drug products and manufacturing processes to meet the desired quality standards. It encourages the use of design space, a concept in QbD that allows flexibility in process parameters while ensuring consistent product quality.

- **Key Elements:**

  - Understanding Product and Process Variables: ICH Q8 encourages the identification of critical material attributes (CMAs) and critical quality attributes (CQAs) and their relationship with process parameters.
  - Risk Assessment: The guideline incorporates a risk-based approach to ensure the product meets quality standards while managing the associated risks.
  - Design Space: The guideline introduces the concept of design space, which is the range of operating conditions where a product or process can operate within acceptable quality limits. This allows for flexibility in production, provided the product consistently meets CQAs.

  ICH Q10 (Pharmaceutical Quality System):

- Definition: ICH Q10 focuses on the pharmaceutical quality system and outlines the principles for implementing a QbD approach across the entire product lifecycle, from development through to commercialization.
- **Key Elements:**

  - Pharmaceutical Quality System (PQS): Q10 highlights the importance of creating a PQS that supports QbD principles, ensuring that every phase of development and manufacturing is designed with quality in mind.
  - **Continuous Improvement**: The guideline advocates for **continuous monitoring** and improvement of processes, utilizing data collected during **development** and **manufacturing** to ensure sustained product quality.

Regulatory Body	Guideline	Focus
FDA	Q8 (R2) Pharmaceutical Development	Emphasis on understanding **CQAs**, **CPPs**, and using **DoE** to optimize formulations and processes.
EMA	Guideline on the Manufacture of Finished Dosage Form	Focus on **robust manufacturing processes** and defining **critical parameters** for consistency.
ICH	Q8 (Pharmaceutical Development)	Introduction of **design space** and emphasis on risk-based approach to optimize product development.
ICH	Q10 (Pharmaceutical Quality System)	Focus on integrating **QbD** principles across the **product lifecycle** to ensure consistent quality.

Key Regulatory Guidelines for Implementing QbD

CHAPTER SEVEN

Packaging Materials in Pharmaceutical Product Development

Packaging is a critical component of pharmaceutical product development, ensuring that the drug remains stable, safe, and effective from the moment it leaves the manufacturer to its use by the patient. The selection of packaging materials is governed by various criteria, including the type of material, stability requirements, and regulatory standards. This chapter will explore the types of packaging materials, their role in stability and patient compliance, and the quality control testing methods used to ensure packaging materials meet safety and efficacy standards.

7.1 Selection of Packaging Materials

The selection of packaging materials is a critical component of pharmaceutical product development, as the packaging plays a significant role in maintaining the stability, safety, and effectiveness of the drug from the manufacturer to the end user. The packaging material protects the drug from various external factors, such as moisture, light, oxygen, and contamination, which could potentially degrade the active pharmaceutical ingredient (API) or compromise the therapeutic efficacy. This section will focus on the different types of packaging materials, the criteria for selecting the appropriate materials, and their role in product stability, safety, and patient compliance.

Types of Packaging Materials

1. Glass

Glass is one of the most commonly used materials in pharmaceutical packaging due to its **inertness** and **durability**. It is particularly suitable for sensitive drugs and injectables where maintaining the **chemical stability** of the API is critical.

- **Properties:**

  - Inert: Glass is chemically stable and does not react with most drugs or excipients, making it ideal for formulations that are prone to degradation by other materials.
  - Transparency: Glass is transparent, allowing for visual inspection of the product inside. This is crucial for detecting any potential contamination or physical changes in the formulation, such as sediment or precipitation.
  - Impermeability: Glass is impermeable to moisture, oxygen, and gases, which provides excellent protection against external elements that could degrade the drug.

- **Advantages:**

  - Chemical Stability: Glass is ideal for drugs that require protection from external influences, particularly injectables and ophthalmic products.
  - Sterility: Glass packaging can be easily sterilized, making it ideal for sterile products like injectables or infusions.
  - Versatility: Glass is suitable for liquid formulations, parenterals, and topical products, offering excellent protection for products that are sensitive to environmental factors.
  - Visual Inspection: Its transparency allows for easy visual inspection of the drug, ensuring the absence of contamination, changes in color, or settling of particles.

- **Disadvantages:**

  - Fragility: Glass is fragile and can break easily during transportation or handling, posing a risk of spillage or product loss.
  - Weight: Glass is relatively heavy, which can increase shipping costs, especially for large-scale distribution.
  - Cost: Glass packaging is often more expensive compared to plastic, both in terms of material costs and manufacturing costs.

- **Applications:**

  - Injectables: Glass is commonly used for vials, ampoules, and pre-filled syringes, where maintaining the integrity of the drug is critical.
  - Ophthalmic Products: Glass containers are often used for eye drops and other ophthalmic solutions to ensure sterility and protect against contamination.
  - Liquid Dosage Forms: Glass bottles are commonly used for oral solutions and syrups, especially for products that need to be light-sensitive or sterile.

2. Plastic

Plastic is a widely used material in pharmaceutical packaging due to its lightweight nature and versatility. It is used for a variety of dosage forms, including tablets, capsules, liquid formulations, and parenteral products. Plastics come in different types such as polyethylene (PE), polypropylene (PP), and polyvinyl chloride (PVC).

- **Properties:**

  - Lightweight: Plastic is significantly lighter than glass, which reduces shipping costs and makes it easier to handle and transport.
  - Flexibility: Plastic is flexible, allowing for the production of a variety of packaging formats, including blister packs, bottles, and ampoules.
  - Barrier Properties: While plastic can be designed to provide moisture and oxygen barriers, certain types of plastic, such as PET (polyethylene terephthalate), offer better barrier properties than others.

- **Advantages:**

  - Cost-Effective: Plastic is generally more cost-effective than glass, especially in terms of manufacturing and shipping.
  - Durability: Plastic packaging is resilient, resistant to breakage, and more robust compared to glass, making it suitable for products that are transported over long distances.
  - Customization: Plastic can be molded into different shapes and sizes, allowing for versatile packaging designs.

- Child-Resistant: Plastic packaging can be easily designed to include child-resistant features, important for products that could be harmful if ingested by children.

- **Disadvantages**:

  - Potential for Chemical Interactions: Some types of plastic can interact with lipophilic drugs or volatile substances, leading to leaching of plasticizers or stabilizers into the drug.
  - Limited Barrier Properties: Not all plastics are impermeable to moisture and oxygen, which can affect the stability of some formulations. In such cases, additional coatings or laminations may be required.
  - Environmental Concerns: Plastic waste is a growing environmental concern, and the industry is under increasing pressure to use more sustainable packaging options.

- **Applications**:

  - Oral Solid Dosage Forms: Plastic bottles and blister packs are commonly used for tablets and capsules due to their lightweight nature and ability to protect against moisture.
  - Liquid Formulations: Plastic is frequently used for oral solutions, syrups, and injectables that require lightweight and flexible packaging options.
  - Topical Products: Plastic tubes and jars are widely used for creams, ointments, and gels.

3. Metal

Metal packaging, such as **aluminum** and **tin**, is commonly used for specific pharmaceutical products that require **strong protection** against light, moisture, and air. It is used in **aerosols, blister packs**, and certain **injectables**.

- **Properties**:

  - Strength: Metal offers superior strength and protection against physical damage compared to glass and plastic.

- ○ Impermeability: Metals are naturally impermeable to moisture, oxygen, and light, making them ideal for preserving sensitive products.
- ○ Light Weight: Some metal materials, like aluminum, are lightweight, making them easier to handle and transport.

- **Advantages:**

  - ○ Protection Against Contamination: Metal packaging offers excellent protection against light, air, and moisture, ensuring the product remains stable.
  - ○ Sterility: Metals are often used in injectable packaging (e.g., vials and ampoules) because they can be easily sterilized and maintain the sterility of the product.
  - ○ Corrosion Resistance: Materials like aluminum are often treated to resist corrosion, making them suitable for long-term storage of sensitive products.

- **Disadvantages:**

  - ○ **Cost:** Metal packaging tends to be more expensive than plastic, both in terms of material costs and manufacturing.
  - ○ **Weight:** While some metals are lightweight, they can still be heavier than plastic, increasing shipping costs.
  - ○ **Environmental Impact:** The production and disposal of metal packaging contribute to environmental concerns, though metals like aluminum can be recycled.

- **Applications:**

  - ○ **Injectables:** Metal vials and ampoules are commonly used for injectable drugs, especially biologics, that require sterility and protection from environmental factors.
  - ○ **Aerosol Products:** Aluminum cans are widely used for aerosol products, such as inhalers and topical sprays, due to their ability to preserve the stability of the active ingredients.

2. Plastic

Plastic is one of the most versatile and widely used materials in pharmaceutical packaging due to its flexibility, lightweight nature, and cost-effectiveness. It is used in a wide variety of forms, such as bottles, bags, blister packs, and syringes, making it suitable for different types of pharmaceutical products, including liquid and solid dosage forms.

Properties of Plastic

- **Lightweight**: Plastic packaging is much lighter than glass, which reduces shipping costs and makes it easier to handle during manufacturing and transportation.
- **Flexibility**: Plastic is moldable into various shapes and sizes, allowing for customized packaging designs. This flexibility is particularly useful for producing blister packs, vials, and syringes.
- Variety: There are different types of plastic, such as polyethylene (PE), polypropylene (PP), and **polyvinyl chloride (PVC)**, each with unique properties. This variety allows for specific applications depending on the needs of the drug.
- **Barrier Properties**: Some plastics, particularly polyethylene terephthalate (PET) and high-density polyethylene (HDPE), have built-in moisture and oxygen barrier properties, which are crucial for maintaining the stability of sensitive drugs.

Advantages of Plastic Packaging

1. **Lightweight:**

   - Plastics are much lighter than glass, making them easier to transport and handle. This results in lower shipping costs, especially for large-scale distribution.

2. **Cost-Effective:**

   - Plastic packaging is often cheaper to produce than glass and metal, both in terms of raw materials and manufacturing costs. This makes it an attractive option for mass production of pharmaceutical products.

3. **Durability:**

- Plastic is more durable than glass and less prone to breakage or chipping, making it suitable for bulk production and transportation.

4. **Versatility**:

- Plastics can be used in both liquid (e.g., oral syrups, injectables) and solid (e.g., tablets, capsules) dosage forms. The variety of plastic types offers tailored flexibility for different product requirements.

5. Barrier Properties:

- Certain plastics offer barrier properties for moisture, oxygen, and light. For instance, PET is used in bottles for liquids as it offers excellent moisture and oxygen barriers, which are crucial for the stability of many pharmaceutical products.

Disadvantages of Plastic Packaging

1. **Chemical Interactions**:

- Some plastics, particularly PVC, can interact with lipophilic drugs (drugs that are poorly soluble in water but soluble in fats) and may cause degradation or contamination of the drug.
- Plastics are not as inert as glass, meaning they may release plasticizers, additives, or monomers into the drug product, potentially altering its stability or efficacy.

2. **Degradation with UV Light**:

- Certain plastics, especially PVC, are susceptible to degradation when exposed to UV light. This is particularly concerning for light-sensitive drugs, as exposure to light can degrade the active pharmaceutical ingredients (API) in the product.

3. **Migration of Additives**:

- Plastics contain various additives (e.g., plasticizers, stabilizers, flame retardants) that can migrate into the drug, potentially affecting the drug's safety, efficacy, or taste. Migration studies are essential to ensure these additives do not leach into the drug formulation.

Applications of Plastic Packaging

- Oral Solid Dosage Forms:

  - Plastic blister packs and bottles are commonly used to package tablets and capsules. Plastic provides the strength and protection needed while keeping manufacturing costs low.

- Liquid Formulations:

  - Plastic bottles and vials are often used for liquid products like oral syrups, injectables, and oral solutions. Plastic's barrier properties ensure the drug is protected from moisture and air, while its lightweight nature makes it easier to handle.

- Injectables and Parenteral Products:

  - Plastic vials and syringes are frequently used for injectable formulations. Certain plastics, like polypropylene (PP), are biocompatible and suitable for use in medical devices, such as pre-filled syringes.

- Topical Products:

  - Plastic tubes and containers are used for creams, ointments, gels, and lotions, providing ease of application and storage stability.

3. Metal

Metal packaging materials, such as aluminum and tin, are frequently used in pharmaceutical packaging, particularly for blister packs, aerosols, and injectable vials. These materials are valued for their strength, protection, and ability to preserve the stability of sensitive drugs by preventing exposure to harmful environmental factors.

Properties of Metal Packaging

- Strength: Metals like aluminum and tin offer high mechanical strength, making them durable and capable of withstanding physical stress during transportation and handling. This is particularly useful for products that need robust packaging to avoid damage.
- Impermeability: Metals are impermeable to oxygen, light, and moisture, which are key factors that can degrade the active pharmaceutical ingredient (API) in the product. This makes metals highly suitable for packaging light-sensitive and moisture-sensitive drugs.
- Sterility: Metal packaging is ideal for products that need to maintain sterility, such as injectable formulations and inhalers, because metals can be sterilized effectively during the manufacturing process.
- Recyclability: Many metals, especially aluminum, are highly recyclable, which is a significant advantage in terms of environmental impact compared to non-recyclable materials like plastic.

Advantages of Metal Packaging

1. Protection Against Moisture, Oxygen, and Light:

   - Metals like aluminum and tin provide excellent protection against moisture, oxygen, and light, all of which can degrade sensitive drugs. This is especially important for products like aerosol sprays, inhalers, and biological products that are vulnerable to environmental factors.

2. Sterility Maintenance:

   - Metal packaging, such as vials and ampoules, is widely used for injectable drugs and other products requiring sterile conditions. These containers can be easily sterilized through methods such as autoclaving or gamma radiation, ensuring that the product remains free from contaminants.

3. Durability and Strength:

   - The rigidity and strength of metal packaging provide excellent protection during handling, storage, and transportation. This reduces the risk of damage, leaks, or breakage, ensuring the product's integrity.

4. Long Shelf Life:

- Due to the impermeable nature of metals, they offer extended shelf life for drugs that are light-sensitive or oxygen-sensitive. This protection ensures that the drug remains stable over time, maintaining its potency and effectiveness.

Disadvantages of Metal Packaging

1. Weight:

- Metal packaging is generally heavier compared to plastic, which can increase shipping costs and affect handling during distribution. The weight of the packaging can also make it less convenient for consumers in certain drug forms, such as oral doses or topical products.

2. Cost:

- The manufacturing costs of metal packaging are generally higher than that of plastic, especially for materials like aluminum. Additionally, the cost of metal treatment (such as for corrosion resistance) can further increase the price of the packaging.

3. Corrosion Issues:

- Although metals like aluminum are resistant to oxidation, they may still be susceptible to corrosion if not properly treated or coated. Corrosion can compromise the integrity of the packaging and contaminate the product.

  - Solution: Protective coatings, such as lacquer or anodizing processes, are applied to prevent corrosion and ensure the packaging remains effective throughout the product's shelf life.

4. Limited Flexibility:

- Compared to plastic, metal packaging has limited flexibility in terms of shapes and sizes. While plastics can be molded into a variety of designs, metal packaging is often produced in standardized forms like vials and cans, limiting customization options.

Applications of Metal Packaging

1. Injectables:

   - Metal vials and ampoules are widely used for injectable drugs, particularly for sterile medications like biologics, vaccines, and chemotherapeutic agents. The ability to sterilize metal packaging ensures that injectables remain free of contamination.

2. Aerosol Products:

   - Aerosol cans, often made from aluminum, are used for products like inhalers and topical sprays. The metal packaging protects the active ingredients from degradation due to exposure to air, moisture, and light, and allows for the controlled release of the drug.

3. Ophthalmic Products:

   - Aluminum tubes are commonly used for eye drops and ophthalmic ointments, where the drug's sensitivity to light or air requires airtight protection.

4. Topical and Oral Liquid Formulations:

   - Aluminum containers are also used for topical products, such as ointments and creams, that need to be protected from environmental factors. Metal packaging for oral liquid formulations also offers protection for light-sensitive or air-sensitive drugs.

7.2 Quality Control Testing of Packaging Materials

Ensuring that packaging materials meet the necessary safety and performance standards is crucial for preserving the integrity and efficacy of the pharmaceutical product. Packaging materials must not only protect the drug from external factors but also ensure that no harmful substances are introduced into the product. The quality control (QC) testing of packaging materials ensures that the packaging performs as expected and does not adversely affect the quality or safety of the drug product.

This section discusses the key methods for testing the compatibility and safety of packaging materials, ensuring they are suitable for protecting the drug and maintaining its quality throughout its shelf life.

Methods for Testing Compatibility and Safety

1. Material Compatibility Testing

Material compatibility testing is essential to ensure that the packaging material does not negatively affect the drug product. The interaction between the packaging and the API (Active Pharmaceutical Ingredient) or formulation excipients could lead to degradation, contamination, or unwanted chemical reactions that may compromise the safety and efficacy of the drug.

Key Aspects of Material Compatibility Testing:

- Chemical Stability Studies: This test involves evaluating how the drug interacts with the packaging material over time. It checks for any chemical degradation, adsorption, or leaching of substances from the packaging into the drug.

  - Purpose: To ensure that the packaging material does not introduce any foreign chemicals that could alter the drug's composition, safety, or effectiveness.
  - Example: Testing the stability of an oral liquid formulation in a plastic bottle to ensure that plasticizers or stabilizers do not migrate into the drug and alter its chemical composition.

- Migration Tests: Migration studies are conducted to detect whether any molecules from the packaging material, such as plasticizers, additives, or monomers, migrate into the drug. These tests assess the risk of contamination from the packaging.

- Method: A common test is to expose the drug product to the packaging material for an extended period under real-life conditions (e.g., temperature, humidity). The drug is then analyzed for the presence of any substances from the packaging material.
- Example: Testing a polyethylene terephthalate (PET) bottle used for a liquid formulation to ensure that antioxidants or plasticizers from the plastic do not migrate into the solution.

- Extraction Tests: These tests simulate the conditions under which the packaging may interact with the drug. The packaging material is exposed to a solvent, which mimics the potential migration of substances that could be harmful.

  - Purpose: To assess the degree of leaching and determine if any harmful substances are extracted from the packaging into the drug.
  - Example: Exposing a metal container to a solvent to test for the potential migration of coating materials (e.g., lacquer), which might leach into the drug product.

- Example: A plastic bottle containing an oral liquid formulation might undergo testing to ensure that no plasticizers or stabilizers migrate into the drug, altering its composition or affecting its therapeutic efficacy. The testing ensures that the integrity of the drug is maintained and no contaminants are introduced.

2. Barrier Properties Testing
Packaging materials need to protect the drug from **moisture, oxygen, light**, and **other environmental factors** that could degrade the product. Testing the **barrier properties** of packaging materials ensures that they provide **adequate protection** to the drug.

- Oxygen and Moisture Permeability: Oxygen and moisture are two critical factors that can lead to the degradation of drugs, especially sensitive APIs. Packaging materials need to be tested for their barrier properties against oxygen and moisture.

- Test Methods: Water Vapor Transmission Rate (WVTR) and Oxygen Transmission Rate (OTR) tests are commonly used to assess the permeability of packaging materials. These tests measure how much water vapor or oxygen can pass through the packaging material over a specified period under controlled conditions.
- Example: An aluminum foil blister pack would be tested for its ability to block moisture and oxygen from entering and affecting the stability of the drug.

3. Mechanical and Physical Testing

Mechanical testing ensures that the packaging can withstand the physical stresses that occur during manufacturing, storage, and transportation. These tests assess whether the packaging material can maintain its **structural integrity** and **protect** the drug.

- Leakage Testing: Packaging that is used for liquids or injectables must maintain a hermetic seal to prevent leakage and contamination. Leakage testing ensures that the packaging does not allow the drug to escape or be exposed to contaminants.

  - Test Method: Vacuum or pressure decay testing can be performed to detect any leaks in the packaging material.
  - Example: A vial used for injectable drugs will be tested for leakage to ensure the seal is intact and prevents any contamination or product loss.

- Drop Testing and Compression Testing: These tests assess how well the packaging can withstand physical stress during shipping or handling. It ensures that the packaging material will not crack, break, or deform under normal conditions.

  - Test Method: A drop test may involve dropping the packaging from a set height to simulate real-world impact, while compression testing evaluates the material's ability to withstand pressure.
  - Example: A blister pack is subjected to drop tests to ensure the integrity of the packaging and prevent any damage to the drug.

4. Regulatory Requirements for Packaging Materials

Regulatory agencies, including the FDA, EMA, and ICH, have specific guidelines and requirements for testing packaging materials to ensure they meet safety, efficacy, and quality standards.

- FDA Guidelines: The FDA provides specific regulations on packaging materials, including testing for leaching, migration, and compatibility with drug formulations. These guidelines ensure that packaging materials used for drug products are safe and do not compromise the integrity of the product.

  ○ FDA Title 21 CFR Part 177 covers indirect food additives that include packaging materials for pharmaceutical products.

- EMA Guidelines: The European Medicines Agency (EMA) also provides guidelines for testing packaging materials, emphasizing stability and compatibility testing to ensure that packaging materials meet the required safety and quality standards.
- ICH Guidelines: The International Council for Harmonisation (ICH) provides guidelines that outline the testing requirements for packaging materials as part of the Good Manufacturing Practices (GMP) for ensuring consistent product quality throughout its shelf life.

2. Barrier Properties Testing

Barrier properties testing is a critical aspect of quality control for **packaging materials.** The primary function of packaging is to protect the drug from external factors such as **moisture, oxygen,** and **light,** which can lead to **degradation** or **loss of potency** over time. Testing the **barrier properties** of packaging materials ensures that they provide sufficient protection to maintain the **stability** and **effectiveness** of the pharmaceutical product.

Importance of Barrier Properties in Pharmaceutical Packaging

The integrity of pharmaceutical products, especially those sensitive to **moisture, oxygen,** or **light,** relies heavily on the **barrier properties** of the packaging material. If the packaging fails to prevent the ingress of these elements, the **active pharmaceutical ingredient (API)** may degrade, leading to a loss of efficacy, safety, or both. Therefore, assessing the **moisture barrier, oxygen barrier,** and **light barrier** properties is essential for ensuring that drugs remain **stable** and **effective** throughout their shelf life.

Test Methods for Barrier Properties

The following methods are commonly used to evaluate the **barrier properties** of packaging materials:

1. Water Vapor Transmission Rate (WVTR)

- **Purpose:** The **Water Vapor Transmission Rate (WVTR)** measures how much water vapor passes through the packaging material over a specified period. **Moisture** is one of the most significant environmental factors that can degrade drugs, especially for **solid oral dosage forms, liquids,** and **biologics.**
- **Test Method:**

  - The packaging material is exposed to a **moisture gradient**, typically by placing the material in a **sealed chamber.** The chamber on one side is kept **humid**, while the other side is dry. The amount of **water vapor** that permeates through the material is measured.

- **Significance:**

  - Packaging with low **WVTR** indicates that it is **effective** at preventing moisture from reaching the product, helping to maintain **drug stability** and **shelf life.**
  - This test is particularly critical for drugs like **tablets** and **capsules** that are sensitive to moisture, which could lead to **degradation** or **loss of potency.**

- **Example:** A **plastic bottle** used for **oral liquids** is tested for **moisture resistance** to ensure that no moisture enters the bottle, which could lead to **microbial contamination** or **dilution** of the formulation.

2. Oxygen Transmission Rate (OTR)

- **Purpose:** The Oxygen Transmission Rate (OTR) measures the amount of **oxygen** that permeates through the packaging material over a given period. **Oxygen** is a significant cause of **oxidative degradation** for many drugs, especially **biologics, vitamins,** and **some antibiotics.**
- **Test Method:**

○ The test involves placing the packaging material in a controlled **oxygen-rich environment** and measuring the **amount of oxygen** that passes through it. The **OTR** is determined by the difference in oxygen concentration inside and outside the packaging.

- **Significance:**

  ○ Packaging materials with low **OTR** values ensure that the product is shielded from **oxidation**, helping to preserve the **drug's chemical stability** and effectiveness.
  ○ For drugs prone to **oxidative degradation**, such as **vitamin C, biologic formulations**, or **inhalers**, the packaging must effectively prevent oxygen ingress.

- **Example: Aluminum foil** used for **blister packaging** of tablets or **aerosol canisters** is tested for **oxygen barrier properties** to protect sensitive ingredients like **inhaled medications** or **vaccine formulations** from oxidative damage.

3. Light Transmission

- **Purpose: Light transmission testing** measures the amount of light that passes through the packaging material. This is particularly important for **light-sensitive drugs**, such as **biologics, vitamins**, and some **injectables** that can degrade or lose efficacy upon exposure to light.
- **Test Method:**

  ○ In this test, the packaging material is exposed to light of varying intensities, and the **amount of light** transmitted through the material is measured. **UV light** transmission is particularly significant for drugs sensitive to **photodegradation.**

- **Significance:**

  ○ Packaging with **low light transmission** is essential for **photosensitive drugs**, providing a protective barrier against light, especially **ultraviolet (UV)** radiation, which can cause chemical changes or breakdown of the API.

- ○ Light transmission tests help **ensure** that the drug remains **effective** and **stable** during storage and transportation.

- **Example: Amber glass vials** for **injectable medications** are tested to ensure they adequately block light, preventing the drug from degrading due to **UV light** exposure.

Key Tests for Packaging Materials

Ensuring that packaging materials are **safe**, **durable**, and **functional** is critical to maintaining the **integrity** of the pharmaceutical product. Several quality control (QC) tests are conducted to verify that the packaging material meets the required standards for protecting the drug. One of the most important tests is **leakage testing**, which ensures that the packaging provides a secure, **airtight seal** to prevent contamination and degradation of the drug.

1. Leakage Testing

Leakage testing is crucial for verifying that the packaging material can **contain the drug** effectively and prevent any **contamination** or **degradation**. Packaging failures, such as leaks, can lead to the exposure of the drug to harmful environmental factors (e.g., **oxygen, moisture, light**) or external contaminants, compromising the drug's **safety** and **efficacy**.

Purpose of Leakage Testing:

- **Preventing contamination**: Leakage can allow harmful substances to enter the packaging, leading to **contamination** of the drug product.
- **Ensuring stability**: Leaks can expose the drug to **moisture, oxygen**, or **light**, leading to **degradation** or loss of **potency**.
- **Maintaining product integrity**: Packaging must maintain its **seal** during handling, storage, and transportation to protect the drug from environmental factors.

Packaging Types Subjected to Leakage Testing:

- **Aerosol Cans:** Aerosol packaging needs to maintain a **hermetic seal** to avoid leakage of the propellant or active ingredients. **Leakage testing** ensures the **integrity** of the seal and prevents leakage during use.
- **Vials: Injectable vials** are commonly tested for leaks to ensure that the drug remains sterile and is not exposed to contaminants.

- **Blister Packs: Blister packaging** must maintain a **tight seal** to ensure the **tablet** or **capsule** is protected from moisture and air.

Test Methods for Leakage Testing:

1. **Vacuum Leak Testing:**

   - **Principle:** In this method, the **packaging material** (e.g., a vial, aerosol can, or blister pack) is placed under a **vacuum**. The packaging is then checked for any **change in pressure**, which would indicate a **leak**.
   - **Process:** The package is evacuated of air, and the resulting **pressure change** is monitored. If the seal is intact, the pressure should remain constant. A significant drop in pressure suggests a leak in the packaging.
   - **Applications:** Commonly used for **vials, ampoules**, and **aerosol cans** to ensure the **seal integrity**.

2. **Pressure Decay Testing:**

   - **Principle:** This method involves applying **pressurized air** to the packaging and monitoring the **pressure** over time. If the pressure drops, it indicates that there is a **leak** in the packaging.
   - **Process:** The packaging is pressurized, and the **pressure is recorded**. Any decline in pressure within a specified period indicates a **leak**. The magnitude and rate of the pressure decay help identify the size and location of the leak.
   - **Applications:** Often used for **blister packs, ampoules**, and **aerosol products**, where even the smallest leak can lead to contamination or degradation.

3. **Helium Leak Testing:**

   - **Principle:** This is a **highly sensitive** leak detection method that uses **helium** as a tracer gas. Helium, due to its small atomic size, is used to detect even the smallest leaks in packaging materials.
   - **Process:** The package is exposed to a **helium environment**, and the amount of **helium** that escapes from the package is measured. If helium is detected outside the packaging, it indicates a **leak**.

◦ **Applications**: This method is typically used for **injectable vials, ampoules**, and **aerosol cans**, where **sterility** is crucial.

Significance of Leakage Testing

- **Protecting Sterility**: Leakage in **injectable vials** or **ampoules** could lead to **contamination** and compromise the **sterility** of the drug, posing a risk to patient safety.
- **Maintaining Efficacy**: For **aerosol products** and **inhalers**, leakage could lead to the loss of the **propellant** or **active ingredient**, reducing the drug's efficacy and making it unusable.
- **Ensuring Patient Safety**: If the packaging fails, the drug may be exposed to harmful environmental factors, leading to **degradation, toxicity**, or **ineffectiveness**, which could compromise patient health.

2. Stability Testing

Stability testing is crucial in the pharmaceutical industry to ensure that both the **product** and **packaging materials** maintain their **integrity** and **effectiveness** throughout their **shelf life**. Packaging plays a key role in protecting the drug from environmental factors such as **temperature, humidity**, and **light**, which can degrade both the drug and the packaging material. Stability testing evaluates whether the packaging can withstand various storage conditions and ensure that the drug remains **safe, effective**, and **high-quality** until it reaches the end user.

Importance of Stability Testing for Packaging Materials

- **Ensures Product Safety**: Packaging materials must protect the drug from exposure to **moisture, oxygen**, and **light**, which can compromise its **safety, efficacy**, and **shelf life**.
- **Prevents Degradation**: Environmental conditions such as **temperature fluctuations** and **high humidity** can lead to the breakdown of the drug or the packaging material. Stability testing ensures that the packaging can **resist** these environmental stresses.
- **Regulatory Compliance**: Stability testing is a regulatory requirement by agencies like the **FDA, EMA**, and **ICH** to verify that the product meets **safety** and **quality** standards for its entire shelf life.

Test Methods for Stability Testing of Packaging Materials

One of the key methods used in **stability testing** is **accelerated stability testing**, which is designed to simulate long-term storage conditions by subjecting packaging materials to extreme environmental conditions. This helps to predict how the packaging will perform over time, under real-life storage conditions.

1. Accelerated Stability Testing

- **Purpose:** Accelerated stability testing is used to simulate the **long-term storage** of products by subjecting them to **extreme conditions of temperature** and **humidity**. This method helps determine how packaging materials will perform over an extended period of time and predict the **product's shelf life.**
- **Test Method:**

  - **Temperature:** Packaging materials are exposed to **elevated temperatures** (e.g., **40°C to 60°C**) for a specific period of time to simulate the effects of **heat** on the packaging material and drug product.
  - **Humidity:** The packaging is subjected to **high humidity** (e.g., **75% to 90% RH**) to test its ability to resist **moisture ingress. Moisture** is a common cause of **degradation** in both drugs and packaging materials.
  - **Light:** Some accelerated testing includes exposure to **light** (particularly **UV light**) to simulate **photodegradation** of both the drug and the packaging material.

- **Analysis:** After exposure to the accelerated conditions, the packaging material is examined for any changes in its **physical integrity**, such as **cracking, brittleness,** or **deformation.** Additionally, any **chemical degradation** or **migration of additives** from the packaging material into the drug is analyzed.
- **Significance:**

  - **Shelf-life Prediction:** The data obtained from accelerated stability testing is used to predict the **shelf life** of the packaging material and drug product under real storage conditions. This is crucial for determining expiration dates and ensuring that the packaging will continue to protect the drug throughout its shelf life.

- ○ **Material Performance**: The test helps ensure that the packaging material remains **stable** and **functional** over time, providing consistent protection to the drug.

- **Example:**

  - ○ A **plastic bottle** containing an **oral liquid formulation** might undergo accelerated stability testing by subjecting it to **40°C** and **75% relative humidity (RH)** for **six months**. The test would evaluate the bottle's **moisture barrier** and **chemical compatibility** to ensure that no harmful substances leach into the drug and that the packaging maintains its **integrity** over time.

2. Long-Term Stability Testing

- **Purpose**: Long-term stability testing is conducted under normal storage conditions (e.g., **room temperature, ambient humidity**) for extended periods, usually up to **12 months or more**.
- **Test Method**: The product is stored under real-life conditions, and the packaging is monitored for **physical changes**, such as **deformation, discoloration**, or **leakage**. The **drug** is also tested periodically to ensure that it maintains its **potency, dissolution rate**, and **other quality attributes**.
- **Significance**: Long-term stability testing provides the most accurate representation of how the packaging will perform during the product's **actual shelf life** in **real-world conditions**.

3. Environmental Stress Testing

- **Purpose**: This test evaluates the **performance** of the packaging material under more extreme environmental conditions, such as **extreme heat, cold**, or **fluctuating temperature** conditions.
- **Test Method:**

  - ○ The packaging material is subjected to rapid **temperature fluctuations**, such as from **-20°C to 50°C**, to simulate the effects of **shipping** or **storage in non-ideal conditions**.

○ The material is also exposed to extreme **light exposure**, particularly UV light, to simulate the potential for **photodegradation**.

- **Significance**: This testing ensures that packaging materials can withstand **extreme conditions** without compromising the drug product's **safety** or **quality**.

3. Migration Studies

Migration studies are critical tests used to evaluate the potential for **substances** from packaging materials, such as **plasticizers, resins**, and **additives**, to **migrate** into the drug product. The migration of these substances can compromise the **safety** and **efficacy** of the drug, leading to potential **toxicity, alteration of drug properties**, or even **contamination** of the drug. These studies are designed to ensure that the **packaging material** does not negatively affect the **drug product** over time, especially during storage and transport.

Importance of Migration Studies

- **Safety and Toxicity Prevention**: Certain substances, such as **plasticizers** or **stabilizers**, used in the manufacturing of packaging materials may **migrate** into the drug formulation. This migration could cause **adverse effects, toxicity,** or **alteration** of the drug's chemical composition, rendering it **unsafe** for consumption or use.
- **Maintaining Drug Integrity**: Migration of **chemical additives** from the packaging material into the drug can change its **pharmacological properties**, such as **potency, stability,** and **dissolution rate**. Migration studies ensure that the **integrity** and **efficacy** of the drug are not compromised.
- **Regulatory Compliance**: Regulatory agencies, including the **FDA** and **EMA**, require migration studies to ensure that **packaging materials** are **safe** for use with pharmaceutical products. The tests are crucial for obtaining **market approval** and ensuring that packaging complies with **safety standards**.

Test Method for Migration Studies

Migration studies involve testing to quantify the amount of substance that can **migrate** from the packaging material into the drug product. These tests simulate the **real-life** conditions under which the drug will be stored and transported, such as temperature, humidity, and exposure to solvents.

1. Simulated Migration Testing

- **Purpose**: Simulated migration tests measure the amount of **substances** that migrate from the packaging material into the drug under controlled conditions. These tests help assess the **degree of contamination** that might occur from the packaging material.
- **Test Method**:

  - **Solvent Exposure**: In the test, the packaging material is exposed to a solvent that mimics the **drug formulation** or the **drug itself**. The **solvent** could be a **simulated gastric fluid, phosphate buffer,** or **alcohol**, depending on the nature of the drug.
  - **Environmental Conditions**: The test is conducted under **accelerated conditions**, where the packaging material is exposed to **elevated temperatures, humidity,** or other factors that simulate real-world storage and transportation conditions.
  - **Time and Temperature**: The packaging material is exposed to the drug or solvent over a period, typically ranging from **a few days to several weeks,** to simulate long-term contact.
  - **Analysis**: After exposure, the **amount of migration** is measured using various analytical techniques, such as **high-performance liquid chromatography (HPLC)** or **gas chromatography (GC),** to detect any harmful migration of **additives** or **plasticizers** from the packaging material into the drug.

- **Example**: A **plastic bottle** used for **oral liquid formulations** might be exposed to a **simulated gastric fluid** for **two weeks** at **37°C**. The migration of **plasticizers** or **antioxidants** from the plastic into the drug is then measured to determine if any **harmful substances** have leached into the formulation.

2. Migration Testing with Drug Formulation

- **Purpose**: To test how the packaging material interacts with the **actual drug** rather than a simulated solvent, ensuring the **compatibility** and **safety** of the packaging with the drug product.
- **Test Method**:

- ○ **Real-Drug Testing**: The packaging material is filled with the actual **drug formulation** and stored under **normal** or **accelerated conditions.**
- ○ **Monitoring**: The packaging is periodically checked for any **changes** or **leakage** of substances into the drug. The drug's **chemical stability, content uniformity**, and **toxicity** are assessed over time.
- ○ **Analytical Testing**: After a specified period, the formulation is tested for the presence of any **foreign substances** that may have migrated from the packaging material. Methods such as **spectroscopy** or **HPLC** can detect trace amounts of **migrated components.**

- **Example**: A **plastic blister pack** containing **tablets** may be exposed to **light** and **humidity** for **six months**. The **migration of plasticizers** from the blister pack into the tablet formulation would then be evaluated to ensure that there is no **adverse effect** on the **tablet's dissolution rate** or **potency.**

Significance of Migration Studies

1. **Maintaining Drug Safety:**

- ○ Migration studies ensure that packaging materials do not **release harmful substances** that could affect the **drug's safety** and **efficacy.** Substances like **plasticizers, resins,** and **stabilizers** can **alter** the drug's composition, leading to **toxicity** or reduced **therapeutic effect.**

2. **Ensuring Drug Stability:**

- ○ Packaging materials must prevent the **degradation** of sensitive drugs. **Migration of additives** from packaging materials could alter the **chemical structure** or **physical properties** of the API, leading to **stability issues.**
- ○ For **light-sensitive drugs, plasticizers** migrating from packaging into the drug could **alter its degradation rate** when exposed to light.

3. **Regulatory Compliance:**

○ Regulatory agencies like the **FDA** and **EMA** require **migration studies** to ensure that **packaging materials** used for pharmaceutical products meet strict **safety standards**. These studies help demonstrate that the packaging material is **safe** and **compatible** with the drug formulation.

4. **Improved Product Quality:**

○ By performing migration studies, manufacturers can ensure that their packaging materials do not negatively affect the drug's **quality**, allowing for **consistent product performance** and **patient safety**.

Regulatory Requirements for Packaging Materials

Regulatory bodies like the **FDA**, **EMA**, and **ICH** have established comprehensive guidelines to ensure that **packaging materials** used in pharmaceutical products are **safe, compatible,** and **meet quality standards.** These regulations are designed to protect both the **integrity** of the drug product and the **safety** of the consumer. Packaging materials must meet strict specifications to ensure that they do not **contaminate** or **degrade** the drug, while also providing adequate protection from **moisture, light,** and **oxygen.**

Below are some of the **key regulatory guidelines** for packaging materials:

1. FDA Title 21 CFR (Code of Federal Regulations)

The **FDA's Title 21 CFR** outlines the **regulatory requirements** for packaging materials used in food and drug products. It establishes **material specifications, testing requirements,** and **labeling standards** that pharmaceutical packaging materials must meet to ensure **safety, compatibility,** and **quality.**

Key Points:

- **Material Specifications:** Title 21 CFR specifies the **types of materials** that are allowed for use in food and drug packaging, ensuring that only **safe, non-toxic,** and **non-reactive** materials are used. The guidelines cover materials such as **glass, plastic, metal,** and **paper.**
- **Testing Requirements:** The regulation sets standards for **migration testing, compatibility testing,** and **leakage testing** to ensure that packaging materials do not introduce harmful substances into the drug formulation.

- **Labeling Standards**: Packaging materials must also comply with **labeling regulations**, which include **information about the contents, handling instructions**, and **storage conditions** to ensure safe use and storage of the drug.

Example: A **plastic bottle** used for an oral solution would need to meet FDA requirements for **chemical stability** and **moisture barrier properties**. This ensures that no harmful **plasticizers** or **additives** migrate into the drug formulation.

2. EU Regulation 1935/2004

The **EU Regulation 1935/2004** governs materials and articles intended to come into contact with food, and it is also relevant for pharmaceutical packaging materials. This regulation ensures that packaging materials used for food and drug products do not **release harmful substances** into the product, ensuring **consumer safety**.

Key Points:

- **Safety of Materials**: The regulation specifies that materials used for packaging must be **safe** for their intended use, meaning they must not release any **toxic substances** or **contaminants** that could endanger public health.
- **Testing and Compliance**: It requires that packaging materials undergo **migration testing** to ensure they do not release harmful substances into the food or drug product. The regulation also mandates that materials comply with specific **composition** requirements, ensuring that packaging does not alter the quality or integrity of the product.
- **Labeling**: It also establishes labeling requirements, such as the need to include statements that the packaging material complies with the regulation's safety requirements.

Example: Aluminum blister packs used for tablets must comply with EU regulations to ensure that the aluminum does not release harmful substances like **aluminum salts** into the drug formulation. This ensures the **drug's safety** and **stability**.

3. ICH Guidelines (International Council for Harmonisation)

The **International Council for Harmonisation (ICH)** provides guidelines for ensuring the **compatibility** and **safety** of pharmaceutical packaging materials. One of the key ICH guidelines related to packaging is the **ICH Q3C** guideline, which addresses the acceptable levels of **organic impurities** in packaging materials.

Key Points:

- **Organic Impurities**: ICH Q3C specifies the **acceptable levels of organic impurities** that can be present in packaging materials. This is critical because certain **organic compounds** from packaging materials can **migrate** into the drug product, potentially altering its **stability** or **safety**.
- **Testing Requirements**: The guideline also sets the standards for **migration testing** and **compatibility testing** to ensure that no **toxic** or **harmful impurities** are introduced into the drug from the packaging.
- **Global Harmonization**: ICH guidelines promote **global consistency** in the standards for packaging materials, making it easier for pharmaceutical companies to comply with regulatory requirements across different regions.

Example: The **polymeric materials** used in **plastic vials** must meet ICH Q3C guidelines to ensure that no **plasticizers** or other organic compounds leach into the drug product, maintaining its **chemical stability** and **therapeutic efficacy**.

CHAPTER EIGHT

Regulatory Considerations in Pharmaceutical Packaging

Pharmaceutical packaging is not only critical for protecting the drug and ensuring its stability, but it also plays a significant role in regulatory approval and market access. Various regulatory bodies, including the FDA, EMA, and others, have established guidelines to ensure that packaging materials meet quality, safety, and compliance standards. These guidelines are pivotal in ensuring that pharmaceutical products are safe for consumers, and that packaging does not negatively affect the efficacy, stability, or safety of the drug.

This chapter will explore the regulatory frameworks for packaging, the role of packaging in product registration, and its impact on market approval.

8.1 Regulatory Frameworks for Packaging

Pharmaceutical packaging is an essential aspect of the product development process, not only serving as a protective barrier for the drug but also playing a vital role in regulatory approval and market access. Various regulatory bodies have established guidelines to ensure that packaging materials meet stringent standards of quality, safety, and compliance, which are crucial for protecting consumer health. The FDA (Food and Drug Administration), EMA (European Medicines Agency), and other global regulatory agencies ensure that packaging materials protect the drug from degradation, contamination, and physical damage while maintaining the drug's stability, efficacy, and safety throughout its shelf life. This section explores the role of these regulatory bodies and their guidelines for pharmaceutical packaging materials.

Role of FDA, EMA, and Other Regulatory Bodies

FDA (Food and Drug Administration)

The FDA plays a pivotal role in overseeing the safety and effectiveness of pharmaceutical packaging materials in the United States. The FDA ensures that packaging materials meet strict regulatory standards that guarantee the protection of the drug's integrity during storage, transportation, and use. The FDA's regulatory framework for packaging materials is outlined in Title 21 of the Code of Federal Regulations (CFR), which covers food contact substances, including materials used in pharmaceutical packaging.

- **FDA Regulations:**

  - **Title 21 CFR:** This part of the regulation addresses the **safety** of packaging materials and establishes the conditions under which these materials may be used in contact with pharmaceutical products. It ensures that packaging materials do not introduce **toxic substances** into the drug formulation.
  - **Chemical Stability:** The FDA requires manufacturers to demonstrate that the packaging materials do not release **harmful substances** into the drug, such as **plasticizers, solvents,** or **monomers,** that could degrade the drug's **chemical stability** and **therapeutic efficacy.**
  - **Barrier Properties:** The FDA also mandates that packaging materials provide adequate **protection** against external elements such as **moisture, light,** and **oxygen,** which could compromise the stability and potency of the drug.
  - **Regulatory Compliance:** Packaging materials must comply with the FDA's **material specifications, testing requirements,** and **labeling standards** for pharmaceutical products. This includes ensuring the **packaging** maintains the **drug's integrity** and does not cause any **adverse reactions** or **toxicity** to the end user.

- **FDA Labeling Standards:**

  - The **FDA** also enforces strict **labeling standards** for packaging materials, ensuring that all **drug packaging** includes clear instructions for **handling, storage,** and **disposal** to maintain **product safety** and **efficacy.**
  - These instructions also ensure that consumers and healthcare professionals understand how to properly store and use the product to avoid degradation or contamination of the drug.

EMA (European Medicines Agency)

The **EMA**, which oversees pharmaceutical regulations across the European Union (EU), has established similar guidelines for **pharmaceutical packaging** that prioritize **drug safety** and **product quality**. The **EMA** collaborates with national regulatory authorities within the EU to harmonize packaging requirements and ensure compliance with **global standards**.

- **EMA Regulations:**

  - **Directive 2001/83/EC:** This directive addresses the **packaging** of **medicinal products** for human use, specifying that packaging must be **safe, compatible**, and **effective** in maintaining the drug's **integrity** throughout its shelf life. It also sets the requirements for **child-resistant** packaging for products that could be dangerous to children.
  - **Regulatory Requirements:** The **EMA** requires that packaging materials meet specific criteria for **moisture resistance, light protection**, and **oxygen impermeability**. The material should not interact with the drug formulation, ensuring that it does not alter the **drug's chemical stability, dissolution**, or **bioavailability**.

- **Packaging Safety and Compatibility:**

  - The **EMA** emphasizes the need for **compatibility testing** of packaging materials to ensure that no **migration** of harmful substances from the packaging into the drug occurs. Testing is conducted to evaluate the packaging's **chemical** and **physical stability** over time.

Other Regulatory Bodies

In addition to the **FDA** and **EMA**, several other global regulatory bodies provide guidance on pharmaceutical packaging:

- **Health Canada:** Health Canada sets the standards for packaging materials used in the pharmaceutical industry within Canada. The regulations ensure that packaging is **safe** and provides **protection** against factors that may degrade drug products.
- **Australian Therapeutic Goods Administration (TGA):** The TGA ensures that **pharmaceutical packaging** used within Australia complies

with strict **safety, efficacy,** and **quality** standards.

- **WHO (World Health Organization):** The **WHO** provides international guidelines on pharmaceutical packaging, focusing on **safety, stability,** and the **environmental impact** of packaging materials.

EMA (European Medicines Agency)

The European Medicines Agency (EMA) plays a key role in regulating pharmaceutical packaging in the European Union (EU). The EMA ensures that packaging materials are compatible with the drug formulation and do not compromise the drug's safety, efficacy, or stability. The agency provides detailed guidelines and regulations for packaging materials used in the pharmaceutical industry, as well as overseeing the use of novel packaging technologies that can enhance drug protection and patient safety.

EMA Guidelines for Pharmaceutical Packaging

1. **Directive 2001/83/EC for Medicinal Products for Human Use:**

   - This directive outlines the **requirements** for packaging **medicinal products** within the EU. It specifies that the packaging must meet strict **safety** and **compatibility** standards, ensuring that the packaging protects the drug from degradation and contamination.
   - The **Directive** mandates that the packaging material does not **react** with the drug or affect its **stability**, ensuring that the drug remains effective throughout its **shelf life.**
   - **Key Provisions:**

     - Packaging materials must not release any **toxic** or **harmful substances** into the drug.
     - **Child-resistant packaging** is required for certain products to prevent accidental ingestion by children.

2. **Regulation (EC) No 1935/2004 for Materials in Contact with Food:**

   - While primarily aimed at materials used in food packaging, this regulation is also relevant for **pharmaceutical packaging** as it ensures that **materials** intended to come into contact with food (and medicines) do not release harmful substances into the product.

- The regulation outlines **requirements for safety** and **compatibility** for materials used in packaging to prevent any harmful interactions between the packaging and the drug formulation.
- **Key Points:**

  - Packaging materials must be **safe**, meaning they must not alter the drug's **composition** or **effectiveness**.
  - The materials should be **non-reactive** and must not release **toxic chemicals** that could compromise the safety or quality of the pharmaceutical product.

EMA's Emphasis on Compatibility of Packaging Materials

The **EMA** places significant emphasis on the **compatibility** of packaging materials with the drug formulation. Packaging materials must not **interfere** with the drug's **therapeutic action** or cause **chemical degradation**. The compatibility testing ensures that there are no unwanted **chemical interactions** between the packaging and the active pharmaceutical ingredient (API).

- **Important Considerations:**

  - Chemical Stability: Packaging materials must prevent any migration of additives, such as plasticizers or stabilizers, into the drug product. These additives could change the drug's stability or cause harmful reactions.
  - Physical Stability: Packaging materials must maintain the structural integrity of the product, ensuring it does not break, degrade, or leak, which could compromise the drug's quality.
  - Barrier Properties: Packaging must provide adequate protection against moisture, light, and oxygen that could degrade the API or change its properties.

EMA's Monitoring of Novel Packaging Technologies

The **EMA** also plays a role in overseeing the **use of novel packaging technologies**, which are designed to provide **additional safety features** and enhance the **patient experience**. These technologies can improve packaging functionality and provide greater control over the drug's **environmental conditions**.

1. **Smart Packaging:**

   - **Smart packaging** refers to packaging materials that are equipped with technology to provide real-time monitoring of the drug's **environment**. This can include monitoring conditions like **temperature, humidity,** and **pressure** to ensure that the drug is stored and transported under optimal conditions.
   - **Example: Temperature-sensitive packaging** can alert patients or healthcare providers if the drug has been exposed to temperatures that could compromise its **stability** or **efficacy**.

2. **Intelligent Packaging:**

   - Intelligent packaging incorporates features that provide added functionality, such as tamper-evidence, tracking, and authentication.
   - Tamper-evident packaging ensures that any unauthorized access to the product is easily detectable, preventing counterfeiting and tampering.
   - Example: RFID (Radio Frequency Identification) or QR codes integrated into the packaging can be used to verify the authenticity of the product and track the drug's supply chain.

3. **Monitoring and Control Features:**

   - Packaging with built-in **monitoring** and **control features** helps to ensure that the drug is stored and used under the **appropriate conditions**, providing both **patient safety** and **product integrity**.
   - **Example: Time-temperature indicators (TTIs)** are used to show if a product has been exposed to **excessive heat** during transit or storage, indicating whether the product remains **safe** to use.

Other Regulatory Bodies

In addition to the **FDA** and **EMA**, several other global regulatory bodies oversee pharmaceutical packaging standards to ensure that packaging materials meet safety, **compatibility**, and **quality** standards. These organizations provide crucial guidelines that help pharmaceutical companies maintain product integrity, comply with international regulations, and ensure the safety and **efficacy** of their products for global markets.

Health Canada and Australian Therapeutic Goods Administration (TGA)

Health Canada

- **Health Canada** regulates packaging materials for pharmaceutical products in Canada. The organization ensures that packaging **materials are safe** and **compatible** with the drug, preventing any adverse effects on the **drug's quality** and **efficacy**.
- **Key Regulations:**

  - Health Canada mandates that packaging materials must meet strict **chemical compatibility** and **migration** testing to prevent harmful substances from leaching into the drug product.
  - The **Food and Drug Act** and the **Medical Devices Regulations** outline the requirements for packaging materials used for both **drugs** and **medical devices**, including **safety** and **stability** testing to prevent degradation.

Australian Therapeutic Goods Administration (TGA)

- The **TGA** is the Australian regulatory authority responsible for ensuring the **safety**, **quality**, and **efficacy** of medicines and medical devices, including their packaging.
- **Key Regulations:**

  - **TGA guidelines** require packaging materials to be tested for **compatibility** with the drug formulation, ensuring that they do not compromise **stability** or **safety**.
  - Packaging must also meet specific standards for **moisture resistance**, **light protection**, and **barrier properties** to prevent product degradation during transportation and storage.
  - The **TGA** also enforces labeling standards for pharmaceutical packaging, ensuring that products are properly marked with usage instructions and safety precautions.

World Health Organization (WHO)

The **World Health Organization (WHO)** provides global standards for pharmaceutical packaging, ensuring that packaging materials used for medicines comply with international safety and quality standards. WHO guidelines are crucial for **global market access** and ensure that packaging materials help maintain the **stability** and **integrity** of the drug.

Key WHO Guidelines:

- **WHO Good Manufacturing Practices (GMP):** WHO's **GMP guidelines** for packaging materials focus on **material selection, compatibility testing**, and **quality control** to ensure that packaging is appropriate for various pharmaceutical products, including **injectables, oral formulations**, and **topical products.**
- **Drug Regulatory Guidelines:** The **WHO Prequalification Program** sets guidelines for packaging materials to ensure **quality control** and **regulatory compliance.** Packaging must prevent **degradation** and **contamination** while maintaining **product stability** during storage and transit.
- **Migration and Leaching Testing:** WHO guidelines require **migration studies** and **leaching tests** to ensure that **additives** or **plasticizers** from packaging materials do not migrate into the drug, which could affect the drug's quality.

International Council for Harmonisation (ICH) Guidelines

The **International Council for Harmonisation (ICH)** is a global body that provides harmonized standards for the development, registration, and manufacture of pharmaceutical products. The ICH plays a critical role in providing **internationally recognized guidelines** for pharmaceutical packaging, which help manufacturers navigate **regulatory requirements** across different regions.

Key ICH Guidelines:

- **ICH Q3C Guidelines:** The **ICH Q3C** guideline specifies the acceptable levels of **organic impurities** in packaging materials, ensuring that these materials do not introduce harmful contaminants into the drug product.

  - This is particularly important for **biologics, injectables,** and **drugs** that are sensitive to **plasticizers, solvents,** or other substances that could migrate from packaging into the drug.

- **ICH Q10 Pharmaceutical Quality System**: This guideline emphasizes the **integration** of quality practices in **pharmaceutical manufacturing** and the importance of **quality control** in packaging materials. It ensures that packaging materials are part of the **overall quality system** to maintain the **drug's stability, safety**, and **efficacy**.
- **Harmonization Across Regions**: ICH provides **harmonized standards** for packaging materials, ensuring that manufacturers can meet **global regulatory requirements** efficiently. This reduces the complexity of compliance for pharmaceutical companies that want to sell their products in multiple regions.

Packaging Regulations for Different Dosage Forms

Packaging materials for pharmaceutical products are not **one-size-fits-all**; they vary depending on the **dosage form** of the drug. The **packaging** must provide the necessary protection for the product to ensure that it remains **stable, effective**, and **safe** throughout its shelf life. Packaging is tailored to meet the **specific requirements** of each dosage form, such as protecting against **moisture, light, oxygen,** and **temperature** variations. Below are the packaging requirements for **oral dosage forms**, with a focus on the regulations for **tablets** and **capsules**.

Oral Dosage Forms

Oral dosage forms, such as **tablets** and **capsules**, require packaging that ensures **drug stability, ease of handling**, and **patient compliance**. The main objective is to prevent the **drug** from **degradation** caused by external factors like **moisture, light**, and **oxygen** while ensuring that the packaging is **convenient** for consumers.

Tablets and Capsules

- **Packaging Requirements**:

  - **Protection from Moisture and Light**: Tablets and capsules are sensitive to moisture and light, both of which can degrade the **active pharmaceutical ingredient (API)**. Packaging must provide a **moisture barrier** to prevent **hydration** and **light** protection to prevent **photodegradation**.
  - **Convenient Handling**: Packaging must allow **easy dispensing**, accurate dosing, and provide information on **drug use**. For example, **unit-dose packaging, blister packs**, and **bottles** are commonly used

for **tablets** and **capsules.**

- ○ **Tamper-Evidence:** Packaging must be tamper-evident to ensure that the drug remains safe and **unaltered** from manufacturing to the point of **use.**

- **Common Packaging Types:**

  - ○ **Blister Packs:** These are widely used for **tablets** and **capsules.** Blister packaging allows for **individual doses** and provides excellent **moisture** and **light protection.**
  - ○ **Bottles: Plastic or glass bottles** are commonly used for **capsules** and **oral tablets.** Bottles typically provide **protection from light** (when **amber glass** is used) and can accommodate larger quantities of **tablets** and **capsules.**
  - ○ **Unit-Dose Packages:** These are often used in institutional settings to ensure that a **single dose** is provided in a **safe and convenient** form. This packaging is particularly beneficial for **elderly** or **pediatric** patients who may require pre-measured doses.

FDA and EMA Regulations for Oral Dosage Forms Packaging

Both the **FDA** and **EMA** impose strict guidelines to ensure that **oral dosage forms** maintain their **stability, safety,** and **efficacy** throughout their shelf life. Packaging materials must undergo several **testing procedures** to demonstrate their **compatibility** with the drug and ensure that they do not negatively affect the **drug's performance.**

Key Tests and Regulations:

1. **Migration Studies:**

   - ○ Both the **FDA** and **EMA** require migration studies to ensure that **substances** in the packaging material (e.g., **plasticizers, stabilizers,** or **adhesives**) do not **migrate** into the drug formulation. Migration of harmful substances could lead to **drug contamination** or alter its **chemical stability.**
   - ○ **Test Method:** Packaging materials are exposed to solvents or the actual drug formulation to test if any **harmful substances** are leached into the drug.

2. **Leakage Testing:**

   - This test is crucial for packaging like **bottles** or **blister packs** that contain multiple doses of **tablets** or **capsules**. Packaging must prevent **leakage** or **exposure to contaminants** that could degrade the drug.
   - **Test Method: Vacuum leak testing** or **pressure decay testing** is used to detect any potential **leaks** in the packaging, ensuring that the drug remains sealed until it is dispensed for use.

3. **Barrier Properties Testing:**

   - Packaging materials for oral dosage forms, especially **blister packs** and **bottles**, must have adequate **barrier properties** to protect the drug from external factors such as **moisture, oxygen**, and **light**.
   - **Test Method: Water Vapor Transmission Rate (WVTR)** and **Oxygen Transmission Rate (OTR)** are commonly used to measure how well the packaging prevents moisture and oxygen from entering and affecting the drug.
   - **Importance:** Ensuring **moisture protection** is particularly crucial for drugs like **antibiotics** or **hormonal therapies**, where exposure to moisture can cause degradation.

Injectables

Injectable pharmaceutical formulations, such as **vials, ampoules,** and **pre-filled syringes**, require **sterile packaging** to maintain their **sterility** and **effectiveness**. These packaging materials not only protect the drug from **microbial contamination**, but also safeguard it against **oxidation, light exposure,** and **chemical degradation** during storage and transport. Ensuring the **integrity** of injectable packaging is crucial, as any **compromise** in packaging could result in **safety concerns, product instability,** and **inefficacy**.

Packaging Requirements for Injectables

Injectable drugs, particularly those administered **parenterally** (i.e., through routes other than the digestive tract, such as **intravenous, intramuscular,** or **subcutaneous injections**), require **specialized packaging** to ensure that the drug remains **sterile** and **safe** for administration. Packaging materials must provide adequate protection from **contamination, oxidation,** and **physical damage**.

1. Sterility Maintenance:

- **Vials, ampoules,** and **pre-filled syringes** used for injectable formulations must be **hermetically sealed** to maintain **sterility** and prevent **microbial contamination.**
- These packaging materials are designed to protect the drug product from exposure to **microorganisms** and other external contaminants, ensuring that the product remains safe for patient use.

2. Protection from Oxidation:

- Many injectable drugs, particularly **biologics** and **proteins**, are sensitive to **oxidation**, which can degrade the active ingredient and reduce **potency.**
- Packaging materials such as **glass vials** and **ampoules** often feature **oxidation-resistant coatings** or are made of materials that are **impermeable to oxygen**, preventing **oxidative degradation** of the drug.

3. Protection from Physical Damage:

- The packaging must also protect injectable products from **physical damage**, such as **breakage** or **leaks**, which could lead to contamination or loss of drug efficacy.

4. Ease of Use:

- **Pre-filled syringes** and **ampoules** are designed for easy **administration** by healthcare professionals, ensuring that the drug can be delivered safely and efficiently with minimal risk of **error** or **wastage.**

FDA and EMA Guidelines for Injectable Packaging

Both the **FDA** and the **EMA** provide **strict guidelines** for injectable packaging materials to ensure that the **sterility, stability,** and **quality** of injectable formulations are maintained. These guidelines focus on the **container closure systems**, which include the **vials, ampoules, syringes,** and other packaging components used to contain injectable drugs.

FDA Guidelines for Injectable Packaging:

- Sterile Container Closure Systems: The FDA requires injectable products to be packaged in sterile containers that maintain their sterility throughout the product's shelf life. The packaging must also prevent microbial contamination and protect the drug from external environmental factors such as moisture and oxygen.
- Packaging Material Safety: The FDA also mandates that the packaging material must not interact with the drug in a way that could alter its chemistry, efficacy, or stability. For example, the plastic components used in pre-filled syringes must be compatible with the drug formulation to prevent the leaching of plasticizers or other additives into the drug product.
- Glass Packaging: When using glass containers (e.g., vials and ampoules), the FDA requires that glass be free from defects and imperfections that could affect the drug's stability or the safety of its administration.

EMA Guidelines for Injectable Packaging:

- Container Closure Systems for Parenteral Products: The EMA mandates that packaging systems for injectable drugs must be able to maintain the drug's sterility and chemical stability. These systems include vials, ampoules, and pre-filled syringes that are designed to prevent contamination and oxidation.
- Biocompatibility and Leachability Testing: The EMA requires that injectable packaging undergo rigorous compatibility testing to ensure that no harmful substances (e.g., plasticizers, resins) migrate from the packaging into the drug formulation. For biologics or injectable formulations that are sensitive to oxidative degradation, the packaging must be oxygen impermeable and prevent chemical changes.
- Sterilization Process Validation: The EMA ensures that the sterilization process used to prepare the packaging materials (e.g., gamma radiation, ethylene oxide) is validated to prevent contamination and ensure the integrity of the injectable formulation.

Key Packaging Types for Injectables

1. **Vials:**

- **Glass Vials**: Commonly used for **injectables**, especially when the drug is sensitive to **light** or **oxygen**. Glass vials offer excellent protection against **oxidation** and are easy to sterilize. **Amber glass** is often used to protect the drug from **light-sensitive degradation**.

2. **Ampoules**:

- **Glass Ampoules**: These are typically used for **single-dose injectable products**. The **ampoule's sealed closure** ensures the product remains **sterile** and **protected** from contamination. The **breakable nature** of ampoules requires careful handling, but they are ideal for **light-sensitive** formulations.

3. **Pre-filled Syringes**:

- **Plastic and Glass Syringes**: These syringes are pre-filled with the drug formulation and are often used for biologics, vaccines, and other injectable products. **Pre-filled syringes** provide convenience, reduce dosing errors, and offer **tamper-evidence** features.

4. **Cartridges**:

- **Glass or Plastic Cartridges**: Used for **multi-dose injectable systems**, these are commonly employed in devices such as **insulin pens**. They allow patients to administer their own injections with ease, ensuring **consistent dosing** and **ease of use**.

8.2 Impact of Packaging on Product Registration

The packaging of a pharmaceutical product plays a crucial role in the product registration process with regulatory bodies like the FDA, EMA, and other international agencies. Packaging is not only essential for protecting the drug but also for ensuring that it remains safe, effective, and high-quality throughout its shelf life. The packaging material must meet stringent regulatory requirements to obtain market approval. The following outlines the role of packaging in product registration and its impact on market approval.

Role of Packaging in Product Registration

1. Compliance with Safety Standards

One of the primary roles of packaging in product registration is ensuring **compliance with safety standards**. Regulatory bodies require that the **packaging materials** used in pharmaceutical products are **safe** and **do not interact with the drug** in ways that could affect its **stability** or **safety**.

- Safety Requirements: The FDA, EMA, and other regulatory agencies mandate that packaging materials be non-toxic and non-reactive with the drug formulation. The packaging must not leach any harmful chemicals such as plasticizers, solvents, or resins that could potentially alter the drug's chemical composition, potency, or safety.
- Migration Studies: As part of the safety assessment, packaging materials undergo migration testing to ensure that no harmful substances migrate into the drug product. This is particularly important for plastic packaging materials, which could release additives into the formulation.

2. Quality Assurance

Packaging plays a significant role in **quality assurance** by maintaining the **stability** of the drug during its **storage, transport**, and **use**. The **FDA** and **EMA** require that packaging materials effectively protect the drug from **moisture, light, oxygen**, and **temperature fluctuations** that could lead to degradation.

- **Barrier Properties**: Packaging must offer effective **barrier properties** to prevent **moisture**, oxygen, and light from compromising the drug's efficacy and stability. This is especially important for drugs that are light-sensitive, oxygen-sensitive, or hygroscopic (i.e., prone to absorbing moisture from the environment).

- Stability Studies: Extensive stability testing is required to ensure that the packaging material does not interfere with the drug's shelf life. Accelerated stability tests and real-time stability testing are used to evaluate how the packaging performs under extreme environmental conditions (e.g., high temperature, high humidity).
- Testing for Compatibility: Packaging materials must also undergo compatibility testing with the drug formulation to ensure that the drug is not negatively affected by chemical reactions or physical interactions with the packaging. Glass vials, for example, must be tested for compatibility with injectable formulations to ensure they do not react with the drug.

3. Regulatory Approval

Packaging is a key factor in obtaining **market approval** for pharmaceutical products. Regulatory bodies require that **packaging materials** meet **specific standards** for each region, such as **FDA** approval for the U.S., **EMA** approval for Europe, and **Health Canada** approval for Canada. These standards ensure that the packaging is **safe** and **protective** throughout the drug's shelf life.

- **Regulatory Requirements**: In addition to safety and stability testing, regulatory bodies require packaging materials to undergo **leakage testing**, **barrier properties testing**, and **migration studies**. Any failure to meet these requirements can lead to **delays** in approval or, in some cases, **rejection** of the drug product.
- **Packaging Design and Materials**: The packaging design, **materials used**, and **closure systems** (e.g., vials, ampoules, pre-filled syringes) are all evaluated for their ability to protect the drug while maintaining **sterility** and **integrity**. Packaging designs that are difficult to open or prone to damage may delay approval until **modifications** are made.

Impact on Market Approval

The packaging of a pharmaceutical product significantly impacts its **market approval**. Regulatory agencies evaluate packaging in the **initial approval process** and continue to monitor it during **post-market** surveillance.

1. Initial Approval

During the **initial approval process**, the regulatory agency evaluates the **packaging materials** to ensure they meet the required **safety, stability**, and **compatibility** standards. This process includes:

- **Evaluation of Packaging Design**: Regulatory bodies review the **design** of the packaging, including its **materials, closure systems**, and **tamper-evident features**. These must ensure that the drug remains **secure, protected**, and **stable** throughout its shelf life.
- **Packaging Performance Testing**: The **FDA** and **EMA** review **testing data** on **leakage, migration, barrier properties**, and **compatibility** to ensure that the packaging will not interfere with the drug's **efficacy** or **safety**.
- **Compliance with Regulatory Standards**: The packaging must meet the **specific regulations** set by the **FDA, EMA**, or other relevant regulatory bodies for the region in which the drug is being marketed. Packaging that does not meet these standards can result in **delays** or **rejection** of market approval.

2. Post-Approval Monitoring

After the product has been approved, **post-market surveillance** is conducted to monitor the packaging's performance in the real world. This phase ensures that the packaging continues to **protect** the drug and **maintain its quality** under actual storage, transportation, and handling conditions.

- **Packaging Integrity**: The packaging is monitored for any signs of **damage, leakage**, or **compromise** in its **barrier properties**. If any issues are detected, it may result in **recalls, modifications to packaging design**, or further **testing**.
- **Patient Safety**: If post-market surveillance reveals that packaging issues have impacted **patient safety** (e.g., due to **contamination** or **degradation** of the drug), the **product may be recalled**, and packaging changes may be mandated.

CHAPTER NINE

Advanced Drug Delivery Systems (NDDS)

9.1 Introduction to NDDS

The development of **Novel Drug Delivery Systems (NDDS)** has revolutionized the way drugs are delivered to the body. These systems are designed to address the limitations of traditional drug delivery methods, offering more efficient and effective ways to enhance the **therapeutic effectiveness, bioavailability**, and **safety** of drugs. This section introduces the **concept** of NDDS, explores its **historical context**, and highlights the **technological advancements** that have enabled its growth.

Overview of NDDS

Definition of NDDS

Novel Drug Delivery Systems (NDDS) refer to advanced **pharmaceutical technologies** designed to optimize the way drugs are delivered to the body. NDDS aim to overcome challenges associated with **poor bioavailability, inconsistent drug release**, and **systemic side effects** by providing **targeted, controlled,** or **sustained release** of the **active pharmaceutical ingredient (API)**.

NDDS include a variety of advanced drug delivery technologies that ensure that drugs are delivered in a **precise manner**, with improved **efficacy, patient compliance**, and minimized **side effects**. They are designed to:

- **Enhance the bioavailability** of poorly soluble or poorly absorbed drugs.
- **Target drug delivery** to specific tissues or organs to improve therapeutic outcomes.
- Provide **controlled release** to extend the duration of the drug's effect and reduce dosing frequency.

- **Improve patient compliance** by offering more convenient or non-invasive delivery methods, such as **oral tablets, patches, inhalers,** or **implants.**

NDDS technologies are a significant advancement over conventional drug delivery methods, offering precise **drug release profiles**, the ability to **target** specific sites, and improvements in **bioavailability** and **therapeutic outcomes.**

Historical Context of NDDS

The **concept of NDDS** has evolved over several decades, driven by advances in **biotechnology, polymer science,** and **pharmaceutical technology.** Traditional drug delivery systems, such as **oral tablets** and **injectable formulations,** have limitations in terms of **drug absorption, release control,** and **targeting** specific tissues.

The shift toward **NDDS** began with an increasing understanding of **drug pharmacokinetics**—the movement of drugs within the body—and how **drug release rates** and **bioavailability** impact therapeutic outcomes. The key milestones in the development of NDDS include:

1. **Early Development:**

   - The initial use of **controlled-release formulations** in the 1950s and 1960s aimed to reduce the need for frequent dosing of medications.
   - The introduction of **liposomal formulations** in the 1970s paved the way for **targeted drug delivery** using **lipid-based systems.**

2. **Polymer Science and Biotechnology:**

   - In the 1980s and 1990s, the development of **biodegradable polymers** and **microsphere technologies** allowed for the development of **long-acting injectable formulations,** which extended the duration of action of many drugs.
   - **Nanotechnology** also emerged as a significant field, enabling the creation of **nanoparticles** and **nanocarriers** that could deliver drugs directly to **targeted cells** or tissues.

3. **Advancements in Smart Delivery Systems:**

- The advent of **smart drug delivery systems** in the late 1990s and early 2000s led to the creation of systems that could respond to **environmental stimuli**, such as **pH, temperature**, or **enzymes**. These systems provided more precise control over **drug release.**
- **Gene therapies** and **biologics** also benefited from these advancements, allowing for more effective delivery of **therapeutic proteins** and **RNA-based drugs.**

4. **Recent Developments:**

- More recently, the focus has been on creating **personalized drug delivery systems** that are tailored to individual patient needs, such as **smart pills, implants,** and **wearable patches** that provide continuous **drug delivery** based on real-time monitoring of the patient's condition.
- Advances in **biomaterials, nanotechnology,** and **3D printing** are enabling the development of **highly sophisticated drug delivery systems,** offering new possibilities for **targeted, controlled,** and **personalized drug delivery.**

Significance in Modern Drug Delivery

The significance of **Novel Drug Delivery Systems (NDDS)** in modern pharmaceutical development lies in their ability to overcome many of the challenges associated with conventional drug delivery methods. NDDS offer innovative solutions to enhance **drug efficacy, targeted delivery,** and **controlled release.** Below is an exploration of the key significance of NDDS, particularly in improving **bioavailability,** which directly impacts the **therapeutic outcomes** of drug treatments.

Improved Bioavailability

Bioavailability refers to the proportion of the **active pharmaceutical ingredient (API)** that reaches the bloodstream and is available to exert its therapeutic effects. Drugs with **poor solubility** and **low bioavailability** often face challenges in achieving **effective therapeutic levels** when administered through conventional delivery methods like **oral tablets** or **capsules.**

One of the most significant benefits of NDDS is their ability to enhance the **bioavailability** of **poorly soluble** drugs. This is particularly important for drugs that are **insoluble** or **poorly absorbed** in the **gastrointestinal** tract. NDDS can utilize several mechanisms to improve **drug solubility, absorption**, and ultimately **bioavailability**.

How NDDS Improve Bioavailability:

1. **Enhancing Solubility:**

   - NDDS, such as **liposomes, nanoemulsions**, and **solid dispersions**, can significantly improve the solubility of poorly soluble drugs. **Nanotechnology** is commonly used to create **nano-sized particles** or **microparticles** that have a much larger surface area, making it easier for the drug to dissolve in the body.
   - **Cyclodextrins**, a class of molecules that can form inclusion complexes with drugs, are often used in NDDS to **increase solubility** and improve **bioavailability** of hydrophobic drugs.

2. **Targeted Delivery:**

   - NDDS allow for **targeted delivery** of the drug to the **desired site of action**, thereby minimizing **systemic side effects** and enhancing the therapeutic effect. For example, **liposomes** or **micelles** can encapsulate drugs and **target specific tissues**, such as **cancer cells**, allowing for higher local concentrations of the drug and improving its effectiveness.
   - **Targeted delivery** also helps to bypass the **first-pass metabolism** (the metabolism of a drug by the liver before it reaches systemic circulation), which can limit the bioavailability of many oral drugs. For example, **nanoparticles** can be engineered to bypass the **liver** and directly release the drug at the **target site**, reducing the **dose** needed to achieve therapeutic levels.

3. **Controlled and Sustained Release:**

   - NDDS can provide **controlled release** of the drug, ensuring that it is delivered steadily over time. This **sustained release** helps maintain consistent **blood drug levels**, improving **patient compliance** and reducing the frequency of **dosing**.
   - **Polymeric formulations**, like **hydroxypropyl methylcellulose (HPMC)**-based systems, are often used to achieve controlled release

of drugs, allowing them to be absorbed more efficiently over time, improving **bioavailability** compared to **immediate-release** systems.

4. Improving Permeability:

- Some NDDS, such as **transdermal systems** or **oral nanocarriers**, can improve the **permeability** of the drug across **biological barriers** (e.g., the **skin** or **gastrointestinal epithelium**), enhancing drug absorption and bioavailability.
- **Penetration enhancers** like **dimethyl sulfoxide (DMSO)** or **fatty acid derivatives** are used in **transdermal systems** to facilitate the **absorption** of poorly permeable drugs through the **skin**, allowing for improved bioavailability without the need for invasive injections.

Impact on Therapeutic Outcomes

Improved **bioavailability** directly enhances the **therapeutic outcomes** of a drug, ensuring that the **right amount** of drug reaches the **site of action** in the **correct concentration**. By improving solubility and absorption, NDDS can:

- **Increase Drug Effectiveness:** By improving **bioavailability**, NDDS can help drugs achieve the desired therapeutic effect with a **lower dose**, reducing the risk of **adverse effects**.
- **Reduce Side Effects: Targeted delivery** systems can minimize **off-target effects** and **toxicity** by directing the drug to the intended site of action, such as a **tumor** or **inflammatory tissue**.
- **Improve Patient Compliance: Sustained release** formulations and **non-invasive delivery methods** (such as **transdermal patches** or **inhalable systems**) can reduce the need for frequent dosing, leading to improved **patient adherence** to treatment regimens.

Targeted Delivery in NDDS

Targeted drug delivery is one of the most significant advantages of **Novel Drug Delivery Systems (NDDS)**. Traditional drug delivery methods often result in the distribution of the active pharmaceutical ingredient (API) throughout the entire body, which can lead to **systemic side effects** and reduced **therapeutic efficacy**. In contrast, **NDDS** are designed to **deliver drugs directly to the site of action**, ensuring that the drug exerts its effect where it is most needed, while minimizing exposure to other parts of the body. This has a profound impact on improving **efficacy** and reducing **side effects**, particularly for **complex diseases** such as **cancer, diabetes, and neurodegenerative disorders.**

Benefits of Targeted Delivery

1. Improved Efficacy

- **Precision targeting** allows the drug to **concentrate** in the **affected area,** increasing the **local concentration** of the drug and improving its therapeutic effect.
- By focusing on the **specific site of action,** the drug can exert a stronger and more **effective therapeutic response,** even when used at **lower doses,** thereby **enhancing its overall efficacy.**

2. Minimizing Side Effects

- In traditional therapies, drugs often affect **healthy tissues** in addition to the targeted site, leading to **adverse effects.** For example, **chemotherapy drugs** are known to cause significant **side effects** because they indiscriminately attack both **cancer cells** and **healthy cells.**
- **Targeted delivery systems,** such as **liposomes, nanoparticles,** and **monoclonal antibodies,** can be engineered to recognize **specific receptors** or **pathological cells** (e.g., **tumor cells** or **inflammatory sites).** This **selective targeting** reduces **systemic exposure** to the drug, lowering the risk of **side effects** and **toxicity.**

3. Treatment of Complex Diseases

- **Cancer:** One of the most prominent applications of **targeted drug delivery** is in the treatment of **cancer. Chemotherapy** and **targeted therapies** can be combined with **liposomal formulations** or **nanoparticles** to **directly deliver drugs** to **tumor cells.** This improves **drug penetration** into the **tumor,** enhances its **potency,** and reduces damage to surrounding **healthy tissue.**
- **Diabetes:** For chronic conditions like **diabetes, insulin** and other **anti- diabetic drugs** can be delivered using **targeted delivery systems** that release the drug in response to specific signals, such as **blood glucose levels.** This enables more **precise dosing** and **enhanced control** over

disease management.

- **Neurological Diseases**: For **neurodegenerative diseases** like **Alzheimer's** or **Parkinson's**, **brain-targeted delivery systems** (e.g., **nanoparticles** or **liposomes**) can be used to cross the **blood-brain barrier (BBB)**, ensuring that drugs reach the **brain** where they are needed the most.

Mechanisms of Targeted Delivery

1. **Ligand-Receptor Targeting:**

   - This strategy involves **functionalizing** the drug carrier (e.g., **nanoparticles, liposomes**) with **specific ligands** (such as **antibodies** or **peptides**) that can recognize and bind to **receptors** on **target cells**. This ensures that the drug is delivered to the **right location**.
   - **Example: Herceptin** (trastuzumab), a monoclonal antibody, targets the **HER2 receptor** on **breast cancer cells**, providing **precise drug delivery** to **tumor cells**.

2. **Stimuli-Responsive Targeting:**

   - Stimuli-responsive systems release the drug in response to specific **environmental triggers** like **pH, temperature,** or **enzymes** present at the site of action. This enables **controlled release** and **localized drug delivery**.
   - **Example: pH-sensitive nanoparticles** can release their drug payload in the **acidic environment** of a **tumor** or **inflammatory tissue**, where the **pH** is lower than in healthy tissues.

3. **Passive Targeting:**

   - **Passive targeting** exploits the **physiological characteristics** of the disease site, such as the **leaky blood vessels** present in **tumors** (also known as the **Enhanced Permeability and Retention (EPR) effect**). Drugs encapsulated in **nanocarriers** can accumulate at the tumor site, where they passively **penetrate** through these leaky vessels.
   - **Example: Doxil**, a **liposomal formulation** of **doxorubicin**, uses the **EPR effect** to accumulate in **tumor tissues**, allowing for **targeted**

chemotherapy.

4. **Active Targeting:**

    - **Active targeting** involves the **direct interaction** between the drug carrier and specific **cell receptors** on the target tissue. This method is more **precise** than passive targeting.
    - **Example: Antibody-drug conjugates (ADCs)** use **monoclonal antibodies** to deliver drugs directly to **cancer cells.** The **antibody** binds to specific receptors on **cancer cells,** allowing for **targeted delivery** of the cytotoxic drug.

Applications of Targeted Drug Delivery in NDDS

1. **Cancer Therapy:**

    - **Targeted drug delivery** in cancer therapy is a major advancement that aims to deliver chemotherapeutic agents specifically to **cancer cells** while avoiding healthy tissues. This reduces **toxicity** and enhances **treatment efficacy.**
    - **Example: Nanoparticles** such as **liposomes** are often used to encapsulate **chemotherapeutic drugs** like **doxorubicin** and deliver them directly to **tumors,** improving drug accumulation at the tumor site.

2. **Chronic Diseases (e.g., Diabetes):**

    - For chronic diseases like **diabetes, targeted drug delivery systems** like **smart insulin patches** and **controlled-release systems** offer more efficient management by releasing **insulin** in response to **blood glucose levels.**
    - **Example: Nanocarriers** that release **insulin** in response to **elevated blood glucose levels,** helping to **maintain stable glucose levels.**

3. **Neurological Disorders:**

    - In diseases like **Alzheimer's, Parkinson's,** or **multiple sclerosis,** delivering drugs directly to the **brain** is challenging due to the **blood-**

brain barrier (BBB). **Targeted drug delivery systems** like **liposomes, nanoparticles,** and **hydrogels** are designed to cross the BBB and deliver drugs directly to the **central nervous system (CNS).**

- **Example: Nanoparticles** designed to deliver **dopamine** for **Parkinson's disease** can cross the BBB and release the drug at the **brain** where it's needed.

Controlled Release in NDDS

Controlled Release is one of the most important features of **Novel Drug Delivery Systems (NDDS).** These systems are designed to release the **active pharmaceutical ingredient (API)** at a **predetermined rate,** thereby optimizing the therapeutic effects of the drug while minimizing side effects and the need for **frequent dosing.** The goal of **controlled release systems** is to maintain **consistent drug levels** in the bloodstream over an extended period, which helps **improve patient compliance** and reduce the variability seen with conventional **immediate-release formulations.**

Benefits of Controlled Release Systems

1. Reduced Frequency of Dosing

- **Traditional drug delivery systems** often require patients to take medications multiple times a day to maintain therapeutic drug levels. However, **controlled release systems** allow for **once-daily dosing** or even less frequent administration, which improves **patient convenience** and **compliance.**
- For example, a **controlled-release tablet** may release the drug **over 24 hours,** eliminating the need for patients to take medication multiple times per day.

2. Improved Patient Compliance

- **Patient compliance** is a significant challenge in medication adherence, particularly in chronic diseases that require **long-term treatment.** By reducing the number of doses required, controlled release systems make it easier for patients to stick to their treatment regimen.
- **Extended-release formulations** help patients maintain **consistent drug levels** throughout the day, minimizing fluctuations in **drug concentration** and reducing the risk of **missing doses.**

3. Steady Therapeutic Effect

- Controlled release systems aim to deliver a **consistent amount of the drug** over an extended period, providing a **steady therapeutic effect**. This **steady release** ensures that the drug remains at an **optimal concentration** in the bloodstream, improving the **efficacy** of the treatment and minimizing the risk of **toxic peaks** or **sub-therapeutic troughs** that may occur with conventional drug delivery.
- For example, **sustained-release formulations** of **pain medications** provide **continuous relief** over 12-24 hours, preventing the recurrence of pain while avoiding the risk of drug **overdose** from taking too many doses.

4. Reduced Side Effects

- Many drugs produce **side effects** when their concentration in the body peaks quickly. With **controlled release**, the drug is released gradually, avoiding high drug concentrations and reducing the occurrence of **adverse effects**.
- For instance, controlled-release formulations of **anti-inflammatory drugs** can provide **consistent pain relief** without the risk of the **gastrointestinal issues** often associated with **immediate-release** NSAIDs.

5. Optimized Drug Delivery for Specific Conditions

- For certain **chronic conditions**, such as **hypertension, diabetes,** and **depression**, maintaining **consistent therapeutic drug levels** is crucial. **Controlled release systems** help manage these conditions by releasing the drug gradually and ensuring that it is available when needed, improving the **effectiveness** of the treatment.
- For example, **oral controlled-release formulations** of **antidepressants** provide stable drug levels throughout the day, enhancing therapeutic outcomes and reducing the **rebound effect** often seen with **irregular dosing.**

Mechanisms of Controlled Release

There are several ways in which **controlled release systems** can deliver drugs at a consistent rate, depending on the **drug's properties** and the **formulation design**. Below are the primary mechanisms of controlled release:

1. **Matrix Systems:**

   - In **matrix systems**, the drug is dispersed throughout a **polymeric matrix** that slowly releases the drug as it **diffuses** through the polymer. The rate of release depends on the **drug's solubility** and the **matrix composition**.
   - **Example: Hydrophilic matrices** that swell in the presence of water, releasing the drug gradually as the matrix dissolves.

2. **Reservoir Systems:**

   - **Reservoir systems** consist of a drug core surrounded by a rate-controlling membrane. The drug is released through the membrane at a constant rate, based on the properties of the membrane material.
   - **Example: Coated tablets** where the coating controls the rate at which the drug is released, ensuring sustained release over time.

3. **Osmotic Systems:**

   - **Osmotic pumps** use **osmotic pressure** to control the release of the drug. Water from the surrounding environment enters the system, causing it to expand and push the drug out through a small hole at a controlled rate.
   - **Example: Osmotic pumps** used for **antihypertensive drugs** to maintain consistent **blood pressure** levels throughout the day.

4. **Polymeric Systems:**

   - These systems use **biodegradable or non-biodegradable polymers** to encapsulate the drug. The release rate is controlled by the **polymer's degradation** or **swelling properties**.
   - **Example: Polymer-based microparticles** for **injectable depot formulations** that release the drug over several weeks or months.

Applications of Controlled Release Systems

1. **Pain Management:**

   - **Extended-release formulations** of **opioid analgesics** provide **consistent pain relief** without the need for frequent dosing. These formulations help maintain stable **opioid levels**, reducing the risk of **addiction** and **overdose**.

2. **Diabetes Management:**

   - **Insulin pumps** and **sustained-release formulations** of **insulin** offer **long-term control** over **blood glucose levels**, minimizing the risk of **hyperglycemia** and **hypoglycemia** by providing a consistent dose throughout the day.

3. **Cardiovascular Diseases:**

   - **Controlled-release tablets** of **antihypertensive** drugs help maintain **stable blood pressure** without requiring multiple daily doses, improving **patient adherence** and therapeutic outcomes.

4. **Mental Health Disorders:**

   - **Antidepressant medications** with controlled release reduce the fluctuations in drug levels, ensuring consistent therapeutic effects and reducing the likelihood of relapse or side effects caused by peaks and troughs in drug concentration.

Patient Convenience in NDDS

One of the key benefits of **Novel Drug Delivery Systems (NDDS)** is the significant improvement in **patient convenience**. Traditional drug delivery methods, such as oral tablets or injections, often require **frequent dosing** and may be uncomfortable or inconvenient for the patient. In contrast, **NDDS** offer **alternative routes of drug administration** that are often more **patient-friendly**, offering easier, more comfortable, and less intrusive options. By improving the **ease of use**, **comfort**, and **adherence** to medication regimens, these systems significantly enhance **patient** compliance.

Alternative Routes of Drug Administration

1. Patches

Transdermal patches are one of the most widely used forms of NDDS for providing **controlled release** of drugs over an extended period. These patches are applied directly to the skin and allow the drug to pass through the skin and enter the bloodstream.

- **Benefits:**

  - **Non-invasive:** Unlike injections, **transdermal patches** offer a **painless** method of drug delivery.
  - **Convenience:** Patches can be applied once daily, weekly, or even for longer durations, depending on the medication, providing a convenient alternative to frequent pill-taking.
  - **Continuous Release:** The drug is **slowly released** through the skin, maintaining **consistent blood levels** over time, which helps in reducing fluctuations in therapeutic drug concentrations.

- **Examples:**

  - **Nicotine patches:** Used to help people quit smoking by delivering a controlled dose of nicotine.
  - **Fentanyl patches:** Used for pain management, providing **long-term analgesic effects** without the need for repeated dosing.

2. Inhalers

Inhalable drug delivery systems (such as **metered-dose inhalers (MDIs)** and **dry powder inhalers (DPIs)**) offer an alternative route for administering drugs directly to the **lungs**. This method is particularly beneficial for respiratory diseases like **asthma, chronic obstructive pulmonary disease (COPD)**, and **pulmonary infections**.

- **Benefits:**

  - **Fast Onset of Action:** Inhaled drugs can quickly reach the **lungs** and **enter systemic circulation**, providing rapid relief from symptoms.

- ◦ **Localized Treatment**: Inhalers target the **lungs** directly, providing effective treatment for **respiratory diseases** while reducing side effects that might occur with oral or injectable medications.
- ◦ **Convenient**: Inhalers are small, portable devices, allowing patients to easily carry them and use them as needed throughout the day.

- **Examples**:

  - ◦ **Albuterol inhalers**: Used for quick relief from **asthma attacks**.
  - ◦ **Fluticasone inhalers**: Used for **maintenance therapy** in asthma and COPD patients, providing long-term **anti-inflammatory effects**.

3. Implants

Drug implants are small devices that are implanted under the skin and release drugs over a prolonged period. These systems are often used for conditions that require **constant drug levels**, such as **hormonal therapy, chronic pain management**, or **contraception**.

- **Benefits**:

  - ◦ **Long-term, Controlled Release**: Implants provide sustained drug release over weeks, months, or even longer, reducing the need for frequent dosing.
  - ◦ **Convenience**: Once implanted, the device requires little to no maintenance, allowing patients to continue with their daily lives without worrying about taking medication regularly.
  - ◦ **Non-intrusive**: Implants are typically **small and discrete**, and once implanted, they can remain in place without causing significant discomfort.

- **Examples**:

  - ◦ **Subdermal contraceptive implants**: Deliver hormones over several months to prevent pregnancy.
  - ◦ **Morphine implants**: Used for **chronic pain management**, offering long-term, localized relief without the need for frequent dosing.

4. Oral Disintegrating Tablets (ODTs)

Oral disintegrating tablets (ODTs) dissolve rapidly when placed on the tongue, offering an alternative for patients who have difficulty swallowing traditional tablets or capsules.

- **Benefits**:

  - **Ease of Use**: ODTs dissolve in the mouth without the need for water, making them easier for children, elderly patients, or those with **dysphagia** (difficulty swallowing) to take.
  - **Rapid Onset**: ODTs provide a fast onset of action as the drug is absorbed directly from the mouth or **buccal mucosa** into the bloodstream, bypassing the gastrointestinal tract.
  - **Convenience**: These tablets are easy to carry and can be taken without the need for water, making them ideal for use on the go.

- **Examples**:

  - **Ondansetron ODTs**: Used for nausea and vomiting prevention in chemotherapy patients.
  - **Diphenhydramine ODTs**: Used for **allergy relief** or **sleep aid**, especially in people who have difficulty swallowing pills.

Impact on Patient Compliance

One of the primary challenges in healthcare is ensuring **patient compliance** with prescribed therapies. Many patients fail to take their medications as directed due to factors such as **complex dosing schedules, difficulty swallowing pills**, or **unpleasant side effects**.

NDDS significantly improve **patient adherence** by offering more **convenient, comfortable**, and **patient-friendly** drug delivery options. By reducing the frequency of dosing and improving ease of use, these systems make it easier for patients to follow their treatment regimens, leading to better health outcomes.

9.2 Types of NDDS

Novel Drug Delivery Systems (NDDS) can be categorized based on their **mode of delivery**, with each system offering unique advantages tailored to specific **therapeutic needs**. These systems are designed to **improve drug bioavailability**, **targeted delivery**, **controlled release**, and **patient compliance**. This section highlights various types of NDDS that are currently in use or under development, with a focus on their **mechanisms** and **clinical applications**.

1. **Inhalable Drug Delivery Systems**

Overview

Inhalable drug delivery systems offer a direct route to the **lungs**, allowing for the **rapid absorption** of drugs into the bloodstream through the **pulmonary system**. These systems are widely used for the treatment of **respiratory diseases** such as **asthma, chronic obstructive pulmonary disease (COPD)**, and **pulmonary infections**. However, the potential of inhalable systems extends beyond respiratory conditions, as these systems are increasingly being explored for **systemic drug delivery** to treat a range of **chronic diseases** and even **targeted therapies**.

Key Advantages of Inhalable Drug Delivery Systems

- **Rapid Onset of Action**: Inhaled drugs are absorbed directly through the **lungs**, allowing for faster **onset of action** compared to oral or injectable formulations. This is particularly beneficial for acute conditions such as **asthma attacks** or **COPD exacerbations**.
- **Localized Delivery**: Inhalable systems provide **localized drug delivery** to the lungs, making them ideal for **respiratory diseases**. This localized delivery reduces **systemic side effects** compared to oral administration, as the drug directly reaches the site of action.
- **Non-invasive**: Unlike injections, which can be painful, inhalable systems provide a **non-invasive** method of drug delivery, which can improve **patient compliance**, especially for children or elderly patients who may be averse to needles.
- **Systemic Drug Delivery**: Recent advances have made it possible to use inhalable drug delivery systems for **systemic drug delivery**. Drugs that are poorly absorbed through the gastrointestinal tract or liver can be effectively administered via the **lungs**, offering an alternative to

conventional routes.

Types of Inhalable Drug Delivery Systems

1. **Metered-Dose Inhalers (MDIs)**:

   - **Overview**: MDIs are portable devices that deliver a precise dose of drug in the form of an **aerosol** to the lungs. MDIs are often used to deliver bronchodilators and corticosteroids for **asthma** and **COPD**.
   - **Mechanism**: The device uses a **propellant** to create an aerosol mist of the drug, which is then inhaled into the lungs.
   - **Advantages**: MDIs are **quick, easy to use**, and provide a **controlled dose** of the drug with each inhalation.

2. **Dry Powder Inhalers (DPIs)**:

   - **Overview**: DPIs are used to deliver **dry powdered drugs** to the lungs. Unlike MDIs, DPIs do not require a propellant and rely on the patient's **breath** to generate the flow needed for drug delivery.
   - **Mechanism**: The powder is **breathed in** through a mouthpiece, where it is **dispersed** into the lungs by the **force of inhalation**.
   - **Advantages**: DPIs are **easy to use**, often have fewer components than MDIs, and are **breath-actuated**, meaning there is no need to coordinate pressing a button and inhaling.

3. **Nebulizers**:

   - **Overview**: **Nebulizers** are devices that convert a liquid drug solution into a **fine mist** for inhalation. They are commonly used in hospital settings or for patients who have difficulty using MDIs or DPIs.
   - **Mechanism**: A nebulizer uses **compressed air** or **ultrasonic vibrations** to convert liquid drugs into an aerosol mist that can be inhaled.
   - **Advantages**: Nebulizers are particularly useful for **severe asthma** or COPD attacks and for patients with **chronic conditions** who may need large doses or extended inhalation times.

Clinical Applications of Inhalable Drug Delivery Systems

Inhalable drug delivery systems are primarily used in the treatment of **respiratory diseases**, but their potential is expanding into systemic drug delivery as well.

1. **Respiratory Diseases:**

   - **Asthma: Inhalers** and **nebulizers** are used for the **acute treatment** of asthma symptoms, including **bronchodilators** (e.g., **albuterol**) and **corticosteroids** (e.g., **fluticasone**), to control inflammation and bronchoconstriction.
   - **Chronic Obstructive Pulmonary Disease (COPD):** Similar to asthma, inhalable therapies are commonly used to treat **COPD**, providing long-acting bronchodilators and anti-inflammatory medications to control symptoms and improve lung function.
   - **Pulmonary Infections**: Inhalable antibiotics (e.g., **gentamicin, tobramycin**) are used for the treatment of **lung infections** such as **pneumonia** and **cystic fibrosis**.

2. **Systemic Drug Delivery:**

   - **Peptides and Proteins:** Drugs that are **poorly absorbed** via the gastrointestinal route, such as **insulin** or **hormones**, can be delivered **inhaled** into the bloodstream via the **lungs**. This approach can potentially eliminate the need for **injections** and offer a **non-invasive** alternative.
   - **Pain Management:** **Fentanyl** and other **opioids** can be delivered via inhalation for rapid **pain relief** in patients with **acute pain** or **breakthrough pain** in conditions like **cancer**.

Mechanism of Inhalable Drug Delivery Systems

Inhalable drug delivery systems, such as **inhalers** and **nebulizers**, administer drugs in **aerosol form**, allowing the **active pharmaceutical ingredient (API)** to be absorbed **rapidly** through the **lungs**. These systems are designed to optimize **drug delivery** by taking advantage of the lungs' **large surface area** and **vascularization**, which facilitate the **rapid absorption** of drugs directly into the bloodstream.

Mechanism of Action:

- **Inhalers** and **nebulizers** deliver the **drug in the form of fine droplets** or **particles** that are **breathed into the lungs.**
- Once inhaled, the drug particles or droplets reach the **alveoli**, the tiny air sacs in the lungs where **gas exchange** occurs. From there, the drug can **diffuse** into the **bloodstream** for **systemic circulation**, or remain in the **lungs** to act locally, depending on the formulation.
- This direct delivery method allows the drug to **bypass the gastrointestinal tract** and **first-pass metabolism** (in the case of systemic drugs), leading to **faster onset** of action and potentially lower doses compared to oral or injectable routes.

Types of Inhalable Drug Delivery Systems
1. Metered-Dose Inhalers (MDIs)

- **Mechanism:** Metered-dose inhalers **(MDIs)** deliver a pre-measured dose of **drug aerosol** to the lungs. The MDI uses a **propellant** to push the drug formulation (usually a liquid) out of the canister and into the mouthpiece, where it is inhaled as a fine mist.
- **Advantages:**

  - Provides a **precise dose** of medication with each puff.
  - **Portable** and easy to use, making it convenient for **asthma** and COPD patients.
  - Often equipped with a **dose counter** to track the number of remaining doses.

- **Examples:**

  - **Albuterol MDI:** Commonly used for **acute relief of asthma** symptoms by acting as a **bronchodilator.**
  - **Fluticasone MDI:** Used for **maintenance therapy** in asthma and COPD to control inflammation.

2. Dry Powder Inhalers (DPIs)

- **Mechanism:** Unlike MDIs, **Dry Powder Inhalers (DPIs)** deliver medication in the form of a **powder** that is inhaled directly into the lungs. DPIs rely on the patient's **breathing effort** to generate airflow that

disperses the powder into the airways. DPIs do not require a **propellant**.
- **Advantages:**

  - **Breath-actuated**, meaning no coordination between pressing a button and inhaling is required.
  - **No need for propellants**, making them more environmentally friendly than MDIs.
  - **Easy to use**, with fewer components and maintenance required.

- **Examples:**

  - **Advair Diskus**: A DPI used to treat **asthma** and **COPD**, combining **fluticasone** (corticosteroid) and **salmeterol** (long-acting beta-agonist) for both inflammation and bronchodilation.
  - **Spiriva HandiHaler**: A DPI used for **COPD**, containing **tiotropium bromide**, a long-acting anticholinergic agent.

3. Nebulizers

- **Mechanism: Nebulizers** convert a liquid medication into a **fine mist** that can be inhaled into the lungs. Nebulizers use either **compressed air** or **ultrasonic vibrations** to create the mist, which is then inhaled by the patient over several minutes.
- **Advantages:**

  - **Ideal for patients** who are unable to use MDIs or DPIs effectively, such as **young children**, **elderly patients**, or those with severe **respiratory distress**.
  - **Longer inhalation time** allows for **deeper drug penetration** into the lungs.
  - Nebulizers are **useful for large doses** of medication or for drugs that need to be delivered over an extended period.

- **Examples:**

  - **Salbutamol (Albuterol) Nebulizer Solution**: Used for **acute asthma attacks** or exacerbations of **COPD**, allowing rapid bronchodilation.

- ○ **Pulmicort Respules**: A nebulized **budesonide** formulation used for **maintenance therapy** in asthma and **COPD**, providing anti-inflammatory effects.

2. Transdermal Drug Delivery Systems

Overview

Transdermal Drug Delivery Systems (TDDS) are **non-invasive systems** designed to deliver drugs through the **skin** directly into the **systemic circulation**. These systems offer a **controlled release** of drugs over a prolonged period, improving **therapeutic outcomes** and enhancing **patient compliance**. Unlike oral medications, which need to be absorbed through the gastrointestinal tract and subjected to **first-pass metabolism** by the liver, **transdermal systems** allow the drug to bypass the digestive system and enter the bloodstream directly.

Transdermal delivery is particularly useful for **chronic diseases** where **consistent drug levels** are required throughout the day, as well as for **acute conditions** where rapid, sustained drug delivery is necessary. The **controlled release** mechanism in TDDS ensures that the drug is delivered gradually, reducing the need for **frequent dosing** and maintaining **steady plasma drug levels**.

Mechanism of Action

TDDS work by using the **skin** as a pathway for **drug absorption**. The skin consists of several layers, and the most important layer for drug penetration is the **stratum corneum** (the outermost layer of skin). Transdermal systems are designed to overcome the skin's natural **barriers** to allow drugs to pass through and reach the **dermis**, where they can be absorbed into the **bloodstream**.

Key steps in the mechanism:

1. **Drug Diffusion**: The drug is usually incorporated into a **patch** or **gel** that is applied to the skin. The drug diffuses through the **epidermis** and **dermis** layers.

2. **Controlled Release**: TDDS are often designed with a **rate-limiting membrane** or other release mechanisms that control the amount of drug released into the bloodstream. This ensures **continuous drug delivery** over time.

3. **Absorption into Bloodstream**: Once the drug reaches the **dermis**, it enters the **capillaries** and eventually enters the **systemic circulation**.

Advantages of Transdermal Drug Delivery Systems

1. **Non-Invasive:**

   - Unlike injections, which require a needle, **transdermal patches** provide a **painless** method of drug delivery, making them suitable for patients who dislike needles or have **fear of injections.**

2. **Controlled Release:**

   - TDDS provide a **continuous** and **controlled release** of the drug, maintaining **steady drug levels** in the bloodstream, which is particularly beneficial for **chronic conditions** requiring **long-term management.**

3. **Bypasses First-Pass Metabolism:**

   - Drugs delivered via TDDS bypass the **liver** and the **first-pass metabolism**, which is common with oral drugs. This means that a **larger proportion** of the active drug reaches the bloodstream in its active form.

4. **Improved Patient Compliance:**

   - TDDS often require **fewer applications** (e.g., a patch that can be worn for a **week** or **a month**), reducing the need for **frequent dosing** and improving **patient adherence** to treatment regimens.

5. **Localized Drug Delivery:**

   - In some cases, transdermal delivery can be used to deliver drugs to **localized areas** of the body (e.g., **topical analgesics** for **muscle pain**).

Types of Transdermal Drug Delivery Systems

1. **Transdermal Patches:**

- **Overview**: Transdermal patches are the most common type of **TDDS**. They consist of a drug reservoir or matrix that is applied directly to the skin. The drug is released slowly from the patch and diffuses through the skin into the bloodstream.
- **Mechanism**: Patches can use different mechanisms, including **rate-controlled membranes** or **reservoir systems**, to deliver the drug at a consistent rate.
- **Examples**:

  - **Nicotine patches**: Used to help people quit smoking by delivering a controlled dose of nicotine.
  - **Fentanyl patches**: Used for pain management, providing **sustained analgesic effects** over several days.

2. **Transdermal Gels**:

- **Overview**: **Gels** are another form of transdermal delivery. They are typically applied to the skin and form a thin film that facilitates the release of the drug.
- **Mechanism**: These systems rely on **skin penetration enhancers** to increase the permeability of the skin and promote drug absorption.
- **Examples**:

  - **Testosterone gel**: Used for **hormone replacement therapy** in men with low testosterone levels.
  - **Nitroglycerin ointment**: Used for **angina** (chest pain), providing continuous release of the drug to manage heart conditions.

3. **Transdermal Sprays**:

- **Overview**: **Sprays** offer a convenient way to deliver drugs through the skin. The drug is aerosolized and applied to the skin, where it is absorbed over time.
- **Mechanism**: Sprays work similarly to gels, with the drug being absorbed through the skin, aided by penetration enhancers that facilitate the drug's passage into the bloodstream.
- **Examples**:

- **Sumatriptan nasal spray**: Used for **acute migraine treatment.**

Challenges in Transdermal Drug Delivery

1. **Skin Permeability:**

   - One of the primary challenges in **transdermal drug delivery** is the **skin's natural barrier**, which can limit the absorption of certain drugs, especially large or hydrophilic molecules.
   - To overcome this, **penetration enhancers**, such as **DMSO (dimethyl sulfoxide)** or **ethanol**, are often used to improve skin permeability.

2. **Drug Molecular Size:**

   - Large molecules, such as **proteins, peptides**, and **hormones**, are often difficult to deliver via transdermal systems because they do not easily pass through the skin.
   - However, advances in **nanotechnology** and the use of **microneedles** are helping to improve the **transdermal delivery** of larger molecules.

3. **Skin Irritation:**

   - Prolonged use of **transdermal patches** can cause **skin irritation** or **sensitization**. To minimize this risk, patches are designed with **hypoallergenic materials** and **controlled adhesion** to reduce adverse reactions.

Mechanism of Transdermal Drug Delivery Systems

Transdermal drug delivery systems (TDDS) provide a **controlled and sustained release** of drugs through the **skin**. These systems typically involve **patches** that are applied to the skin, where they deliver a **consistent dose** of the drug over an **extended period**. The mechanism involves several key steps to ensure that the drug reaches the **bloodstream** efficiently while maintaining a **steady drug level** throughout the treatment period.

Key Mechanism of Action

1. **Skin Penetration:**

- **Stratum Corneum**: The outermost layer of the skin, known as the **stratum corneum**, serves as the primary barrier to drug absorption. **Drugs** must penetrate this layer to reach the **dermis**, where the **blood vessels** are located.
- **Rate-Limiting Step**: The **stratum corneum** acts as the rate-limiting step in transdermal drug absorption. Drugs must pass through this layer before they can enter the **systemic circulation**.

2. Drug Diffusion:

- Once the drug reaches the **stratum corneum**, it diffuses through the layers of the skin (epidermis and dermis) via **passive diffusion**.
- **Drug concentration gradient**: The **drug concentration** in the **patch** is higher than the concentration in the **skin**, driving the drug from the patch through the skin and into the bloodstream.

3. Controlled Release:

- **Transdermal patches** are designed with a **rate-controlling mechanism** that allows the drug to be released **gradually** over time. The patch's formulation and the material used (e.g., **membranes** or **matrix systems**) ensure that the drug is released at a consistent rate.
- **Types of Release Mechanisms**:

  - **Reservoir Systems**: These patches contain a drug **reservoir** surrounded by a **rate-controlling membrane** that regulates the drug's release.
  - **Matrix Systems**: The drug is embedded within a **polymeric matrix**, and as the patch is applied to the skin, the drug gradually diffuses out.

4. Absorption into the Bloodstream:

- Once the drug passes through the skin's layers, it enters the **dermis**, where it can then be absorbed into the **capillaries**. From the **capillaries**, the drug enters the **systemic circulation**, delivering the therapeutic effects.

Advantages of the Mechanism

1. **Sustained Drug Release:**

   - The **controlled release** mechanism ensures that the drug is delivered **steadily** over an extended period, eliminating the need for frequent dosing and providing **continuous therapeutic effects**.
   - This is particularly useful for managing **chronic conditions** such as **pain, hormonal imbalances**, and **nicotine addiction**.

2. **Bypassing the Gastrointestinal Tract:**

   - **Oral administration** often faces challenges such as **poor bioavailability** due to **first-pass metabolism** in the liver. With TDDS, the drug is absorbed directly through the **skin**, bypassing the **liver**, which allows for a greater proportion of the drug to enter the **bloodstream** in its **active form**.

3. **Improved Patient Compliance:**

   - Since TDDS typically require fewer doses (e.g., **once daily, weekly,** or **monthly**), patients are more likely to adhere to their treatment regimen, especially in cases where frequent dosing is cumbersome or when taking **oral medications** is difficult (e.g., for **elderly** or **children**).

Examples of Transdermal Drug Delivery Systems

1. **Nicotine Patches:**

   - **Nicotine patches** are used to help **smoking cessation** by providing a consistent **dose of nicotine** over the course of the day. This helps reduce withdrawal symptoms and cravings in individuals trying to quit smoking.

2. **Fentanyl Patches:**

- ○ **Fentanyl patches** are used for **chronic pain management**. These patches deliver **sustained-release fentanyl**, a powerful opioid, over **72 hours**, providing long-term **pain relief** without the need for frequent dosing.

3. Hormonal Patches:

- ○ **Contraceptive patches** deliver **estrogen** and **progestin** in a controlled, consistent manner over a period of time (usually a week or a month), offering an **effective and convenient** birth control option.

4. Testosterone Patches:

- ○ **Testosterone replacement therapy** is commonly administered via **transdermal patches** for men with **low testosterone levels**, allowing for continuous, stable hormone delivery.

3. Other Novel Systems

In addition to **inhalable** and **transdermal** systems, several **novel drug delivery systems (NDDS)** are being developed to improve drug delivery and therapeutic outcomes. These systems aim to **target specific tissues or cells**, enhance **bioavailability**, and provide **controlled release**. One of the most innovative approaches involves the use of **injectable nanocarriers**, such as **nanoparticles** and **liposomes**, which offer significant advantages in the delivery of drugs, particularly for **oncology** and **gene therapy**.

Injectable Nanocarriers

Injectable **nanocarriers** are **nano-sized particles** or **liposomes** designed to deliver **drugs** directly to **targeted cells** or tissues. These systems leverage the small size of nanoparticles, which can enable **enhanced drug penetration** and **direct targeting** of disease sites, such as **tumors**, while minimizing **systemic exposure** and **side effects**.

Overview of Nanocarriers

- **Nanoparticles** are engineered particles with a **size range** of **1-1000 nanometers**. They can be made from a variety of materials, including **lipids, polymers**, or **proteins**, depending on the desired **drug release profile, biocompatibility**, and **targeting ability**.

- **Liposomes** are **lipid-based nanocarriers** that encapsulate the drug inside a lipid bilayer. They can be used for both **intravenous injection** and **local drug delivery**, and they can enhance the **solubility, stability,** and **bioavailability** of poorly soluble drugs.

Mechanisms of Action

- **Targeted Drug Delivery**: Nanocarriers are typically functionalized with **targeting ligands** (e.g., antibodies, peptides, or small molecules) that can specifically bind to **receptors** or **molecules** found on the surface of **target cells**, such as **cancer cells**. This allows the drug to be delivered **precisely** to the desired tissue, reducing **off-target effects** and enhancing therapeutic efficacy.
- **Enhanced Permeability and Retention (EPR) Effect**: Tumors and other diseased tissues often have **leaky blood vessels**, allowing **nanocarriers** to passively accumulate in these areas through the **EPR effect**. This mechanism enables **passive targeting** of drugs to **tumors** and **inflammatory tissues**.
- **Controlled Release**: Many nanocarriers are designed to release their drug payload in response to specific conditions at the **target site**, such as **pH changes, temperature**, or the presence of **enzymes**. This enables **sustained** or **localized release** of drugs, improving efficacy and minimizing toxicity.

Applications of Injectable Nanocarriers
1. Oncology (Cancer Therapy)

One of the most promising applications of injectable **nanocarriers** is in the treatment of **cancer**. Traditional chemotherapy often lacks specificity, affecting both **cancerous** and **healthy cells**, leading to severe **side effects**. **Nanocarriers** offer a way to deliver **chemotherapeutic drugs** specifically to **cancer cells**, improving efficacy and reducing toxicity.

- **Liposomes**: Liposomal formulations, such as **Doxil (liposomal doxorubicin)**, encapsulate the drug **doxorubicin**, a commonly used chemotherapy agent, within a lipid bilayer. This formulation helps to **target the drug** to the **tumor site**, reducing the toxic effects on healthy tissues.

- **Polymeric Nanoparticles: Polymeric nanoparticles** can encapsulate **hydrophobic drugs** and **improve solubility,** allowing for more efficient delivery to **tumor tissues.** These nanoparticles can be engineered to release their drug payload in response to the **acidic microenvironment** of tumors.
- **Targeted Cancer Therapy:** By modifying the surface of nanoparticles with **targeting ligands,** such as **antibodies** or **peptides,** these systems can specifically bind to receptors expressed on **cancer cells.** This allows for more **precise drug delivery** to the tumor site, minimizing **systemic exposure** and **side effects.**

2. Gene Therapy

Gene therapy involves the delivery of genetic material (e.g., **DNA, RNA,** or **gene-editing tools** like **CRISPR-Cas9**) to target cells in order to treat genetic disorders. **Nanocarriers** are used to safely transport and deliver these therapeutic genes into cells.

- **Liposomes:** Liposomes are widely used to encapsulate **DNA** or **RNA** molecules and deliver them to the **target cells.** The lipid bilayer of liposomes protects the genetic material from **degradation** by **enzymes** and ensures efficient **cellular uptake.**
- **Polymeric Nanoparticles: Polymeric nanoparticles** are also used to deliver **genetic material.** These nanoparticles can be engineered to carry **plasmid DNA** or **mRNA** for gene therapy applications. Additionally, they can be functionalized with **targeting ligands** to ensure that the **genetic material** is delivered to the correct cells.
- **RNA Delivery:** Nanocarriers are used to deliver **RNA-based therapies,** such as **siRNA (small interfering RNA)** and **mRNA vaccines,** which play a crucial role in **gene silencing** and **protein production.** Nanocarriers protect the fragile RNA from **enzymatic degradation** and help to deliver it efficiently to the **target cells.**

3. Other Applications

- **Inflammation and Autoimmune Diseases:** Injectable **nanocarriers** can deliver **anti-inflammatory drugs** or **immunomodulatory agents** directly to sites of **inflammation** (e.g., **rheumatoid arthritis, inflammatory bowel disease)** or **autoimmune diseases,** ensuring a more **localized** treatment while minimizing side effects.

- **Neurodegenerative Diseases: Nanoparticles** can be used to deliver drugs across the **blood-brain barrier (BBB)** for the treatment of **neurodegenerative diseases** such as **Alzheimer's disease** and **Parkinson's disease**. Nanocarriers can be designed to **cross the BBB** and deliver therapeutic agents directly to the **brain**.

Examples of Injectable Nanocarriers

1. **Doxil:** A **liposomal formulation** of **doxorubicin**, a chemotherapy drug, used for **cancer treatment**. This formulation helps to reduce the **toxicity** associated with **doxorubicin** by targeting the **tumor site**.
2. **Abraxane:** A **nanoparticle albumin-bound formulation** of **paclitaxel**, used for the treatment of various cancers, including **breast cancer, non-small cell lung cancer,** and **pancreatic cancer.** This formulation improves the **bioavailability** of paclitaxel and **reduces side effects.**
3. **Onpattro:** A **lipid nanoparticle formulation** of **patisiran**, used for **gene silencing** in the treatment of **hereditary transthyretin-mediated amyloidosis (hATTR).** This nanocarrier delivers **siRNA** to the liver, where it silences the mutated gene.
4. **Ciluprevir:** A **nanoparticle-based drug** used in the treatment of **hepatitis** C. This nanocarrier enhances the **drug's solubility** and **bioavailability.**

Implants in Novel Drug Delivery Systems (NDDS)

Drug-loaded implants or **microspheres** are advanced **drug delivery systems** designed to provide **sustained** and **controlled release** of drugs over extended periods, ranging from **weeks to months.** These systems are typically implanted under the skin, where they release the drug gradually, allowing for continuous treatment with minimal intervention. Implants are especially beneficial for patients who require **long-term medication** or for **drugs** that need to be delivered at **specific doses** over an extended period.

Overview of Drug-loaded Implants

Implants are typically **solid dosage forms** that contain a specific amount of drug, which is **gradually released** into the body. They are typically small in size, **biocompatible,** and designed to be **implanted** into the **subcutaneous** tissue or **other tissues** where they can **deliver drugs** directly to the bloodstream over a long period without the need for **frequent dosing.**

- **Biodegradable Implants**: Some implants are made from **biodegradable materials** that dissolve naturally over time as the drug is released. These types of implants gradually break down in the body, leaving no need for surgical removal once the drug has been fully released.
- **Non-biodegradable Implants**: These implants do not degrade in the body and must be removed after the drug is fully delivered.

Mechanism of Action

1. **Controlled Drug Release:**

   - The drug is embedded within the implant or microsphere and is released **gradually** through a **diffusion process** or **erosion** of the implant material. The rate of drug release can be controlled by adjusting the **polymer composition**, **implant size**, and **structure**.
   - For **biodegradable implants**, the **implant material** breaks down over time, and the drug is **released** as the material degrades.

2. **Drug Absorption:**

   - After the drug is released from the implant, it diffuses through the **tissues** or **blood vessels** at the implantation site, and from there, it enters the **systemic circulation**.

3. **Sustained Delivery:**

   - The drug is released over a prolonged period, providing **continuous therapeutic effects** without the need for multiple doses. This **extended release** ensures that the drug maintains **steady blood levels** throughout the desired treatment period.

Advantages of Implants

1. **Sustained Drug Release:**

   - Implants provide a **consistent release** of the drug over an extended period, reducing the need for **frequent dosing** and ensuring **constant drug levels** in the bloodstream.

- This is particularly useful for **chronic conditions** that require **long-term treatment**, such as **pain management, hormonal therapies,** or **cancer treatment.**

2. **Improved Patient Compliance:**

- With **long-acting implants,** patients do not need to take **daily medications** or schedule frequent visits to healthcare providers for injections. This enhances **compliance,** particularly in cases where the patient may have difficulty adhering to complex drug regimens.

3. **Reduced Side Effects:**

- By delivering the drug at a **controlled rate,** implants help to minimize the peak-and-trough fluctuations in **drug levels** that are common with oral or injectable forms. This steady release can reduce the risk of **drug toxicity** and **side effects** associated with high drug concentrations.

4. **Non-invasive:**

- Implants provide a **non-invasive** and **pain-free** method of drug administration, offering an alternative to injections or frequent oral medications. Once implanted, they can provide **weeks or months** of **continuous drug delivery** with minimal patient intervention.

Applications of Implants

1. **Pain Management:**

- **Drug-loaded implants** are commonly used in **chronic pain management,** particularly in patients with **cancer** or **post-surgical pain.** They offer a **long-term solution** for pain relief, especially in patients who require **opioid analgesics.**
- **Example: Morphine implants** are used for **persistent pain** relief by providing **continuous release** of morphine directly at the **pain site.**

2. **Hormonal Therapies:**

- Hormonal implants are used in **contraception** and **hormone replacement therapy** (HRT). For example, **contraceptive implants** provide a **continuous release of progestin**, offering **long-term birth control** with minimal side effects.
- Example: **Subdermal contraceptive implants** provide continuous **hormonal release** to prevent pregnancy for up to **three years.**

3. Cancer Therapy:

- Implants are used in **oncology** to provide **local** or **systemic delivery** of **chemotherapy drugs.** These implants can be placed directly near a **tumor** to deliver high drug concentrations directly to the cancerous tissue, minimizing damage to healthy tissue.
- Example: **Chemotherapy drug-eluting implants** provide continuous drug delivery at the **tumor site**, improving efficacy while minimizing systemic side effects.

4. Gene Therapy:

- In **gene therapy**, implants or **microspheres** can deliver **genetic material** (e.g., **DNA, RNA**) directly to specific tissues or cells, offering targeted delivery for the treatment of **genetic disorders.**
- Example: **Gene therapy implants** are used to deliver **viral vectors** or **gene-editing tools** to targeted cells for **gene correction** or **gene silencing.**

Examples of Drug-loaded Implants

1. Norplant (Contraceptive Implants):

- **Norplant** is a **subdermal implant** that delivers **levonorgestrel**, a synthetic hormone, for **long-term contraception.** The implants release the hormone slowly over **five years**, providing continuous contraception with minimal patient intervention.

2. Zoladex (Goserelin Implants):

◦ **Zoladex** is a **drug-loaded implant** used in the treatment of **prostate cancer, breast cancer,** and **endometriosis.** The implant releases **goserelin,** a **hormone therapy,** continuously over **28 days,** suppressing hormone levels to treat cancer and reduce symptoms.

3. **Gliadel Wafer (Carmustine Implants):**

◦ **Gliadel** wafers are used in **brain cancer treatment.** These **biodegradable implants** release **carmustine,** a chemotherapy drug, directly at the tumor site, offering local treatment while minimizing systemic side effects.

4. **Bioness (Neuromodulation Implants):**

◦ **Bioness** is an example of a **neuromodulation implant** used to treat **chronic pain** or **spinal conditions** by delivering **electrical stimulation** directly to the **nerves.**

4. Smart Drug Delivery Systems

Smart Drug Delivery Systems (SDDS) represent an innovative class of **Novel Drug Delivery Systems (NDDS)** that are designed to **respond dynamically** to specific **environmental stimuli** at the target site, such as **pH, temperature,** or the presence of **enzymes.** These systems offer precise control over drug release, allowing drugs to be delivered **only when and where** they are needed, improving therapeutic outcomes while minimizing side effects and enhancing **patient compliance.**

Overview of Smart Drug Delivery Systems

Smart drug delivery systems are designed with the ability to **monitor** and **respond** to **changes** in their **environment,** making them "intelligent" in terms of their ability to **control the release** of drugs based on specific conditions. This **adaptive release mechanism** ensures that the drug is delivered only under specific **conditions** such as a change in **pH, temperature,** or **enzyme concentration** in the body, which are often unique to the **target site.**

Mechanisms of Smart Drug Delivery

1. **pH-sensitive Systems:**

- **pH-sensitive** drug delivery systems are designed to release the drug when they encounter **specific pH conditions** that are characteristic of certain **tissues** or **pathological sites** (e.g., **tumors, inflammatory sites,** or the **gastrointestinal tract**).
- **Example: Enteric-coated tablets** that release the drug only when the **pH** increases in the **small intestine**, ensuring that the drug does not release prematurely in the acidic stomach.

2. Temperature-sensitive Systems:

- **Temperature-sensitive drug delivery systems** respond to changes in **temperature.** These systems are particularly useful for **targeted delivery** in **localized** or **deep tissues** where **temperature** changes occur due to **inflammation, infection,** or **tumors.**
- **Example: Hydrogel-based formulations** that undergo a **phase transition** and release the drug at **higher temperatures,** ideal for localized drug release in inflamed tissues.

3. Enzyme-sensitive Systems:

- **Enzyme-sensitive drug delivery systems** are designed to release their drug payload in the presence of specific **enzymes** found in certain tissues or organs. This method is especially useful for targeting **cancer cells,** where certain **proteases** are overexpressed.
- **Example: Liposomes** or **nanoparticles** functionalized with **peptide sequences** that are cleaved by **cancer-associated enzymes,** resulting in the release of the drug specifically at the **tumor site.**

4. Magnetic Field-responsive Systems:

- Some smart drug delivery systems incorporate **magnetic nanoparticles** that can be directed to the target site using an **external magnetic field.** Once at the desired site, the drug can be released via an **external stimulus,** such as **temperature change** or **magnetic field.**
- **Example: Magnetic nanoparticles** for **targeted cancer therapy,** where the **magnetic field** guides the nanoparticles to the **tumor site,** and the drug is released in response to localized **temperature changes.**

Advantages of Smart Drug Delivery Systems

1. **Targeted and Controlled Release:**

   - Smart drug delivery systems enable **precise control** over when and where the drug is released. This ensures **optimal drug concentrations** at the **target site**, reducing systemic side effects and improving the **efficacy** of the treatment.

2. **Minimized Side Effects:**

   - By releasing the drug only at the **target site, smart systems** can reduce the exposure of healthy tissues to the drug, minimizing side effects that are often associated with **traditional drug delivery** methods.

3. **Improved Bioavailability:**

   - These systems can enhance the **bioavailability** of drugs that are otherwise poorly absorbed or unstable, by protecting the drug from degradation or providing **localized delivery** where absorption is optimal.

4. **Personalized Medicine:**

   - Smart drug delivery systems can be tailored to respond to individual patient characteristics, such as specific **biomarkers, disease states,** or **tissue conditions**, making them suitable for **personalized treatment**.

Applications of Smart Drug Delivery Systems

1. **Cancer Therapy:**

   - **Smart drug delivery** is particularly useful in **oncology**. These systems can release chemotherapeutic agents specifically at the **tumor site**, reducing damage to surrounding healthy tissues and minimizing side effects.

- ○ **Example: pH-sensitive nanoparticles** that release chemotherapeutic drugs when they encounter the **acidic environment** of **tumors**, improving drug targeting and reducing systemic toxicity.

2. **Gene Therapy:**

- ○ **Gene delivery** systems use **smart technologies** to deliver **genetic material** to specific tissues in response to **enzymatic activity** or **external stimuli**, such as **light** or **temperature**. This is useful in **gene-editing** therapies or **RNA-based treatments.**
- ○ **Example: Polymeric nanoparticles** that release **RNA-based drugs** in response to specific **enzymes** at the **site of action**, offering precision in **gene therapy** applications.

3. **Chronic Disease Management:**

- ○ **Smart drug delivery systems** are ideal for managing **chronic diseases** such as **diabetes** or **hypertension**, where drugs need to be delivered over a long period.
- ○ **Example: Insulin delivery systems** that release **insulin** in response to changes in **blood glucose levels**, ensuring that the patient receives the right amount of medication when needed.

4. **Localized Pain Management:**

- ○ **Smart transdermal patches** can deliver **analgesic** drugs in response to localized **pain** or **inflammation**, providing targeted relief without the risk of systemic side effects.
- ○ **Example: Temperature-sensitive patches** that release **pain-relieving drugs** when the skin temperature increases due to **inflammation.**

Challenges of Smart Drug Delivery Systems

1. **Complexity in Design:**

- ○ Designing **smart drug delivery systems** that respond to specific stimuli requires **complex formulations** and precise control over the release mechanisms. Ensuring that the drug is delivered at the correct time and in the right dose can be technically challenging.

2. **Cost:**

   - The development of smart systems is often more expensive than traditional drug delivery methods due to the need for **advanced materials, specialized equipment,** and **customized formulations.**

3. **Regulatory Approval:**

   - Regulatory approval for **novel drug delivery systems** can be more challenging, as these systems require extensive **testing** to ensure that they meet **safety** and **efficacy standards.**

Examples of Smart Drug Delivery Systems

1. **Smart Insulin Delivery:**

   - Systems that release **insulin** in response to **blood glucose levels.** These systems ensure that **insulin is delivered only when necessary,** offering more **precise control** over blood glucose levels in **diabetic patients.**

2. **Nanoparticle-based Targeted Therapy:**

   - **Smart nanoparticles** that release drugs in response to **enzymatic cleavage** or **pH changes** at **cancer sites,** improving the precision of **chemotherapy** while minimizing systemic side effects.

3. **pH-sensitive Drug Release for Gastric Conditions:**

   - **Polymeric systems** that release **anti-ulcer drugs** when they encounter the **acidic environment** in the **stomach,** ensuring **localized drug delivery** for conditions like **gastritis** or **peptic ulcers.**

9.3 Excipients for NDDS

Excipients are non-active ingredients used in the formulation of **Novel Drug Delivery Systems (NDDS)** to **enhance** the drug's **delivery, stability, and release** characteristics. These **inactive substances** play a key role in ensuring that the **Active Pharmaceutical Ingredient (API)** is delivered effectively to the **target site**, and that it maintains its **therapeutic effect** over the appropriate time frame. The inclusion of the right excipients can significantly **improve the bioavailability, targeting**, and **controlled release** of the drug, making NDDS an essential tool for modern drug delivery.

1. Role of Excipients in NDDS

Enhance Stability

One of the primary roles of excipients in NDDS is to **enhance the stability** of the **active pharmaceutical ingredient (API)**, ensuring that the drug remains **effective** and **safe** during storage and after administration.

- **Stabilization of APIs**: Many drugs, particularly biologics or **poorly soluble drugs**, can be unstable in their raw form. **Excipients** such as **antioxidants, chelating agents**, and **preservatives** are included in NDDS to protect the API from **oxidation, degradation**, or **hydrolysis** that might occur during storage or transit.

  - **Example: Vitamin C** (ascorbic acid) is highly **susceptible to oxidation. Excipients like sodium metabisulfite** are added to formulations to protect it from **oxidative degradation.**

- **Preventing Degradation**: Certain excipients like **stabilizing agents** help to **maintain the integrity** of the drug by creating a **protective environment** that prevents **light exposure, moisture absorption,** or **temperature fluctuations.**

  - **Example: Liposomes** used in **chemotherapy** protect the **drug** from **enzymatic degradation** while **targeting** cancer cells.

Improve Bioavailability

Excipients are crucial in improving the **bioavailability** of drugs, especially for **poorly soluble** or **poorly absorbed drugs**. They can enhance the **dissolution rate, solubility,** or **penetration** of drugs through biological barriers.

- **Solubilizers and Surfactants**: These excipients can improve the **solubility** of **hydrophobic drugs**, enabling their **absorption** in the **gastrointestinal tract** or **skin**.

  - **Example: Cyclodextrins** are often used to **increase the solubility** of hydrophobic drugs, thereby enhancing their **bioavailability**.

- **Permeation Enhancers**: In **transdermal systems**, excipients like **DMSO (dimethyl sulfoxide)** or **ethanol** are used to enhance the **skin permeability** of drugs, ensuring that they reach the **systemic circulation** effectively.

  - **Example: Penetration enhancers** in **transdermal patches** help **insulin** pass through the skin and maintain **steady glucose control**.

Control Drug Release

Excipients play a central role in controlling the **rate** and **pattern** of drug release in NDDS, ensuring **timed release** and minimizing the **need for frequent dosing**.

- **Rate-Controlling Polymers**: Excipients such as **hydrophilic polymers, lipid matrices,** and **polymers** are used in formulations to control the **drug release** profile, providing **sustained** or **controlled release**.

  - **Example: Hydroxypropyl methylcellulose (HPMC)** is commonly used in **controlled-release tablets** to slow down the release of the active ingredient over time, ensuring prolonged therapeutic effects.

- **Biodegradable Polymers**: In **injectable nanocarriers** or **microspheres, biodegradable polymers** such as **poly(lactic-co-glycolic acid) (PLGA)** are used to provide a **controlled and sustained release** of drugs over days, weeks, or months. These systems are often used in **oncology** and **hormonal therapy**.

- ○ **Example: PLGA-based implants** for **oncology** drugs provide **long-term drug release**, reducing the need for frequent injections.

Ensure Drug Targeting

Excipients are also used to **target drugs** to specific tissues or organs, which is a key feature of NDDS. They help to enhance **selectivity** and **avoid off-target effects**.

- Targeting Ligands: Excipients can be functionalized with **targeting ligands** (e.g., **antibodies, peptides,** or **small molecules**) that **bind specifically** to **receptors** on **target cells**. This ensures that the drug is delivered to the intended site, such as **tumors** or **inflammatory tissues**.

  - ○ **Example: Antibody-drug conjugates (ADCs)** use **monoclonal antibodies** to selectively deliver **cytotoxic drugs** to **cancer cells** expressing specific **cell surface markers**.

  2. Common Types of Excipients Used in NDDS

1. Solubilizers and Surfactants:

   - ○ **Cyclodextrins, polyethylene glycol (PEG),** and **sodium lauryl sulfate** improve the **solubility** of poorly water-soluble drugs.
   - ○ **Function:** Enhance **bioavailability** by increasing **drug solubility** in aqueous environments.

2. Polymers:

   - ○ **Hydroxypropyl methylcellulose (HPMC), polyvinyl alcohol (PVA), PLGA** are used for **controlled release** of drugs.
   - ○ **Function: Rate-controlling** excipients that provide **sustained release** by slowing down the drug's dissolution or absorption.

3. Stabilizing Agents:

   - ○ **Antioxidants** like **ascorbic acid, sodium metabisulfite,** and **EDTA** are used to stabilize drugs that are sensitive to **oxidation** or **degradation**.

- ◦ **Function:** Prevent **drug degradation** during storage or when exposed to environmental factors such as **light** and **oxygen**.

4. **Penetration Enhancers:**

   - ◦ **DMSO, ethanol,** and **propylene glycol** are used to increase the **skin permeability** of drugs in **transdermal systems.**
   - ◦ **Function: Facilitate drug absorption** through biological barriers such as the **skin** or **gastrointestinal lining.**

5. **Targeting Ligands:**

   - ◦ **Antibodies, peptides,** or **small molecules** that specifically bind to **target receptors** on **diseased tissues.**
   - ◦ **Function:** Ensure **targeted delivery** of drugs to specific cells or tissues (e.g., **tumor targeting** in **cancer therapies**).

Facilitate Drug Absorption: Role of Excipients in NDDS

One of the key roles of excipients in **Novel Drug Delivery Systems (NDDS)** is to **facilitate drug absorption.** Many **poorly soluble** or **poorly absorbed drugs** face significant challenges in terms of **bioavailability.** These drugs often do not dissolve efficiently in the **gastrointestinal tract (GI)** or **do not cross biological barriers** (like the skin or mucosal lining) effectively. Excipients are incorporated into NDDS to **improve drug solubility** and **permeability,** thereby ensuring that the drug is absorbed effectively and reaches its **target site.**

How Excipients Facilitate Drug Absorption

1. **Enhancing Solubility:**

   - ◦ Many drugs, especially **lipophilic** or **poorly soluble drugs,** face challenges in **dissolving** in the **aqueous environment** of the **GI tract.** Excipients such as **solubilizers** and **surfactants** are included in the formulation to improve the solubility of the drug.
   - ◦ **Solubilizers** like **cyclodextrins, polyethylene glycol (PEG),** and **sodium lauryl sulfate** are widely used to improve the solubility of **poorly soluble drugs.**

- These excipients can **increase the surface area** of the drug or **form inclusion complexes** that enhance its ability to dissolve in the gastrointestinal fluids, facilitating better absorption in the **small intestine.**

2. **Improving Permeability:**

- Even after a drug dissolves in the GI tract, it may struggle to cross the **biological barriers** (like the **intestinal epithelium** or **skin**). Excipients can aid in improving the **permeability** of these barriers, ensuring that the drug enters the **systemic circulation.**
- **Penetration enhancers** like **dimethyl sulfoxide (DMSO), ethanol,** and **propylene glycol** are commonly used in **transdermal systems** and **oral formulations.** These excipients temporarily **disrupt the skin barrier** or **increase cell permeability,** allowing the drug to pass through more easily.
- For **oral formulations,** excipients like **lipids, bile salts,** and **surfactants** help improve the **intestinal permeability** of the drug, ensuring better absorption into the bloodstream.

3. **Promoting Absorption via Nanocarriers:**

- **Nanocarriers,** such as **liposomes, micelles,** and **nanoparticles,** can encapsulate the drug, enhancing its **solubility, stability,** and **absorption.** These **nano-sized carriers** increase the **drug's surface area,** which enhances **solubility** in the **GI tract** and promotes **intestinal absorption.**
- For **poorly soluble drugs, nanoparticles** can also be modified to have **targeted delivery** properties, improving drug absorption at specific sites in the body.
- **Example: Nanoparticle formulations** of poorly soluble drugs such as **taxanes** for **cancer therapy** are designed to enhance their **bioavailability** and **targeted delivery** to **tumors.**

4. **Optimizing the Drug Release Profile:**

- By carefully selecting excipients that control the **release rate** of the drug, NDDS can optimize the drug's **absorption** in the **GI tract.**

Matrix systems, osmotic pumps, and **liposomal formulations** allow for **controlled release,** ensuring that the drug is delivered **slowly** and **consistently,** improving its **absorption efficiency** over time.
- This is especially beneficial for drugs that need to be released at a specific location or over a prolonged period, such as **extended-release** or **sustained-release formulations.**

Examples of Excipients Facilitating Drug Absorption

1. **Cyclodextrins:**

   - **Cyclodextrins** are cyclic oligosaccharides that **enhance the solubility** of poorly soluble drugs. They form **inclusion complexes** with the drug, increasing its **water solubility** and **bioavailability.** Cyclodextrins are particularly useful for **oral formulations** of drugs that are poorly soluble in water.
   - **Example: Hydrocortisone** and **warfarin** are often complexed with **cyclodextrins** to enhance their **solubility** and absorption.

2. **Polysorbates (e.g., Tween 80):**

   - **Polysorbates** are surfactants used to enhance the **solubility** of hydrophobic drugs, particularly in **injectable formulations.** They also improve the **stability** of the drug in solution and aid in **drug absorption** by enhancing the drug's interaction with the **biological membrane.**
   - **Example: Paclitaxel,** a chemotherapy drug, is often formulated with **polysorbates** to improve its **bioavailability** and reduce **toxicity.**

3. **Lipids and Bile Salts:**

   - **Lipids,** such as **phospholipids** or **glycerides,** and **bile salts** are commonly used in drug formulations to improve the **intestinal permeability** of poorly absorbed drugs. These excipients **mimic natural biological processes,** helping drugs cross the **intestinal epithelium** more efficiently.
   - **Example: Fenofibrate** (a cholesterol-lowering drug) is often formulated with **bile salts** to improve its **absorption** and

bioavailability.

4. **Penetration Enhancers (e.g., DMSO, Ethanol):**

   - **Dimethyl sulfoxide (DMSO)** and **ethanol** are commonly used in **topical formulations** and **transdermal drug delivery systems** to enhance **skin permeability**. These excipients work by temporarily disrupting the **lipid bilayers** of the skin, allowing drugs to penetrate deeper layers.
   - **Example:** DMSO is often used in **transdermal patches** for **pain relief** and **anti-inflammatory** treatments.

Controlled Release: Role of Excipients in NDDS

Controlled release is a critical feature of **Novel Drug Delivery Systems (NDDS)** that allows for the **regulated release** of a drug over an extended period. Excipients play a fundamental role in controlling the **rate** at which the drug is released, enabling **sustained** or **targeted delivery**. By tailoring the release profile of a drug, controlled release systems can enhance **therapeutic outcomes** and minimize the **side effects** commonly associated with **rapid drug absorption** or **fluctuating drug levels** in the body.

Role of Excipients in Controlled Release

1. **Modification of Drug Release Rate:**

   - Excipients are used to **modify** the **drug release rate** by forming a **matrix** or **barrier** around the drug. The release rate is determined by the properties of the excipients, such as **polymer composition, solubility, film thickness,** and **pore size.**
   - **Example:** Hydroxypropyl methylcellulose (HPMC) is often used in **controlled-release tablets** to slow down the drug's release by forming a gel-like matrix around the drug.

2. **Targeted Drug Delivery:**

   - Excipients are also used to **target drug delivery** to specific sites in the body, such as the **stomach, intestines,** or **tumors.** This can be achieved by designing formulations that respond to **specific environmental stimuli** like pH, **temperature,** or **enzymes,** ensuring that the drug is released precisely at the site of action.

- **Example: Enteric coatings** (e.g., **methacrylic acid copolymers**) prevent drug release in the **acidic stomach** and allow it to dissolve in the **alkaline small intestine.**

3. **Sustained Release:**

- **Sustained-release formulations** use excipients that control the **rate of drug release** over extended periods, typically ranging from **hours to days.** This approach helps in maintaining **steady therapeutic drug levels** in the bloodstream, improving **patient adherence** and **minimizing peak-to-trough fluctuations.**
- Example: Polymer-based formulations (e.g., PLGA (poly(lactic-co-glycolic acid))) used in **injectable implants** provide **long-term drug release** for conditions like **chronic pain** or **hormonal therapy.**

4. **Reduced Side Effects:**

- By maintaining **steady drug concentrations** over a prolonged period, controlled release formulations help to **minimize fluctuations** in drug levels that can lead to **side effects.** This is particularly important for drugs that have a **narrow therapeutic window** or cause **toxicity** at high concentrations.
- Example: **Sustained-release morphine tablets** provide consistent pain relief over a 12-hour period, reducing the risk of **opioid overdose** or **addiction** from frequent dosing.

Mechanisms of Controlled Release Using Excipients

1. **Matrix Systems:**

- **Matrix-based controlled release** systems use excipients like **hydrophilic** or **hydrophobic polymers** to form a **solid matrix** in which the drug is embedded. The drug is released by **diffusion** through the matrix or by **erosion** of the polymer over time.
- Example: **Polyvinyl alcohol (PVA)** or **carbopol** are used in **tablet matrices** to release the drug in a controlled manner by diffusion and polymer erosion.

2. **Reservoir Systems:**

   - **Reservoir systems** consist of a **drug core** surrounded by a **rate-limiting membrane.** The drug is released through this membrane at a **constant rate.** The membrane can be designed to control the release of the drug over an extended period.
   - **Example: Osmotic pumps,** such as the **Osmotic pump tablet,** release the drug through an **osmotic pressure-driven mechanism** by pushing the drug out through a **semi-permeable membrane.**

3. **Coated Systems:**

   - In **coated formulations,** excipients like **polymers** or **lipids** are used to **coat** the drug, forming a protective layer. The coating controls the release of the drug by **dissolution, erosion,** or **osmotic forces.**
   - **Example: Enteric-coated tablets** ensure that the drug is protected from acidic environments in the stomach and is only released in the **alkaline small intestine.**

4. **Hydrogels:**

   - **Hydrogels** are networks of **polymeric** materials that swell in the presence of water, forming a gel. The drug is incorporated into the hydrogel and is released as the gel **swells** or **degrades** over time.
   - **Example: Polyethylene glycol (PEG)-based hydrogels** are often used in **topical drug delivery** for **controlled release** of **anti-inflammatory drugs** or **wound healing agents.**

Examples of Excipients Used in Controlled Release Systems

1. **Hydroxypropyl Methylcellulose (HPMC):**

   - **Function:** HPMC is a **hydrophilic polymer** widely used in **matrix-based** controlled release systems. It swells in the presence of water, creating a gel that releases the drug slowly over time.
   - **Example: Extended-release tablets** of **metformin** use HPMC to control the release of the drug and reduce side effects associated with high peak plasma levels.

2. **Poly(lactic-co-glycolic acid) (PLGA):**

- ○ **Function:** PLGA is a **biodegradable polymer** that is commonly used in **injectable nanocarriers** and **microspheres** for sustained release. As the polymer degrades, the drug is released gradually over time.
- ○ **Example: Leuprolide acetate** implants use PLGA to provide **sustained drug release** over a period of **months** for the treatment of **prostate cancer.**

3. **Ethylcellulose:**

- ○ **Function: Ethylcellulose** is used in **coating systems** to control the release of drugs. It is **insoluble in water** and serves as an **excellent barrier** to prevent the rapid release of the drug.
- ○ **Example: Aspirin tablets** with **ethylcellulose coating** ensure that the drug is released gradually, providing longer-lasting pain relief.

4. **Polyethylene Glycol (PEG):**

- ○ **Function:** PEG is a **hydrophilic polymer** used in **controlled release formulations** due to its ability to **form hydrogels** and control the drug's release by **diffusion** or **erosion.**
- ○ **Example: PEG-based drug-loaded implants** provide **long-term** release for the treatment of **chronic pain** or **hormonal therapy.**

2. Types of Excipients in NDDS

Excipients are essential components in **Novel Drug Delivery Systems (NDDS),** providing crucial functions such as **drug release control, bioavailability enhancement,** and **targeted delivery.** One of the most important classes of excipients used in NDDS are **polymeric excipients.** These excipients are **polymers** that help **control the release** of the active pharmaceutical ingredient (API), provide **biocompatibility,** and enhance **stability.** Polymers can be used in a variety of formulations, such as **tablets, patches, microspheres,** and **nanoparticles,** making them versatile for **sustained release, targeted delivery,** and **local drug delivery.**

Polymeric Excipients in NDDS

Hydroxypropyl Methylcellulose (HPMC)

- **Overview**: Hydroxypropyl methylcellulose (HPMC) is a **hydrophilic polymer** widely used in **controlled-release formulations**. It has excellent **film-forming properties** and is highly soluble in water, making it ideal for **matrix-based drug delivery systems**.
- **Function in NDDS**:

  - **Controlled Drug Release**: HPMC is commonly used in **tablet formulations** to control the **release rate** of the drug by forming a gel-like matrix around the drug. It swells in the presence of water, which **regulates the diffusion** of the drug from the matrix over time.
  - **Bioavailability Enhancement**: It can enhance the **bioavailability** of poorly soluble drugs by improving their dissolution rate.

- **Applications**:

  - **Sustained-release tablets**: HPMC is often used in **extended-release formulations** like **metformin** and **glipizide**, ensuring that the drug is released gradually, improving **patient compliance** by reducing the frequency of dosing.
  - **Oral tablets** and **capsules**: HPMC is also used to formulate tablets with a **controlled release profile**, improving the drug's efficacy by maintaining **steady plasma levels**.

Polyethylene Glycol (PEG)

- **Overview**: Polyethylene glycol (PEG) is a **hydrophilic polymer** with a wide range of molecular weights. It is used in various drug delivery systems, including **microspheres, nanoparticles, creams**, and **implants**. PEG is biocompatible and can also be used to improve the **solubility** and **stability** of poorly soluble drugs.
- **Function in NDDS**:

  - **Controlled Release**: PEG is often used in **hydrogel-based systems** for **sustained drug release**. It can form a gel matrix that swells in the presence of water, allowing for the gradual release of drugs.
  - **Improved Solubility**: PEG is commonly used as a **solubilizing agent**, particularly for hydrophobic drugs that have poor solubility in water.

- **Applications:**

  - **Injectable formulations:** PEG is used in **injectable nanoparticle formulations,** such as **liposomes,** to enhance the **bioavailability** of the drug and ensure its **controlled release** over a prolonged period.
  - **Controlled-release implants:** PEG-based drug-loaded **implants** can deliver drugs over weeks or months, making them ideal for **long-term treatments** like **hormonal therapy** or **oncology.**

Chitosan

- **Overview: Chitosan** is a **biodegradable, biocompatible** polymer derived from **chitin,** which is found in the exoskeleton of shellfish. It has gained popularity in **drug delivery applications** due to its **low toxicity, controlled release properties,** and ability to improve **drug solubility.**
- **Function in NDDS:**

  - **Controlled Release:** Chitosan can form **microspheres** or **nanoparticles** that encapsulate drugs, providing **sustained release.** The drug is released by **diffusion** or **erosion** of the polymer.
  - **Targeted Drug Delivery:** Chitosan is used to enhance **drug absorption** through the **intestinal mucosa** and to **target** specific tissues, such as **cancer cells,** when functionalized with targeting ligands.

- **Applications:**

  - **Microspheres:** Chitosan-based microspheres can be used to deliver drugs **locally** to the **target site (e.g., tumor** or **inflammatory tissues).**
  - **Oral drug delivery:** Chitosan is used in **oral formulations** to enhance the **absorption** of drugs through the **intestinal wall** and protect the drug from degradation in the stomach.
  - **Gene therapy:** Chitosan is used in **gene delivery systems** to deliver **DNA** or **RNA** molecules to target tissues, especially in **cancer therapy.**

Advantages of Polymeric Excipients in NDDS

1. **Controlled Drug Release:**

   - **Polymeric excipients** provide the ability to deliver drugs at a **controlled rate** over an extended period. This results in **steady drug levels** in the bloodstream and helps avoid the **side effects** associated with **peak concentrations.**

2. **Targeted Drug Delivery:**

   - By modifying the properties of **polymers** or functionalizing them with **targeting ligands,** it is possible to create drug delivery systems that **target specific tissues,** reducing the **systemic exposure** and improving **efficacy** at the **site of action.**

3. **Biocompatibility and Biodegradability:**

   - Many **polymeric excipients,** such as **chitosan** and **PLGA,** are **biocompatible** and **biodegradable,** making them ideal for **implantable systems** and other **long-term delivery systems.** Once the drug is fully delivered, the polymer breaks down and is safely metabolized by the body.

4. **Improved Stability:**

   - **Polymeric systems** can help **stabilize drugs,** protecting them from **degradation** due to environmental factors (e.g., **moisture, light,** and **oxygen**) and enhancing their shelf-life.

Lipids and Liposomes in NDDS

Lipids and **liposomes** are pivotal components in the development of **Novel Drug Delivery Systems (NDDS),** providing **targeted drug delivery,** enhanced **bioavailability,** and improved **stability** for a variety of formulations. Liposomes, in particular, are highly **versatile** and are used extensively for **injectable** and **oral drug delivery,** offering an innovative approach for drugs that require controlled release or specific targeting to **diseased tissues.**

Lipids in NDDS

Lipids are naturally occurring **fatty substances** that play a crucial role in many biological processes, including **drug absorption, membrane structure,** and **cell signaling.** In drug delivery systems, **lipid-based formulations** help improve the **solubility** and **stability** of poorly soluble drugs, allowing them to be delivered more efficiently to the target site.

Role of Lipids in NDDS:

- **Enhancing Drug Solubility:** Many drugs, especially **lipophilic** (fat-soluble) compounds, have poor water solubility. Lipids can encapsulate these **hydrophobic drugs** to improve their solubility and **bioavailability.**
- **Improving Drug Stability:** Lipids can protect **unstable drugs** from degradation by forming protective layers around them, ensuring that the drug remains **effective** throughout its shelf life.
- **Targeted Delivery:** Lipid formulations can be engineered to **target specific cells** or tissues by attaching **targeting ligands** (e.g., antibodies, peptides), allowing drugs to be delivered directly to the desired site of action, such as **tumors** or **inflamed tissues.**

Liposomes in NDDS

Liposomes are **nano-sized vesicles** made from **lipid bilayers,** which can encapsulate both **hydrophilic** and **hydrophobic drugs.** Liposomes are one of the most widely used **lipid-based drug delivery systems** in **injectables** and **oral formulations** due to their ability to **improve drug solubility, stability,** and provide **controlled release.**

Structure of Liposomes:

- **Liposomes** are spherical structures composed of one or more **phospholipid bilayers** surrounding an **aqueous core.** The hydrophobic drugs can be embedded in the lipid bilayer, while hydrophilic drugs can be enclosed in the aqueous core.
- **Liposome Composition:** Common components of liposomes include **phospholipids** (e.g., **phosphatidylcholine**) and **cholesterol** (which helps stabilize the lipid bilayer).

Mechanism of Action of Liposomes

1. **Encapsulation:**

- **Liposomes** encapsulate the **drug** either in the lipid bilayer (for **lipophilic drugs**) or in the aqueous core (for **hydrophilic drugs**), which protects the drug from degradation and allows for controlled and sustained release.

2. **Targeted Delivery:**

- **Liposomes** can be modified with **targeting ligands** (e.g., **antibodies, folic acid**, or **peptides**) that bind to specific receptors on the target cells. This enables the **selective delivery** of the drug to the **site of action**, such as **tumors** or **inflammatory tissues**.

3. **Controlled and Sustained Release:**

- Liposomes provide a **sustained release** of the encapsulated drug, allowing it to be delivered over a prolonged period. The release profile can be controlled by modifying the **liposome composition, size**, and **surface characteristics**.
- **Liposomes** can also be used for **triggered release**, where the drug is released in response to changes in the **environment** (e.g., **pH, temperature**, or **enzymatic activity**).

Advantages of Liposomes in NDDS

1. **Enhanced Drug Delivery:**

- Liposomes provide **enhanced solubility** for poorly water-soluble drugs and can improve **drug stability** during storage and administration.

2. **Reduced Toxicity:**

- Liposomes can **encapsulate toxic drugs** and reduce their exposure to healthy tissues, thereby minimizing side effects. This is particularly useful in **chemotherapy**, where **liposomal formulations** can **target cancer cells** while sparing healthy tissues.

3. **Controlled Release:**

- Liposomes can provide **sustained and controlled drug release** over extended periods, reducing the need for **frequent dosing** and improving **patient compliance.**

4. **Targeted Drug Delivery:**

- Liposomes can be engineered to target specific tissues or cells, which is particularly beneficial for the **treatment of cancer, infectious diseases,** and **autoimmune disorders.** This **targeted delivery** improves the **efficacy** of the drug while reducing **systemic side effects.**

Applications of Lipid-based Drug Delivery Systems

1. **Injectable Liposomes for Cancer Therapy:**

- **Doxil (liposomal doxorubicin)** is a well-known example of a **liposomal formulation** used in **cancer chemotherapy.** Liposomes encapsulate **doxorubicin**, a potent chemotherapy drug, and target it specifically to **tumor cells**, reducing the **toxicity** to healthy tissues and enhancing the therapeutic effect.

2. **Liposomes in Vaccine Delivery:**

- Liposomes are used as **adjuvants** in vaccines, enhancing the **immune response** by delivering the vaccine antigens directly to immune cells, improving **vaccine efficacy.**
- **Example:** Liposomal formulations of **influenza vaccines** improve **immune response** and provide **extended protection.**

3. **Targeted Delivery for Inflammatory Diseases:**

- Liposomes can deliver anti-inflammatory drugs directly to the **site of inflammation,** providing **localized** and **controlled drug release,** reducing systemic side effects and enhancing treatment outcomes.
- **Example: Liposomes** loaded with **steroids** are used for **local treatment of joint inflammation** in **rheumatoid arthritis.**

4. Gene Delivery Systems:

- Liposomes are also used for **gene therapy**, where they encapsulate **genetic material** (e.g., **DNA, RNA**) and deliver it directly to the target cells for **genetic correction** or **gene editing.**
- **Example: Liposomal carriers** are used to deliver **siRNA** or **mRNA** in gene therapies targeting **genetic disorders.**

Challenges with Liposomes and Lipid-based Systems

1. Stability Issues:

- Liposomes can **leak** their contents over time, leading to **drug loss** and reduced **efficacy.** Maintaining the **structural integrity** of liposomes is critical for their effectiveness in controlled-release systems.

2. Scalability:

- Producing liposomal formulations at a **large scale** can be challenging due to **variability** in **size** and **encapsulation efficiency,** which can affect product quality and consistency.

3. Cost:

- The **manufacturing process** for liposomal formulations can be more **costly** compared to traditional drug delivery systems, limiting their widespread use in certain therapeutic areas.

Surfactants in NDDS

Surfactants are a class of excipients widely used in **Novel Drug Delivery Systems (NDDS)** to improve **drug solubility, stability,** and the overall performance of the delivery system. They are primarily used to enhance the **solubility** of poorly water-soluble drugs, stabilize **emulsions,** and assist in the formulation of **nanoparticles** for **targeted drug delivery.**

Surfactants reduce the **surface tension** between two substances, enabling the creation of more stable formulations and enhancing the **absorption** and **bioavailability** of drugs. They are commonly found in **oral, injectable, transdermal,** and **topical** drug delivery systems.

Role of Surfactants in NDDS

1. **Improving Drug Solubility:**

   - Many drugs, especially **lipophilic (fat-soluble)** drugs, face poor **solubility** in water, which limits their **bioavailability**. Surfactants help to **increase the solubility** of these drugs by **reducing surface tension** and forming **micelles** that encapsulate hydrophobic drugs, making them more **soluble** in aqueous solutions.
   - **Example:** Surfactants like **Tween 80** and **sodium lauryl sulfate** are often used in **oral formulations** to improve the solubility of drugs like **cyclosporine** and **poorly soluble vitamins**.

2. **Stabilizing Emulsions:**

   - Surfactants play a key role in **emulsions**, which are mixtures of two immiscible liquids (e.g., oil and water). Surfactants reduce the **interfacial tension** between the two phases and stabilize the formulation by preventing **phase separation**.
   - **Example: Polysorbates** like **Tween 80** are commonly used in **parenteral emulsions** to stabilize **lipid-based formulations** and ensure that the **drug** is delivered efficiently without separation.

3. **Formulating Nanoparticles:**

   - In the formulation of **nanoparticles** or **liposomes**, surfactants are used to **stabilize** the nanoparticles and prevent **aggregation**. They help in **controlling the size, surface charge**, and **drug encapsulation efficiency**, ensuring that the nanoparticles are suitable for **targeted delivery** and provide **controlled release**.
   - **Example: Polyethylene glycol (PEG)-coated surfactants** are used to **stabilize nanoparticles** and increase their **circulatory half-life** by preventing **immune system recognition**.

Types of Surfactants Used in NDDS

1. **Polysorbates (e.g., Tween 80):**

- **Polysorbates**, such as **Tween 80**, are **non-ionic surfactants** that are widely used in pharmaceutical formulations, especially in **lipid-based systems** like **liposomes** and **micelles.**
- **Role**: They improve **solubility, stabilize emulsions**, and enhance the **drug loading** in nanoparticle formulations.
- Applications:

  - Used in **injectable emulsions** and **oral liquid formulations.**
  - Used in **liposomal formulations** for chemotherapy drugs like **doxorubicin.**

2. **Sodium Lauryl Sulfate:**

- **Sodium lauryl sulfate (SLS)** is an **anionic surfactant** that is commonly used to enhance **drug solubility** and **stabilize emulsions.**
- **Role**: SLS reduces the **surface tension** between the drug and aqueous phase, increasing the **drug's solubility** and helping in the formation of **micelles** for the drug delivery.
- Applications:

  - Used in **oral formulations**, such as **syrups** or **liquid suspensions**, to improve solubility and **dissolution rate.**
  - Used in **topical formulations** like **shampoos** and **skin care products.**

3. **Cremophor (e.g., Cremophor EL):**

- Cremophor EL is another **non-ionic surfactant** used to **solubilize hydrophobic drugs** and enhance their **bioavailability.**
- **Role**: It is used to **formulate poorly soluble drugs** and enhance **drug delivery** by improving **solubility** and **dispersion** in aqueous solutions.
- Applications:

  - Used in **parenteral formulations** to solubilize **chemotherapeutic agents** and improve their **drug delivery.**
  - Used in **oral formulations** for solubilizing **lipophilic drugs** such as **paclitaxel.**

Advantages of Surfactants in NDDS

1. **Improved Drug Bioavailability:**

   - Surfactants increase the **solubility** of poorly soluble drugs, leading to **improved absorption** and **bioavailability** in the body. This is particularly important for **oral** and **parenteral formulations** of **hydrophobic drugs**.

2. **Stabilization of Formulations:**

   - Surfactants help in the **stabilization of emulsions, nanoparticles,** and **liposomes**, ensuring that the drug remains stable and **effective** throughout its shelf life.
   - They prevent **aggregation, crystallization,** or **phase separation,** ensuring uniform drug delivery.

3. **Enhanced Drug Targeting:**

   - Surfactants can be used to **modify** the **surface properties** of nanoparticles and liposomes, allowing them to be **functionalized** with **targeting ligands** for **specific tissue targeting**.
   - **Example:** By coating nanoparticles with **PEGylated surfactants**, the **circulatory stability** and **targeting efficiency** are enhanced, particularly in **cancer therapies**.

4. **Versatility:**

   - Surfactants can be used in a wide range of **drug delivery systems**, including **oral, injectable, topical,** and **transdermal** formulations. Their ability to enhance **drug solubility, stability,** and **release profiles** makes them a vital component in NDDS.

Challenges in Using Surfactants

1. **Toxicity:**

- Some surfactants, particularly **ionic surfactants** like **sodium lauryl sulfate**, may cause **irritation** or **toxicity** in sensitive patients, especially when used in high concentrations.
- Careful formulation is necessary to ensure that the surfactant concentration is within **safe limits**.

2. **Formulation Stability:**

- While surfactants help stabilize formulations, their inclusion can sometimes cause **instability** in certain **lipid-based systems** (e.g., **liposomes** or **nanoparticles**), leading to **drug leakage** or **premature release**.

3. **Cost:**

- Some high-performance surfactants (e.g., **Cremophor EL**) can be **expensive** and may not be suitable for large-scale commercial production due to **cost constraints**.

Solubilizers in NDDS

Solubilizers are excipients used in **Novel Drug Delivery Systems (NDDS)** to enhance the **solubility** of poorly soluble or hydrophobic drugs. These excipients improve the **bioavailability** and effectiveness of drugs by enabling them to dissolve in aqueous solutions, making them suitable for **oral, injectable,** and **other delivery systems**. Solubilizers work by either **increasing the solubility** of the drug in the gastrointestinal tract or **stabilizing the drug** in its dissolved form, thus improving the **drug's absorption** and **therapeutic action**.

Role of Solubilizers in NDDS

1. **Enhancing Drug Solubility:**

- Many drugs have **poor water solubility**, which limits their **bioavailability** and **therapeutic effect**. Solubilizers increase the **solubility** of these hydrophobic drugs, allowing them to be delivered more effectively through **oral** or **injectable routes**.

2. **Improving Bioavailability:**

○ Poorly soluble drugs often fail to reach therapeutic concentrations in the bloodstream due to insufficient absorption. By enhancing solubility, solubilizers **improve the drug's absorption** and **bioavailability**, ensuring the drug reaches its intended site of action effectively.

3. **Stabilizing the Drug:**

○ Solubilizers can also **stabilize** drugs that are prone to degradation in their insoluble form. By keeping the drug in a **dissolved state**, solubilizers prevent the drug from **precipitating out** or undergoing **chemical degradation**.

4. **Facilitating Injectable and Oral Formulations:**

○ Many **injectable drugs** and **oral formulations** require **high solubility** to ensure that the drug can be administered in appropriate doses and absorbed effectively. Solubilizers are crucial in enabling these formulations to achieve the required solubility and stability.

Types of Solubilizers Used in NDDS

1. **Cyclodextrins:**

○ **Cyclodextrins** are **cyclic oligosaccharides** composed of **glucose units**. They form **inclusion complexes** with hydrophobic drugs, improving their solubility and stability in aqueous solutions.
○ **Mechanism:** The **hydrophobic drug** is encapsulated within the **hydrophobic cavity** of the **cyclodextrin molecule**, protecting it from degradation and increasing its solubility in water.
○ **Applications:** Cyclodextrins are commonly used in **oral** formulations (e.g., **tablets**, **capsules**) and **injectables**, especially for **poorly water-soluble drugs**.
○ **Example: Itraconazole**, an antifungal drug with poor solubility, is often formulated with **cyclodextrins** to improve its solubility and enhance its **oral bioavailability**.

2. **Surfactants:**

- Surfactants like **polysorbates (e.g., Tween 80)** and **sodium lauryl sulfate (SLS)** are widely used as **solubilizers** in pharmaceutical formulations. They work by reducing the **surface tension** and increasing the **solubility** of hydrophobic drugs.
- **Applications:** Surfactants are used in **oral, injectable,** and **topical** formulations to **enhance solubility** and **stability.**
- **Example: Paclitaxel,** a chemotherapy drug, is often formulated with **polysorbates** to improve its **solubility** and **bioavailability** in **injectable formulations.**

3. **Co-solvents:**

- **Co-solvents** like **ethanol, propylene glycol,** and **glycerin** are used to **dissolve** hydrophobic drugs, especially when the drug is poorly soluble in water.
- **Applications:** Co-solvents are commonly used in **injectable** solutions, where the drug needs to be dissolved in a **solvent mixture** to ensure proper absorption.
- **Example: Diazepam** injection is formulated using **propylene glycol** as a co-solvent to enhance its solubility for parenteral administration.

4. **Hydrophilic Polymers:**

- Hydrophilic polymers like **polyvinyl alcohol (PVA)** and **hydroxypropyl methylcellulose (HPMC)** are used as **solubilizers** in oral and **injectable drug formulations.**
- **Applications:** These polymers improve **drug solubility** by creating **aqueous solutions** or **dispersions,** and they can also help with **controlled release.**
- **Example: Curcumin,** a poorly water-soluble drug, is often formulated with **hydrophilic polymers** to improve its solubility and bioavailability.

Advantages of Solubilizers in NDDS

1. **Enhanced Bioavailability:**

- By improving the **solubility** of poorly soluble drugs, solubilizers significantly increase the **bioavailability** of drugs, allowing for more **effective treatment** and better **therapeutic outcomes**.

2. **Improved Stability:**

- Solubilizers can help maintain the **chemical stability** of drugs that are unstable in their non-soluble form, preventing **degradation** or **precipitation** during formulation or storage.

3. **Versatility:**

- Solubilizers like **cyclodextrins**, **surfactants**, and **co-solvents** are versatile excipients that can be used in various formulations, including **oral, injectable, transdermal,** and **topical** delivery systems.

4. **Targeted Drug Delivery:**

- Solubilizers, when used in **nanocarriers** or **liposomes**, help **target the drug** to specific sites (e.g., **tumors** or **inflammatory tissues**) by enhancing the drug's **solubility** and ensuring efficient **drug delivery** to the desired location.

Examples of Drugs Using Solubilizers

1. **Cyclosporine:**

- **Cyclosporine** is a poorly water-soluble drug used in **organ transplantation** and **autoimmune diseases**. **Cyclodextrins** are used to **solubilize** cyclosporine, improving its **oral bioavailability** and ensuring consistent therapeutic effects.

2. **Paclitaxel:**

- **Paclitaxel**, a chemotherapy agent, is often formulated with **polysorbates (Tween 80)** to improve **solubility** and **bioavailability** in **injectable formulations**. This increases its **efficacy** while reducing the **side effects** associated with traditional formulations.

3. **Diazepam:**

- **Diazepam**, a sedative and anti-anxiety medication, is formulated with **propylene glycol** as a **co-solvent** to improve its **solubility** for intravenous administration, ensuring that the drug is delivered effectively and safely.

4. **Curcumin:**

- **Curcumin**, a poorly water-soluble **bioactive compound** used for **anti-inflammatory** and **antioxidant** purposes, is often formulated with **hydrophilic polymers** to improve its **bioavailability** and **stability** in **oral formulations**.

Challenges of Using Solubilizers

1. **Toxicity:**

- Some solubilizers, especially **ionic surfactants** like **sodium lauryl sulfate**, can cause **irritation** or **toxicity** when used in **high concentrations** or in **sensitive formulations**.

2. **Compatibility:**

- Solubilizers need to be carefully selected for compatibility with both the **API** and the **other excipients** in the formulation. Some solubilizers may interact with the drug or **affect drug stability**, leading to **inconsistent release profiles**.

3. **Cost:**

- High-performance solubilizers such as **cyclodextrins** and **certain surfactants** can be **expensive**, limiting their widespread use, particularly in large-scale manufacturing.

Applications of Excipients in NDDS

Excipients play a pivotal role in **Novel Drug Delivery Systems (NDDS)**, ensuring the **efficacy**, **stability**, and **controlled release** of the drug. Their applications vary depending on the **delivery system**, and they are essential in optimizing the **drug's performance** and **patient outcomes**. One of the important applications is in **inhalable systems**, where excipients help to enhance the **stability, solubility,** and **effective delivery** of drugs to the **lungs**.

Inhalable Drug Delivery Systems

Inhalable drug delivery systems, such as **dry powder inhalers (DPIs), metered-dose inhalers (MDIs),** and **nebulizers,** provide a direct route of drug delivery to the lungs, which is especially useful for **respiratory diseases** like **asthma,** COPD (chronic obstructive pulmonary disease), and other pulmonary conditions. **Excipients** in these systems ensure that the drug remains **stable, easily inhaled,** and **effectively delivered** to the **lungs**.

Role of Excipients in Inhalable Systems

1. **Ensuring Drug Stability:**

   - Excipients are used to protect the **drug** from **degradation** during storage and delivery. This is particularly crucial for drugs that are sensitive to **moisture, light,** or **oxidation**.
   - **Example: Antioxidants** like **ascorbic acid** or **tocopherol** are often added to protect **inhaled drugs** from **oxidative degradation**.

2. **Improving Drug Flowability:**

   - In **dry powder inhalers (DPIs),** excipients help ensure that the drug is **uniformly dispersed** and that the powder flows easily through the device, providing a consistent dose.
   - **Example: Lactose** is commonly used as a **carrier in DPIs,** as it helps to ensure that the drug is **uniformly distributed** and facilitates the powder's **aerosolization** when inhaled.

3. **Facilitating Aerosolization:**

   - Excipients like **lactose** in **DPIs** and **HFA (hydrofluoroalkane)** propellants in **MDIs** help **formulate** the drug in a manner that allows it to be **aerosolized** and inhaled into the lungs.
   - **Example:** In **MDIs,** the **propellant (e.g., HFA 134a)** helps in **dispensing** the drug in an **aerosolized form,** ensuring that it reaches

the lungs in the correct dose.

4. **Targeted Delivery to the Lungs:**

   - Excipients are used to ensure that the drug reaches the **lung tissue** directly and effectively, without **loss** of the drug during **aerosolization** or **inhalation.**
   - **Example: Pulmonary surfactants** can be included in some inhalable formulations to enhance the drug's **stability** and **targeting** within the **lungs.**

Excipients in Dry Powder Inhalers (DPIs)

1. **Lactose:**

   - **Lactose** is one of the most commonly used **carriers** in **DPIs.** It is a **bulking agent** that helps to increase the volume of the powder formulation, making it easier to handle and use.
   - **Function: Lactose** helps to **disperse** the drug powder uniformly and **facilitates flowability,** ensuring that the correct dose is delivered with each inhalation.
   - **Example: Fluticasone propionate** and **salmeterol** are commonly formulated with **lactose** in **DPI formulations** to treat asthma and COPD.

2. **Magnesium Stearate:**

   - **Magnesium stearate** is often used as a **lubricant** in DPI formulations to improve the **flowability** of the powder and reduce the **friction** during the formulation and **inhalation** process.
   - **Function:** It prevents the particles from sticking together, ensuring **consistent powder flow** through the inhaler.

3. **Trehalose:**

   - **Trehalose, a disaccharide sugar,** is used in **DPIs** as a **stabilizing agent.** It helps protect the drug from **degradation** during storage and **maintains drug stability** during inhalation.

○ **Function:** It also protects **sensitive drugs** like **proteins** or **peptides** that might be present in the formulation.

Excipients in Metered-Dose Inhalers (MDIs)

1. **Propellants:**

   ○ **Hydrofluoroalkanes (HFAs)** are used as **propellants** in **MDIs** to deliver the drug in **aerosolized form** to the lungs.
   ○ **Function:** These propellants are **environmentally friendly** alternatives to the older **chlorofluorocarbons (CFCs)**, ensuring **efficient drug delivery** without contributing to **ozone depletion**.
   ○ **Example:** HFA **134a** is commonly used in **MDI formulations** for **asthma** drugs like **albuterol** and **fluticasone**.

2. **Surfactants:**

   ○ Surfactants such as **Polysorbate 80** are used to stabilize the **drug suspension** in MDIs and ensure that the active ingredient remains **uniformly dispersed**.
   ○ **Function:** Surfactants help to reduce **interfacial tension**, which **prevents settling** of the drug in the container and ensures a consistent dose with every spray.

Excipients in Nebulizers

Nebulizers are devices used to convert liquid drug formulations into an **aerosol** that can be inhaled into the lungs. While the drug formulation for nebulizers is typically in liquid form, excipients are still essential for ensuring the **stability**, **aerosolization**, and **targeted delivery** of the drug.

1. **Isotonic Agents (e.g., Sodium Chloride):**

   ○ **Isotonic agents** such as **sodium chloride** are used to adjust the **osmolarity** of the formulation, ensuring that the solution is compatible with the body's natural environment and prevents **irritation** of the lungs during inhalation.
   ○ **Function:** They ensure that the nebulized drug solution has the correct **osmotic pressure** for comfortable and safe use.

2. **Stabilizing Agents (e.g., EDTA, BHT):**

- **Stabilizing agents** like **EDTA** (ethylenediaminetetraacetic acid) and **butylated hydroxytoluene (BHT)** are used to **stabilize the drug** and **prevent degradation** due to exposure to oxygen or light during nebulization.
- **Function**: They maintain the **efficacy** and **shelf-life** of the drug formulation.

About Authors

1. **Dr. Ramakrishna Malepati working as Vice Principal, HoD, Department of Pharmaceutical Analysis,**Narasaraopeta Institute of Pharmaceutical Sciences (Autonomous), Narasaraopet.

Dr.Ramakrishna holds a Bachelor's and Master's degree in Pharmaceutical Analysis from Tamilnadu Dr. M.G.R. Medical University, Chennai, and a Ph.D. from Career Point University, Kota, Rajasthan. He has over Eighteen years of experience in academics with a strong foundation in pharmaceutical sciences.**Dr.Ramakrishna** has published more than 30 research and review papers, 1Practical Manual and has been actively involved in the scientific community, presenting at various conferences. His contributions have earned him numerous accolades, including the Best Performer Award from the Association of Pharmacy Professionals.He was the life member of APTI, APP.

2. **Mrs. Santhosh Aruna Mamidi** Associate Professor, Department of Pharmaceutics, SIMS College of Pharmacy, Affiliated to Acharya Nagarjuna University Guntur.

Mrs Santhosh Aruna holds a bachelor's degree from JNTU Hyderabad, Master degree from Acharya Nagarjuna University, Guntur, pursuing PhD from Acharya Nagarjuna University, Guntur. She has over 15 years of experience in pharmaceutical drug development, specializing in herbal and novel drugs. Santhosh aruna has published more than 45 research and review papers, 1 book and two book chapters in various reputed journals and has been actively involved in the scientific community. Santhosh Aruna guided 13 M.Pharm and 50 B.Pharm students for their dissertation work. She actively combines with deep knowledge with practical principles including mentorship and leadership to create dynamic environment.

3. **Mrs Lakshmi Devi Gottemukkula** is an Associate Professor and Head of the Department of Pharmaceutics at Joginpally B.R. Pharmacy College. With a strong academic background in pharmaceutical sciences, the author holds a**M. Pharmacy** degree in **Pharmaceutics** and has submitted a **PhD** thesis to **GITAM University**, focusing on advanced drug delivery systems and formulation technologies. She has twelve years of experience in academics with a strong foundation in pharmaceutical sciences; Lakshmi has published 30 research and review papers, 1 practical manual and 2 book chapters, and their research focuses on enhancing the

solubility and bioavailability of poorly water-soluble drugs through innovative strategies such as solid dispersions, nanosuspensions, and self-nano emulsifyingdrug delivery systems (SNEDDS). Additionally, the author is keenly interested in designing and evaluating novel dosage forms to improve therapeutic outcomes and patient compliance. Her contributions have earned the best research presentation award at INDO-US SUMMIT-2024, organized by Sarojini Naidu Vanitha Pharmacy Maha Vidyalaya, Hyderabad.

The author has actively contributed to various research publications and presentations in national and international forums and continues to explore interdisciplinary approaches in pharmaceutical formulation and drug delivery.

4. Dr. Raghavendra Kumar Gunda Associate Professor, Faculty-In-Charge, Department of Pharmaceutics, Narasaraopeta Institute of Pharmaceutical Sciences (Autonomous), Narasaraopet.

Dr. Raghavendra holds a Bachelor's and Master's degree in Pharmaceutics from Acharya Nagarjuna University, Guntur, and a Ph.D. from the School of Pharmaceutical Sciences, Vels Institute of Science, Technology and Advanced Studies, Pallavaram, Chennai. He has over Thirteen years of experience in Pharmaceutical Product Development, specializing in novel drug delivery systems.**Dr.Raghavendra** has published more than 100 research and review papers, 3 Books, 7 Book Chapters and has been actively involved in the scientific community, presenting at various conferences and serving on editorial boards. His contributions have earned him numerous accolades, including the Bharath Shiksha Gaurav Puraskar from KTK Outstanding Achievers & Education Foundation; Global Ambassador of Education ExcellencefromInternational Institute of Education & Management and Best Researcher Award from the Association of Pharmacy Professionals.He maintains active involvement in the pharmacy community as a registered pharmacist and member of several professional bodies (IPA, APTI, IPGA, APP, AAPNA).